Black Women, Citizenship, and the Making of Modern Cuba

BLACK WOMEN, CITIZENSHIP, AND THE MAKING OF MODERN CUBA

Takkara K. Brunson

UNIVERSITY OF FLORIDA PRESS

Gainesville

Publication of this paperback edition made possible by a Sustaining the Humanities through the American Rescue Plan grant from the National Endowment for the Humanities.

First cloth printing, 2021
First paperback printing, 2023

28 27 26 25 24 23   6 5 4 3 2 1

Library of Congress Cataloging-in-Publication Data
Names: Brunson, Takkara K., author.
Title: Black women, citizenship, and the making of modern Cuba / Takkara K. Brunson.
Description: 1. | Gainesville : University of Florida Press, 2021. |
Includes bibliographical references and index.
Identifiers: LCCN 2021007578 (print) | LCCN 2021007579 (ebook) | ISBN
9781683402084 (cloth) | ISBN 9781683402428 (pdf) | ISBN 9781683403739 (pbk.)
Subjects: LCSH: Women, Black—Cuba—History. | Women, Black—Cuba—Social
conditions. | Women revolutionaries—Cuba—History. | Cuba—History.
Classification: LCC HQ1507 .B78 2021 (print) | LCC HQ1507 (ebook) | DDC
173/.40951—dc25
LC record available at https://lccn.loc.gov/2021007578
LC ebook record available at https://lccn.loc.gov/2021007579

University of Florida Press
2046 NE Waldo Road
Suite 2100
Gainesville, FL 32609
http://upress.ufl.edu

UF PRESS

UNIVERSITY
OF FLORIDA

To Amaya, Raul, and my parents, James and Kathleen

Contents

Figures

this journey. It is bittersweet to complete this book after my mother's passing, but I know she would be proud. I also thank my father for our endless conversations and for reading drafts of my work over the years. My sister continues to encourage me to pursue my dreams while not taking myself too seriously; in this regard, she helps carry on the legacy of our late godfather. My husband and I met as I was dissertating. Ten years later, I remain indebted to him for his constant support and optimism as we embrace life's adventures and especially the opportunity to raise our daughter, Amaya.

Introduction

Enacting Citizenship between Abolition and the 1959 Revolution

In 1939, María Dámasa Jova Baró authored a statement of candidacy to represent the Conjunto Nacional Democrático (National Democratic Union) at Cuba's upcoming constitutional assembly. The Black Santa Clara resident had garnered national and global recognition as a poet and educator during the 1920s and 1930s.[1] Having witnessed popular protests that led to the overthrow of President Gerardo Machado y Morales and the establishment of a "new Cuba" in 1934, she set her sights on electoral politics.[2] Dámasa Jova determined that the Conjunto Nacional Democrático offered Cuban citizens the best opportunity to build a truly democratic nation. She appealed "to everyone" in her statement, "colleagues, friends, and supporters" to cast their votes in her favor.[3]

Dámasa Jova offered her biography as evidence of her patriotism and political capabilities. Born during the final decade of Spanish colonialism, she lost her grandparents to the "the redemptive revolution" (*revolución redentora*) for independence.[4] She grew up poor following the deaths of her parents at an early age. Dámasa Jova obtained an education and began teaching at the age of thirteen; she founded a school six years later. These experiences made her especially attuned to the struggles and needs of the underprivileged. She emphasized her lifelong dedication to creating educational opportunities for "applied and studious children" from poor families. Notably, she initiated a workshop that trained students as they published her children's magazine, *Ninfas* (1929–1938), as well as a children's radio program. During a period in which African-descended women confronted few opportunities to publish in the mainstream press, she founded the popular culture magazine *Umbrales* (1934–1937). In her appeal for votes she asserts, "The more culture the people have, the greater capacity they have to fulfill their duties and exercise their rights."[5] Her self-funded initiatives helped launch the artistic careers of individuals who had already achieved financial success, providing those who sought to overcome poverty "with a view of a better future."[6]

Cuban women gained the right to vote under the 1934 Constitution. Subsequently, women of all races drew from their experiences as laborers, mothers, and social welfare advocates to demand government reforms through a range of political institutions. Dámasa Jova was one of several Black women to speak at the 1939 Third National Women's Congress in Havana. That congress drew attendees from across the island who proposed constitutional reforms on behalf of a broad contingent of women. She later attended the International American Teachers Congress "to fight for the needs of Cuban schools, for the highest democratic ideals in favor of children and teachers."[7] In her statement of candidacy for the Conjunto Nacional Democrático, Dámasa Jova emphasizes that she entered formal politics not for financial gain, as she remained poor; rather, she had become "convinced that women have to take an active part in the destinies of our country."[8]

Members of the Conjunto Nacional Democrático elected Dámasa Jova to serve as their regional candidate to the constitutional assembly. However, the Provincial Electoral Board rejected her candidacy for reasons unknown.[9] Dámasa Jova died in 1940 at age forty-nine, five months before the constitutional assembly took place. Her extraordinary career provides insight into how Black women activists navigated a shifting political system. Curiously, she sought to represent a conservative party that affirmed the importance of racial equality while denying the existence of racism. Her candidacy statement avoided the topic of race altogether. Yet several of her published poems and political speeches directly confronted how many Black women remained impoverished due to sexism and racial discrimination. Her statement of candidacy echoed the practice of racial silence employed by African-descended women activists prior to the 1920s, a practice abandoned by Black feminists by the 1930s. In this regard, her approach suggests the complexities of building cross-racial alliances on the eve of the constitutional assembly.

In this study I center African-descended women in its examination of Cuba's political system between abolition in 1886 and the 1959 Revolution. The career of María Dámasa Jova elucidates one of my central arguments, that Black Cuban women who confronted gender and racial exclusion in their efforts to obtain rights and resources played an integral role in forging a modern democracy. By focusing on evolving citizenship practices among a range of social actors, I demonstrate how Black women activists contributed to shape legal reforms, political movements, and social ideologies. These women wrote letters, supported civic organizations and presses, joined political parties and labor unions, and established schools in their efforts to create a more just society. They negotiated the terms of racial integration, Black civic culture, women's public roles, labor rights, and Cuban national identity. Furthermore, the archival records of African-descended women show the interlocking nature of struggles for material resources, civil rights, and social recognition in defining citizenship, struggles that reflected competing strategies and priorities among political factions.

Citizenship on the Margins

What do the citizenship practices employed by Black Cuban women reveal about evolving racial and gender dynamics between abolition and the 1959 Revolution? How did such practices contribute to shaping the nation's political development? Addressing these questions prompts a reconsideration of gendered approaches to Cuban nation formation. The actions of men of all races within the electoral sphere, patronage networks, social scientific institutions, and nationalist discourses have been well documented.[10] Notably, in her foundational study of Cuban racial ideologies, Aline Helg explains that her concentration on men was "not a choice but a consequence of the focus on political and armed struggle, in which men were more directly involved than women." Helg observes, "Afro-Cuban women had a more fundamental role in other, more discreet forms of struggle, such as mutual-help organizations and cultural resistance."[11] Women, in other words, appear on the margins of most narratives of Cuban nation formation due to the forms of action prioritized by scholars: political and institutional leadership. In this study I aim to bring Black women activists from the margins to the center of analysis. I propose a better theorization of their engagement with political processes through the inclusion of Afro-diasporic and Latin American feminist perspectives.

In exploring how women shaped Black activist traditions and broader political processes in post-abolition Latin America and the Caribbean, I

garding women's contributions to national progress. Editors complemented elite Black women's writings with photographs that illustrated their feminine domesticity. In addition, privileged women organized social events that excluded poor Black men and women who failed to adhere to expectations of proper behavior, such as marriage and Eurocentric cultural practices, in order to buttress their own public image. Elite Black women's civic club activities also paralleled the growing influence of women in Lucumí (Yoruba) communities during the early twentieth century, demonstrating that elite ideas of public behavior were unevenly embraced by the broader population of African descent. While privileged Black men limited women's formal leadership throughout the republican era, many Lucumí communities validated women's authority.[22]

Examining how race shaped citizenship practices for women across racial lines shows that evolving racial dynamics underpinned the evolution of the Cuban women's movement. Scholars have tended to examine the women's movement in Cuba and Latin America more broadly from the perspectives of urbane elite and middle-class white women.[23] White Cuban feminists' belief in racial hierarchies shaped their organizational strategies during the early years of the republic. White feminist leaders excluded most laboring (and) Black women yet embraced a race-neutral rhetoric. Further, many of the political strategies employed by elite and middle-class white women remained unavailable to Black women, who often lacked the necessary social connections to publish in the mainstream press, obtain professional employment, or influence politicians. By the mid-1920s, those who sought to build a coalition powerful enough to achieve suffrage expanded their circles to include Black women of all class backgrounds. Incorporating previously excluded groups led white feminists to acknowledge how anti-Black racism created disparate experiences for women of African descent. The rise of a cross-racial coalition of women also shaped the political perspectives of elite Black civic activists and labor groups. Indeed, African-descended women's participation in the women's movement paralleled their emergence as nationally renowned activists across a range of political organizations from the 1930s through the 1950s.

An analysis of Black women's activism contributes to studies of gender in the broader political system especially during the final decades of the republican era. Lynn Stoner convincingly argues that Cuban women drew from their roles as morally superior caretakers to justify their entry into broader discussions regarding political representation and social welfare reforms.[24] Manuel Ramírez Chicharro asserts that after gaining suffrage rights in 1934, most Cuban women turned to public affairs rather than to seeking political office.[25] Michelle Chase's study of gender and the Cuban Revolution demonstrates how women crafted a nonthreatening political identity through discourses of maternalism.[26] These scholars find that even as Cubans embraced modernizing gender norms, women remained on the margins of national politics. Here, I explore the factors that maintained their marginalization, through a comparison of Black women communists and activists who employed a moderate approach to democratic reform following the ratification of the 1940 Constitution. Cubans restructured patriarchal expectations at the very moment that women gained new opportunities in the public sphere.[27] Rather than push for equal representation in electoral politics, women joined auxiliary branches of political parties as well as autonomous women's groups through which they sought to exert influence. And although the communist movement empowered women at local, regional, and national levels of government more than other parties did, women's leadership did not translate into gender equity.

By no means does this study provide a comprehensive examination of Black Cuban women's political activism. Instead, I take an approach of exploring the complexities of their citizenship practices. Rather than focus solely on separate historical periods, I move both chronologically and thematically to emphasize the evolving political strategies employed by African-descended women activists. I begin in the post-abolition years, a period essential for understanding how political movements, particularly the struggle for racial equality among African descendants, unfolded during the ensuing republican era. In the first chapter I examine racial citizenship and the expansion of the Black public sphere during the late colonial period. In chapters 2 and 3 I trace how sexual norms informed Black women's efforts to navigate early republican politics in response to discourses of racelessness through letter writing to Black politicians and self-fashioning. In chapters 4 and 5 I look at African-descended women's feminist perspectives within the context of modernizing gender norms, specifically the evolution of Black feminist thought and racial dynamics within the women's movement. In chapter 6 I focus on the limits of constitutional reforms during the 1940s and 1950s, and in chapter 7 I analyze the communist movement during the same period. Throughout the chapters I follow the processes through which sexism and anti-Black racism persisted even as legal definitions of citizenship evolved. Such definitions remained unstable as African-descended women activists reinterpreted ideas of democracy in ways that recognized their full humanity.

Black Cuban Women and the Practice of Citizenship

One assumption made by some historians of Latin America is that archives lack the sources necessary to construct narratives of Black women's political contributions. I would argue that this challenge lies not in the availability of sources but rather the lens applied to historical documents. I began this project by consulting records examined in previous studies of Cuban nation formation, such as publications and organizational records of African descendants, feminists, laborers, communists, and other major political parties as well as letters and census data. These records revealed a wealth of information regarding the shifting political strategies of hundreds of Black women activists who affirmed and modified dominant expectations of citizenship. At the same time, such sources demonstrated the limits of the archive for fully understanding the public lives of African-descended women. Few sources provided biographical details on the individuals I cite in the following pages. Most social columns published in newspapers listed organization members or election results without documenting participants' ongoing activities. The archive, in this regard, left more questions than answers.

To address these gaps, I devote substantial attention to a small group of urbane women who left an extensive set of records: Cristina Ayala (Güines), Úrsula Coimbra de Valverde (Cienfuegos and Santiago de Cuba), Consuelo Serra (Havana and New York City), María Dámasa Jova (Santa Clara), Ana Echegoyen de Cañizares (Havana), and Esperanza Sánchez Mastrapa (Santiago de Cuba). They were exceptional leaders of various Black, feminist, and labor groups, and their stories capture the complexities of African-descended women's citizenship practices during the period. Some hailed from privileged families. Others were born into poverty. Each woman developed a political philosophy that reflected her personal approach to obtain socioeconomic mobility and community reform. I use their stories to think more broadly about the varied social experiences of Cuban women of African descent.

I center this study on the citizenship practices such figures employed during the island's ambiguous period of democracy that unfolded between the end of the US Occupation (1898–1901) and the 1959 Revolution.[28] The archives offer a more comprehensive picture of the actions of elite male and white female leaders, but how women of African descent enter into historical records also provides insight into the evolving nature of Cuban politics. Women appear throughout the records of the Black public sphere. As slavery came to an end, literate women of African descent wrote articles, poems, and social announcements that detailed their efforts to build positive identities. Many contested anti-Black racism through their writings. Women also established civic associations that promoted racial regeneration. The public-sphere activities of elite and upwardly mobile Black women reflected a tradition of civic engagement that in many ways predated that of their white female counterparts. This tradition evolved throughout the republican era as many African-descended women pursued resources through male-headed institutions in order to affirm their femininity. Documents reveal how they responded to racelessness discourses that discouraged critiques of anti-Black racism and especially those issued by Black women activists. Women's participation in the Black public sphere reflected a complex negotiation of patriarchal expectations as Cubans debated the terms of racial integration in an emergent nation.

I read the press of the times with new questions regarding Black women's political actions. For instance, what aims did published photographic portraits serve in the struggle for racial equality? From this perspective, photographs evidenced Black women's feminine virtue as well as practices of self-fashioning and everyday life. Elite women of African descent and male editors employed photography to craft a positive racial identity. Black female sitters projected images of feminine domesticity in order to counter stereotypes that portrayed them as *brujas* (witchcraft practitioners), sex workers, and impoverished mothers. I read photographic portraits as part of a broader dialogue regarding the role of Black women in national life. I find that elite women affirmed the traditional model of femininity that was used to denigrate African descendants who rejected Eurocentric standards of behavior, even as they called for expanded rights and roles in republican society.

By historicizing Black Cuban women's social thought over a period of seventy-three years, I build on the critical work of scholars who have docu-

have chosen to prioritize racial terminology that draws from categories used in primary sources. "Black," *mulato* and *mulata* (mulatto), and "mestizo" refer to individuals in several instances. *Gente de color* and *raza de color* (colored race) referenced a broader population unified in their experiences with anti-Black racism. I use these designations interchangeably with "African-descended" and "persons of African descent," terms that I believe encapsulate the persistence of race and racism in defining the experiences of Black Cubans.

Finally, I attend to the ways that class dynamics shaped the life experiences of African-descended women. The sources I use primarily speak to the experiences and thoughts of literate and semiliterate women. Most women I discuss represent the activism of elite and upwardly mobile women. I use the term "elite" to denote the social and economic privileges of a select population in comparison to the broader Black population. Few Black elite households reached the level of wealth that affluent white families attained, yet their advanced education and political connections set them apart from the average families of African descent. Elite women tended to be the wives, daughters, and sisters of prominent politicians, professionals, and intellectuals. Some pulled themselves out of poverty and became successful professionals. Many were homemakers, and others entered the labor force as midwives, seamstresses, teachers, stenographers, and doctors. Some actively aspired to upward mobility but had not yet attained the financial stability of their elite and white middle-class counterparts. Upwardly mobile women came from families of more humble backgrounds as artisans, domestics, agricultural laborers, and factory workers. Each group held similar goals: they sought racial integration, legal protections, and social recognition as dignified Cuban women. Occasionally their strategies differed, as more African-descended women participated in labor unions and the Communist Party than in feminist groups or Black civic clubs. Often elite women organized on behalf of poor women rather than with them. These two groups would build complex alliances critical to the democratization of the political sphere, especially as women of all races and class backgrounds entered into nationalist movements of the 1920s and 1930s.

"Look for Progress in Our Moral Perfection"

Racial Regeneration and the Post-Zanjón Black Public Sphere

In 1878, nationalist rebel leaders accepted the terms of peace proposed by the Spanish colonial government, effectively ending a decade of war. These terms, referred to as the Pact of Zanjón, entailed a series of political and economic reforms.[1] The pact granted Cubans new rights to publish in the press and to form associations. New political parties organized to advocate on behalf of an expanding electorate. The government also emancipated enslaved Blacks and indentured Chinese laborers who participated in the war and promised to end slavery altogether; it did so in 1886. Throughout the island, a small but dynamic group of aspirational Black women embraced these reforms as community leaders ready for the task of building a modern society. Writing for the Black press and creating organizations, establishing schools and libraries, and forming nuclear families, they aimed to break with the social stigma of enslavement in order to gain recognition as racial equals.

One such woman was Cristina Ayala.[2] Born into slavery in 1856, the teacher and prolific poet in the town of Güines devoted her life to serving the population of African descent. In 1888 she outlined a vision of uplift in the poem "A mi raza" (To my race).[3] Slavery had ended two years earlier, unifying recently emancipated Blacks and freeborn people of color under the umbrella category *la raza de color* (the colored race) or *clase de color* (colored class). Abolition, she determined, presented all Black men and women with the opportunity to forge new lives. She declared, "Now is the time beloved race that, our servitude having ceased, we give proof of our citizenship and have a life of our own." She called upon African descendants to "look for progress in our moral perfection."[4]

Ayala directed her poem to the Black population, but she also addressed elite whites concerned with the island's social "demoralization" and incapacity for self-governance.[5] "A mi raza" responded to the pamphlet of the Spanish intellectual Francisco Moreno titled *Cuba y su gente* (Cuba and its people), in which he denigrates Blacks and women of all races for their "immoral" behaviors.[6] Ayala challenged Moreno's position as she boldly mandated that whites take responsibility for "the time that had passed."[7] She blamed enslavers for creating the circumstances that hindered Black social advancement; she refuted assertions that African descendants alone were to blame for low marriage rates and levels of education. Yet, even in challenging Moreno, she affirmed his association of "moral perfection" with marriage and the denial of African culture.

Ayala's literary activism highlights the interplay of Cuban national and Black public spheres, both of which expanded following the implementation of Pact of Zanjón reforms.[8] African descendants who previously had limited opportunities to be published in the national press established more than 120 publications during the final decades of the colonial era.[9] Many of these publications served as forums for Black associations. Historians have detailed how elite and upwardly mobile Black men advocated on behalf of the *raza de color* through the public sphere.[10] Men of African descent positioned themselves as community leaders who debated and brought visibility to the racial issues they deemed important; they forged connections between Black social networks and the broader political realm.

Women contributed to the growth of the Black public sphere as well. Their writings and organizational activities helped determine the political goals of the community. Their public-sphere activities included labor, social events, protests, civic clubs, and educational endeavors. Elite and upwardly mobile Black women's public engagement, rather than embrace patriarchal gender norms that relegated women to the home, challenged the gendered public/private dichotomy promoted by white Cuban elites. African-descended women who navigated the public sphere worked to inscribe themselves and their visions of citizenship into nationalist agendas.

Women who entered into the Black public sphere tested the possibilities for racial integration as all Cubans grappled with immigration, economic crises, and urban migrations, dynamics that threw social relations into crisis. As slavery came to an end, elite whites reasserted racial hierarchies and claimed leadership over the modernization of the island. Leaders of the

Liberal Autonomist and Conservative Parties employed slightly different approaches to engaging populations of African descent, but the primarily white membership of both shared the perspective that Blacks needed to prove their capacity for integration while also excluding them from opportunities for socioeconomic advancement. This perspective marginalized African-descended men in the electoral realm. It was deployed to justify discriminatory practices against Black men and women in public spaces and in institutions more broadly. Persons of African descent thus obtained new freedoms of political expression while experiencing attacks on their ability to participate fully in modern life.

Ayala represented a community of elite and upwardly mobile African descendants who responded to such dynamics by formulating a platform of racial "regeneration."[11] Racial regeneration discourses outlined a path for moving beyond the perceived darkness under which African descendants had lived during slavery.[12] Utilizing the Black public sphere, racial regeneration advocates emphasized socioeconomic advancement through racial unity and personal responsibility. Women who embraced racial regeneration principles stressed their feminine virtue as educated and patriotic citizens. As public figures, they formulated a model of political action in which elite women contributed to the moral, economic, and intellectual development of the Black population. Their actions illustrated and expanded dominant definitions of the culturally refined woman to include African descendants. By the late 1880s, elite and upwardly mobile Black women and men protested assaults on their moral character and launched a civil rights movement to demand legal protections in education, employment, and public venues.

Dealing with racialized attacks on their femininity gradually led many African-descended women away from a model of women's political action that had set them apart from their white counterparts. Throughout much of the nineteenth century, Black women's public presence as laborers and activists drew scrutiny as elite whites determined their mobility to be a potential threat to the island's stability.[13] The reforms that characterized the post-Zanjón public sphere prompted women of African descent to realign their public roles with shifting standards of Cuban citizenship. By the 1890s, Black women would be less likely to organize outside of male-headed institutions. Increasingly, they drew on such institutions to address racial exclusion.

"An Integral Part of Society"

In 1888 the educator, musician, and writer Úrsula Coimbra de Valverde echoed Ayala's vision of racial regeneration that would define Black civic activism as slavery came to an end. Writing for the Black newspaper *La Fraternidad* under the pen name Cecilia, the Cienfuegos native declared, "In order to compete with other races more privileged than ours, we need only to develop our capabilities; then our rights will be guaranteed to rest in illustration, and we will once again show the good desires that animate us and make us an integral part of society."[14] Individuals like Coimbra promoted illustration through formal education and elite social customs. In what ways did African descendants need to develop their capabilities following abolition? And how did proving their capabilities shape the political strategies of those like Coimbra, who were freeborn and came to align themselves with recently emancipated Blacks?

The Ten Years' War (1868–1878) engendered critical shifts in how Cubans articulated citizenship. Insurgent leaders envisioned an independent nation without African enslavement. Leaders called for the establishment of a republic in which all men were equal before the law, regardless of race. Racial dynamics, however, remained strained throughout the final decades of the nineteenth century. Enslaved and free men of color joined the Liberation Army in support of the rhetoric of racial equality. Those who rose to high-ranking leadership positions experienced discrimination from white soldiers. Pro-Spanish colonial forces pointed to the large contingent of Black soldiers, who comprised 40–60 percent of the rebel forces, to invoke fears of a race war. Independence intellectuals responded by presenting favorable images of Black insurgents, with whites reinforcing a depoliticized trope of Black male docility. Tensions between racism and antiracism, as Ada Ferrer has asserted, defined Cuban nationalism from its emergence.[15]

Abolition presented Blacks with opportunities to assert control over their daily lives, yet many whites continued to exercise control over the mobility of laboring African descendants. The logic employed by the Spanish colonial government exemplified this dynamic; it established the *patronato* (apprenticeship) in 1880 to provide the remaining enslaved population with, in the words of the minister of Ultramar, "help, protection, defense— in short, guardianship" during a gradual process of emancipation.[16] At the same time, the colonial government encouraged Chinese and Spanish immigration to fill the island's labor force. Employers relied on foreign labor to undermine the rights of native workers.[17]

The paradox of granting Blacks new legal rights while undermining their ability to exercise such rights shaped the electoral sphere as well. The Spanish government permitted men to vote in parliamentary elections in 1878. But the government issued a five pesos tax requirement that excluded most men from formal participation, especially men of African descent. The Constitutional Party (also referred to as the Conservative Party) supported Spanish colonial rule and promoted the rights of white male landowners and businessmen, and the Autonomist Party embraced reforms that appealed to veterans of the Liberation Army. Yet anti-Blackness also characterized the Autonomist Party's inner workings. Some party leaders suggested that persons of African descent become "civilized" before asking for equality. They advocated Spanish immigration as a strategy to ensure national progress through whitening. Practices of discrimination led Blacks in Oriente Province to withdraw from the party by 1894.[18]

Though Úrsula Coimbra de Valverde did not use the word "civilization," she likely had the concept in mind when she called upon African descendants to follow the racial regeneration platform outlined by *La Fraternidad* editor Miguel Gualba. Her life exemplified a path toward regeneration. Born into a prominent family, she received formal training in musical arts, language, and literature, possibly at one of the few private schools that accepted children of color. Her marriage to the tailor and independence activist Nicolás Valverde y Basco sustained her honorable reputation. Coimbra, similar to Cristina Ayala, offered classes to prepare Blacks for employment beyond the agricultural and domestic sectors. She wrote articles that asserted Black women's civil rights and responsibilities. "Who can resist," she asked, "what a complete gentleman [Gualba] demands of us, invoking the *patria*, friendship, and duty?"[19] In her writings she appealed to both elite African descendants and the laboring poor. Abolition's promises of racial integration, Coimbra contended, would remain unfulfilled as long as Blacks failed to avail themselves of the opportunities around them in a modernizing society.

Coimbra's efforts to help Blacks develop their capabilities responded to evolving discussions of citizenship. During the late nineteenth century, discourses of civilization sustained a "new racial etiquette" as racial categorization in public records became less frequent.[20] Cubans gradually shifted from discussions of their identity as Spaniards to articulate a nationalist identity, and elite whites employed civilization discourses to exclude persons of African descent. To be "Cuban" meant to embrace a Spanish-Catholic identity, patriarchy, and loyalty to the colonial state.[21] From this perspective, Blacks, whom whites generally associated with immorality and African barbarity, lacked the characteristics necessary to participate in modern life.

That white political leaders employed the language of civilization to enforce racial divisions demonstrates their reluctance to abandon social hierarchies established during slavery. The white Ten Years' War veteran Manuel Sanguily suggested that persons of African descent "remain in their place" rather than push for racial equality. In his war memoir he attacks the Black newspaper *La Igualdad* for promoting the contributions of persons of African descent to the initial insurrection. Sanguily further dismisses African-descended veterans' participation by suggesting that "the origin, preparation, initiative, program and direction of the Revolution, that the Revolution in its character, essence, and aspirations, was exclusively the work of whites."[22] Staunchly opposed to miscegenation, he also applauded Black men for not attempting to sleep with white women. Sanguily concluded that Black men lacked the capacity to contribute to building an independent nation.

Elite whites contended that Blacks lacked civilized customs to justify discriminatory practices beyond formal politics. Sanguily and other men formed civic institutions that promoted civilization through balls and *tertulias* (salons).[23] Leaders of most elite white mutual aid societies, which provided employment and educational opportunities as well as health care, barred African-descended men from membership. Following abolition, elite whites continued to enforce segregation in hospitals and schools. Business owners denied Blacks access to hotels, cafes, and restaurants. Elite white men thus crafted a Cuban identity in which they assumed the role as its architects and reinforced ideas of Black inferiority through spatial division.[24]

Marginalized within a modernizing society, elite Blacks protested discriminatory acts but affirmed the principles that claimed they needed to reform themselves. Racial regeneration ideals enabled them to interpret civilization discourses to meet the particular goals of the population of African descent. Many Black activists echoed the perspectives of white elites that slavery was an impediment from which the nation needed to redeem itself. The Black loyalist and intellectual Rodolfo de Lagardére rejected the idea that all African descendants lacked the capacity to fulfill standards of citizenship.[25] He contended that elites like himself had met the standards of civilization. Black elites appointed themselves leaders who could help the broader population lift itself out of the darkness of slavery through thrift, hard work, self-help, education, and moral respectability. Similar to Black activists who claimed citizenship in post-abolition societies throughout the Americas, their motivation to gain greater access to rights and respectability fueled this contradictory process.[26]

Racial regeneration activists forged a Black public sphere that sustained their mission. Black magazines and newspapers documented elite and aspiring-class ideas of proper behavior put forth by civic and cultural associations. Editors and contributors recorded in detail baptisms, weddings, onomastic days, carnival celebrations, and religious balls, rituals that reflected Blacks' Catholic devotion.[27] They highlighted graduations and the establishment of schools as evidence of intellectual advancement. African descendants detailed their accomplishments and aspirations not only for each other but also for elite whites. From this perspective, poetry and editorials demonstrated how African descendants promoted intellectual development as a physical undertaking.

Racial regeneration activists used the public sphere to enact a patriarchal vision of citizenship that established complementary duties for men and women.[28] Men held most formal positions within Black associations and as publication editors. They called for the formation of married households in which women dedicated themselves to child-rearing. Women's ability to maintain an image of sexual purity reflected on the honor of their families.[29] In this sense, racial regeneration advocates upheld the standards of feminine domesticity promoted by elite whites. Press contributors frequently heralded women whose civic participation buttressed their racial regeneration goals in practice. They insisted that African-descended women's adherence to such standards reflected on the broader population. Black civic activists criticized African descendants who refused to conform to these standards by remaining unmarried.

Though few women held few formal leadership roles in elite associations, they played a critical role in building a Black public sphere as press contributors. By the close of the 1880s, the poet Lucrecia González Consuegra of Sancti Spíritus had contributed to at least three Black newspapers; she cofounded *La Armonía* (1882–1887) with Juan Rafael Valdés and wrote for *La Aurora* (1887) and *La Antorcha* of Trinidad (1887–1889), a weekly political newspaper "for the defense of the emancipated." González Consuegra was among the most prolific women to write for the Black press during the period.

Most publications served as organs for Black associations. Termed *sociedades de instrucción y recreo* (instruction and recreational societies), or *sociedades de socorros mutuos* (mutual aid organizations), Black associations that emerged after the mid-1870s often sought the full inclusion of African descendants into dominant educational and political institutions. *La Fraternidad* advertised the headquarters of almost twenty civic organizations in Havana alone.[30] Among them, the *mulato* patriot and intellectual Juan Gualberto Gómez established the organization La Fraternidad.[31] Black associations such as La Fraternidad erected buildings, established schools and libraries, provided mortgage and business loans, threw sporting events and elegant balls, and hosted public lectures.

In 1887 Gómez formed the Directorio Central de Sociedades de Color (Central Directory of Colored Societies) to unify Black associations on behalf of racial equality.[32] Association members, committed to "the moral and material well-being of the colored race," launched an island-wide campaign for civil rights.[33] Association members created an organized front in response to anti-Black racism and made use of the courts and the press. City residents emphasized their constitutional rights as they filed discrimination lawsuits against cafes; they litigated for first-class travel seating and the honorific titles of "Don" and "Doña." Colonial officials often ruled in their favor and declared discriminatory acts illegal. These activities had limited success but reflect an evolving political consciousness among freeborn and recently emancipated African descendants who increasingly asserted their identity as a unified *raza de color* or *clase de color*.

Formulating a unified racial identity did not unfold without complications, however. Intraracial tensions emerged during discussions about proper public behavior. Racial regeneration advocates, conscious of how whites used the trope of African barbarity to marginalize them, rejected African cultural practices in order to receive recognition as citizens. Black intellectuals took to the press to complain about those who performed African dances during carnival celebrations.[34] They disparaged members of the *cabildos de nación*

(African ethnic associations) and *socorros mutuos* who promoted African ethnic identities. Many elite Blacks supported government attempts to limit the activities of such groups on the grounds that changing the nature of *cabildos* would help modernize the island.[35] By 1888, mutual aid societies replaced *cabildos* as the standard association model, at least in structure. Although *cabildo* leaders changed the names of their organizations to reflect Catholic saints, many groups no doubt continued their practices under the guise of civilization while maintaining African traditions. Indeed, as David Brown notes, African cultural communities *expanded* during the late colonial period, suggesting that many Black men and women rejected racial regeneration or at least formulated their own visions of it.[36]

With the establishment of a racial regeneration platform came self-appointed leaders of the Black population who, moving between labor, associations, and electoral politics, promoted a unified vision of the race that fit emergent models of civilization. Their vision was unevenly embraced, as Blacks among the laboring poor and those who valued African-based traditions often employed alternative social practices.[37] Racial regeneration activists presented Blackness as an organizing political identity for pursuing racial integration. They articulated their socioeconomic aspirations within the framework of morality. As they claimed rights and promoted self-uplift, they presented a gendered vision of racial citizenship that had yet to be realized. Pact of Zanjón reforms thus allowed for the expansion of a Black public sphere through which African-descended women might respond to broader sociopolitical transformations in ways that reflected their particular experiences.

Gender, Civilization, and Black Women's Labor

The discourses of civilization that shaped debates over the place of African descendants in public life informed ideas of Cuban womanhood as well. During the nineteenth century, elite whites promoted feminine domesticity within the framework of civilization. Expectations of civilized feminine behavior entailed maintaining sexual virtue, becoming good wives, and dedicating themselves to raising children. These ideals had been imposed through Spanish colonial legal codes and customs; men possessed ultimate authority of the family, and a woman's respectability or lack of it reflected on the honor of the patriarchs. Elite norms required that decent women protect their honor by remaining shut in the home. Barred windows created a physical barrier that held women at bay from the dangers of the public realm. A servant or male escort accompanied elite women who left the home, and affluent women rode in carriages to avoid touching the filth of the streets.[38]

By the late nineteenth century, a younger generation of privileged white women began to renegotiate the gendered terms of civilization as they staked claims to public space. Many held new expectations of civic engagement after their participation in the initial independence wars.[39] Shifting market forces also brought Cubans into greater contact with consumer goods and sociopolitical ideas from abroad. The historian Louis A. Pérez has noted that economic transformations paralleled the "emergence of a middle-class *criolla.*"[40] Middle-class *criollas* (women of Spanish descent born in Cuba) blurred public/private distinctions as they embraced writing, contemporary fashion trends, public social events, and formal schooling in greater numbers. Pérez asserts that women who embraced such practices disrupted established moral codes that underpinned colonial social hierarchies.[41]

Elite white standards of civilized feminine behavior stood in stark contrast to the experiences of most women of African descent.[42] Freeborn and emancipated Black women were more likely to work than their white counterparts were. They toiled in fields, factories, marketplaces, and the homes of the privileged classes.[43] Work allowed women of African descent a degree of economic autonomy and mobility unavailable to most elite and middle-class white women. That Black women violated dominant gender norms when they passed through the street often made them the target of elite white anxieties regarding racial mixing.[44]

Laboring women of African descent forged a tradition of claiming public space that continued to evolve following slave abolition. Their participation in civic life predated many of the cultural practices employed by privileged white women who challenged gender norms during the late nineteenth century. African and African-descended women took on leadership positions in *cabildos* throughout the nineteenth century. They acted as *cabildo* "queens" in public processionals and preserved religious knowledge as Lucumí priestesses.[45] Many Black women who lived in the countryside attended masquerade balls on sugar plantations.[46] *Cabildo* activities paralleled those of women of African descent who embraced elite white standards of civilized femininity such as salons and theater performances.

Laboring Black women who contributed to the post-Zanjón public sphere formulated models of womanhood that reflected their particular socioeconomic circumstances. Individuals like the thespian and journalist Catalina Medina (pen names K Lanita and Catana) hailed from elite backgrounds. Medina was the daughter of Antonio Medina y Céspedes, the founder of the Colegio de Nuestra Señora de los Desamparados school for poor children and the first man of color to direct a Cuban newspaper, *El Faro*, in 1842.[47] Elite family ties also benefited the career of Úrsula Coimbra de Valverde. She belonged to an established population of free people of color in Cienfuegos whose men and women labored as successful artisans, business owners, and professionals.[48] Many elite Black women did not work, but Coimbra advertised her services as a teacher of piano, English, and French. Her status as the child of a Black mother and white father who supported his domestic partner and children afforded her access to educational opportunities that solidified her social status.[49] Both Coimbra and Medina chose to help build institutions that provided African descendants with alternatives to the schools and associations that excluded them on the basis of race.[50]

Racial regeneration advocates validated the respectability of women like Coimbra who were excluded by the dominant standards of civilization. Colonial elites limited honor to the children of married couples recognized by the Catholic Church. This code excluded most Cubans. It especially marginalized Black children of enslaved parents or those born into domestic unions between a white father and an African-descended mother.[51] Like Coimbra, the *mulata* Angela Rodríguez de Edreira was the child of a Black mother and white father who were not married. She carried the last name of her white father. Rodríguez de Edreira married a well-respected freeborn tailor, Nicolás Edreira, who was also *mulato*.[52] Although white elites disparaged the social backgrounds of such individuals, privileged African descendants born into domestic unions responded by forming married households and promoting matrimony. Elite Black social events and publications publicly affirmed nuclear families.

Freeborn women of African descent from elite backgrounds also collaborated with formerly enslaved women who fulfilled the principles of civilization. A commitment to racial regeneration through education underpinned their alliances. Angela Storini was enslaved by a "cultured and kind" family who brought her on their travels to the United States, France, Germany, and Italy during the Ten Years' War.[53] These early experiences enabled her to develop as a writer. Other *libertas* (women who obtained freedom from slavery) included Cristina Ayala, who was self-educated. Ayala began to write poetry at the age of seven. She carried out a prolific writing career from 1885 to 1920.[54] Storini and Ayala engaged in literary activism at a time when only 12.3 percent of the population of African descent was literate.[55] Their education qualified them for employment opportunities unavailable to most Black Cubans. Formerly enslaved women like Storini and Ayala thus held elite social positions in comparison to the broader Black population.

Despite the growth of an elite class of African-descended women after abolition, most Black women who worked continued to do so in low-paying positions as domestic servants, laundresses, fieldworkers, and market vendors. Often, agricultural workers remained on the land that they had worked during slavery, and some women migrated between urban centers and rural lands as seasonal laborers.[56] Still others entered the émigré communities of southern Florida and New York City, where they labored as midwives and tobacco stemmers.[57] African descendants remained underrepresented in more prestigious positions like teaching and cigar work that required recommendations.[58]

Many laboring Black women achieved financial success that enabled the mobility of their family members. Women of African descent became a sizable proportion of the landholding class from 1878 into the 1890s.[59] They, along with their domestic partners, built homes and used part of the lands for subsistence farming or growing crops to sell. Landownership led to the formation of *barrios negros* in urban and rural areas. Women were legally required to use male notaries, but they held titles and property rights and passed their lands on to their children through their wills. Black female landholders lent money to family and community members to purchase property.[60] Female business owners also contributed to the economic advancement of African descendants. Notably, Cecilia and Virginia Larrinaga moved to Havana sometime during the late nineteenth century. The *mulata* sisters, likely from Oriente Province, established a hat and dress shop on Calle San Rafael in central Havana. They rented an apartment above the store. The sisters financed their nephew's education in France.[61]

Whether freeborn or *libertas*, laboring women of African descent developed a tradition of public engagement that challenged elite white notions of civilized feminine behavior. Their work led them into the streets and beyond the domestic realm to which proper women were assigned. They supported organizations and engaged in cultural practices that colonial elites deemed indecent. At the same time, many Black women became educators to advance racial regeneration goals. Female business owners and landholders invested their earnings in institutions that served the aspirations of African descendants. Women who formed associations and had their writings published also occasionally took on roles in Black civic life apart from the leadership of prominent men. Their Black public-sphere activities elucidate how elite women in particular adapted dominant ideas of civilization to reflect their lived experiences.

The "Spirit of Fraternity"

The experiences of working women of African descent led them to formulate an alternative vision of what civilized, honorable women might accomplish in the public realm. The historian Joan Casanovas has observed that Black Cuban women were more likely to migrate to urban areas than their male counterparts were and more likely to participate in late nineteenth-century civic life than their white counterparts were. She attributes their civic engagement in part to *cabildos*. Women of African descent who migrated to the city for work often joined the ranks of *cabildos*.[62] By the late 1870s, women's *cabildos* faced increased scrutiny during the colonial government's campaign to modernize the island. African-descended women who aimed to present themselves as respectable feminine subjects continued to organize independent organizations. However, they did so increasingly within mutual aid associations and *sociedades de instrucción y recreo* rather than *cabildos*.

After the Pact of Zanjón granted new freedoms of association, African-descended women of central Cuba began to form independent groups that adhered to dominant standards of organizational life. In 1879, the free *pardas* (*mulatas*) Ramona Lombillo and Flora Borrell de Águila founded the Cienfuegos mutual aid society La Caridad (Charity).[63] The organization promoted "the spirit of fraternity" and provided "moral assistance" to its members. Associates contributed ten centavos weekly for dues; members gained access to medical services and funeral expenses. In Sagua La Grande, Adelaida Ponce de León established La Concordia in 1880 to mobilize Black women on behalf of collective moral reform. Ponce de León asserted women's duty: "My sisters, particularly mothers, prepare your children for the present. You must not abandon them even for a moment on the path that we propose and that will lead to glorious moments of happiness."[64] The organizational activities of La Concordia members reinforced women's domestic duties as caretakers dedicated to collective uplift.

The spirit of fraternity guided a broad agenda for moral and intellectual uplift among members of Hijas de Progreso (Daughters of Progress). A group of "distinguished women" from Trinidad and Cienfuegos founded the instruction and recreation society in 1884.[65] Its members included the African-descended educators Ana Joaquina Sosa y González, Quintana Valle de Vega, Juana Bautista Zerquera, Trinidad Domenech, Edelmira Sosa, Mercedes Garavito, and Mercedes Borrell. The women raised and contributed money for schools in the region. Sosa edited and Valle administered the group's biweekly newsletter, La Familia, the first Cuban newspaper published by women of any race. Initially, newsletter contributors focused on literary and religious issues in poetry and social announcements. They later broadened their platform to discussions regarding education and families. In one issue, La Familia issued a call for the establishment of a benevolent society in Cienfuegos.[66] Hijas de Progreso members utilized such actions to stake claims in regional debates over educational access, especially for youths of African descent.

Hijas de Progreso formed connections between its membership and the broader public sphere through the publication of La Familia. Editors collaborated with elite African-descended men including the poet and educator Antonio Medina y Céspedes and Juan Gualberto Gómez. They exchanged articles with Black newspapers across the island such as El Profesorado de Cuba, El Crisol, and La Amistad of Cienfuegos, El Ejemplo of Sancti Spíritus, and La Aurora of Bayamo.[67] Such collaborations in turn enhanced the public profile of Hijas de Progreso members who sought to demonstrate their feminine virtue as learned women committed to the advancement of Cuban society. Their engagement with men like Gómez, who supported the Liberal Party, buttressed the authority of African-descended men within the political system.

For reasons unknown, Sosa later severed ties with Hijas de Progreso.

Subsequently, she founded the Hijas de Progreso school to educate girls of African descent. The institution offered a range of courses: reading, literature, religion, Spanish and Cuban geography, mathematics, sewing, embroidery, needlework, stenciling, and more. The school, similar to others run by Black associations, aimed to balance students' socialization according to elite culture with the practical skills training necessary to earn a living.[68] It filled a necessary void as many African-descended families struggled to achieve racial integration within Cienfuegos schools.[69]

Black women's associational activities evolved throughout the nineteenth century as they responded to post-Zanjón expectations for civic engagement. Their organizations departed from elite white standards of public engagement that encouraged women to remain in the home. By establishing schools, organizations, and publications, women across the island joined elite Black men in carrying out racial regeneration initiatives. Elite women of African descent used literary venues to articulate a more expansive vision of women's public roles from a Black female standpoint.

To "Bring Their Effort into the Public Eye"

Elite and upwardly mobile women forged a collective identity as respectable figures through the Black public sphere. Emphasizing their experiences with racial and sexual oppression in post-abolition Cuba, they identified a range of obstacles women and African descendants confronted as they pursued personal autonomy. While progressive in their understanding of women's roles in civic life, they often reinforced conservative sexual mores that separated them from poor African descendants.

A noteworthy example of this dynamic is the Havana publication *Minerva: Revista Universal Dedicada a la Mujer de Color* (Minerva: Universal biweekly magazine dedicated to the woman of color, which was published from 1888 to 1890). *Minerva* was the first publication devoted to women of African descent. Edited by the Black intellectual Enrique Cos, the magazine featured contributions from men and women living throughout the island. Writers included Cristina Ayala, Úrsula Coimbra de Valverde, Natividad G. González, América Font, and Etelvina Zayas (pen name E. T. Elvira). The magazine was touted in its inaugural issue as "a vehicle through which our sisters who have studied literature can develop a literary vocation, bring their effort into the public eye, and thus encourage women to pursue further studies."[70] *Minerva* circulated within Cuba and in the émigré communities of Florida, New York City, and Jamaica.[71]

Minerva's female contributors collaborated with prominent men but also asserted the capabilities of Black women in a post-abolition society.[72] Contributors disputed assumptions of women's intellectual inferiority when they insisted that women had the capacity to participate in public life. One issue reprinted a Peruvian man's feminist article in which he asserts, "Women are born with the right to work, like men, in all social spheres." The writer insisted that proper work reinforced an "active life of virtue."[73] Yet pursuing such work required that women claim their right to become educated. *Minerva* writer Laura Clarens cited the Cuban-Spanish writer Gertrudis Gómez de Avellaneda and Cuban author Condesa de Merlin as pillars of intellectual attainment who confronted gender discrimination. "The woman, in this fight," Clarens insisted, "has for her part the reason, justice of her cause, and trust in her work with new forces . . . , and will achieve the end that has been proposed."[74] Clarens put forth a cosmopolitan vision of womanhood that connected the discrimination faced by elite white women to the experiences of Black Cubans. Most African descendants, Clarens lamented, feared pursuing an education due to the "blood codes," which until 1878 denied them an education beyond primary schooling. She implored Blacks to move beyond their fears and to look for educational opportunities.[75]

Clarens's call for education underscored the history of African enslavement that shaped Black women's collective identity after abolition. A woman writing under the pen name África Céspedes, perhaps to mark herself as the African counterpart of the independence leader Carlos Manuel de Céspedes, may have agreed with her. África Céspedes celebrated that Blacks' "inalienable rights that for so long had been usurped have been restored to civil status," a change that allowed them to be recognized "as an integral part of the human family." She asserted, "Some compensation had to reach the Black family for the heroic sacrifice of the generous blood spilled by so many martyrs, in the holocaust of the homeland in the epic ten-year [war]."[76] Céspedes viewed abolition as a right earned by the men and women of African descent who fought for their freedom during the independence movement and contributed to the nationalist cause. Céspedes concluded that Cuba would be "blessed for eternity" now that its children who once "groaned in the cruelest servitude" would be in constant study to benefit "the family, society, and homeland."[77]

Writings by *Minerva* contributors fostered a political consciousness among elite Black women at a moment when many still crossed paths with their former enslavers. No doubt they recalled how slavery deprived African-descended women of autonomy over their bodies. The elite Black women's literary activism challenged racism and sexism that characterized Blacks (and) women as inherently inferior. For elite women of African descent, the very act of writing illustrated their moral virtue and intellectual advancement in a society that remained hostile to their existence.

Asserting bodily autonomy in a post-abolition society came with stipulations. E. T. Elvira documented the events of Black organizations in her social column, "Notas Quincenales" (Biweekly notes). She wrote about conferences, baseball games, classes for boys and girls, and local dances that women would have attended.[78] Most events offered respectable social spaces for African descendants committed to racial regeneration. Yet on one occasion, Elvira used column space to scold some Black socialites for placing too much emphasis on dances. She lamented that many parents prioritized dances over formal schooling. One female pupil missed more than twenty classes because, her parents explained, "the girl lacked a clean or new *tuniquito*." Yet the same girl "is on time for [dance] rehearsals every night and her parents have been fully enabling her so she could attend the dance." Such "moral and physical decadence," Elvira surmised, would prove "disastrous" for the present generation.[79]

Minerva provided a vague sense of the activities of its contributors and readers within the broader Black public sphere. Elvira did not note if women contributed to social events as organizers, though she cited women's roles as teachers of the classes offered by Black organizations. By the 1890s, social columns published in *La Igualdad* and *La Fraternidad* suggest that women began to formalize their roles in male-headed associations when they established formal *comités de honor*. These committees, consisting solely of women, elected leaders and raised dues among the general membership. Members organized concerts, dances, and conferences for associations. In this sense, women consolidated their public roles under the umbrella of male-headed institutions. This shift suggests how persons of African descent became more conservative in their organizations, at least in their formal leadership structures.

"A Race That Has Been Plunged into Degradation"

During the late nineteenth century, the government relaxed its ban on interracial marriage among the upper classes as slavery came to an end in Cuba.[80] Subsequently, many white intellectuals aimed to reform the "sexual economy of race" through the family.[81] They hoped that interracial relationships would lead to the whitening of the general population as the Black population disappeared. Intellectuals of African descent expressed fears that this outcome would lead to the extinction of the Black population. Further, they suggested that most Black women who entered into interracial relationships were sex workers and concubines who lacked moral virtue. They lamented that too few of these women married their white partners, and they admonished African-descended women who formed domestic partnerships with white men.[82]

Debates over miscegenation reveal intersections between the Black and elite white public spheres. To some extent, Blacks' preoccupation with interracial unions responded to tropes of the *mulata* that pervaded Cuban popular culture. In 1882, the publication of Cirilo Villaverde's satirical novel *Cecilia Valdés o la loma del ángel: Novela de costumbres cubanas*, a first version of which was published in 1839, called attention to the forms of gender and racial violence that characterized the slave society; in it he criticizes the material superficiality of elite white Creoles. Literary scholars credit the narrative with initiating a series of short stories, novels, and plays centered on the trope of the *mulata*, the daughter of a Black mother and a wealthy white father, whose exotic beauty and aspirations toward whiteness prompted her to climb the social ladder. The *teatro bufo* (Cuban popular theater) playwright José María Quintana reproduced this narrative in *La mulata de rango* (The ranking *mulata*). The Basque artist Victor Patricio Landaluze depicted racial miscegenation in his lithographs and paintings, many of which circulated in popular magazines.[83] In most cases, the *mulata* represented a "symbolic container" whose sexual appeal threatened the boundaries of racial purity necessary to maintain white patriarchal power in a slave society.[84] She appeared as a deceitful character. The stain of her Black racial heritage, despite her attempts to integrate into white society, consistently undermined her success.

Some white intellectuals viewed miscegenation as a path toward civilization; others used pseudoscience to reinforce racial divisions. In 1888, the medical doctor Benjamin de Céspedes published his study *La prostitución en la Ciudad de la Habana* (Prostitution in the city of Havana), in which he employed pseudoscientific methods to reinforce assumptions of Black women's sexual inferiority. Céspedes used prostitution to diagnose larger social and moral diseases that afflicted Cuba as an emergent nation.[85] A supporter of the independence movement, Céspedes faulted Cuba's colonial history for its degradation. He argued,

> The Cuban nation, despite its glorious political and social revolution; despite the energy, honor, and illustriousness of its principal leaders; is today as yesterday and always: the great sewer of Spain, where all classes of dissolute peoples disembark, like a dumping and breeding ground for toxic fish. Cuba remains, as before, a depository of Blackness that dishonors us, reproducing the same savage customs of those countries in this ruinous factory that floats in the confines of the Atlantic, like a broken-down ship that runs aground and sinks further and further, weighed down by its historic iniquities.

Thus, as pro-independence Cubans actively imagined a sovereign republic, and as persons of African descent assumed roles in the development of the nation as anticolonial and racial progress activists, Céspedes placed them outside the bounds of moral respectability. He constructed the ideal patriot as male, honorable, and Cuban-born. Blacks dishonored the nation by their association with Africa and were thus unworthy of full citizenship. Céspedes also asserted that Black women prostitutes represented the "unnatural" crossing of public and private boundaries and the breakdown of gender norms. He labeled the *mulata* in particular as the product of a contagion of Cuba's social crisis. He characterized African-descended women as a social virus that undermined the metaphorical health of the nation.[86]

Céspedes's study became a popular sensation; copies of it filled the shelves of bookstores and newsstands throughout the island. As if the work had not done enough to disparage the colored race, the defenses of Céspedes by mainstream newspapers like *El Progreso* demonstrated the refusal of many whites to stand against anti-Black racism. Céspedes amplified Blacks' frustrations when he submitted a letter to newspapers in which he claimed to be considered "a friend of Blacks." One man of African descent submitted a letter to *Minerva* asserting that Black women should avoid reading Céspedes's study. *La Fraternidad* launched a campaign against it and its supporters throughout 1888. The writers criticized his intention to "aggregate the entire race."[87] The Spanish loyalist, intellectual, and *sociedad* leader Rodolfo Lagardére asserted in his 1889 text *Blancos y negros: Refutación al libro "La prostitutión,"* "There is no superior or inferior race, only a race that has been held back, a race that has been plunged into degradation, and steeped in servility."[88]

África Céspedes's angry defense of Black womanhood appeared in *Minerva*: "Cruelly treated by her vile exploiters, the Black woman has been targeted more prominently where the white man more saliently directs his poison arrows, by the very same people who trafficked with her noble blood during the tragic days of slavery." Céspedes pointed out that although slavery had ended, former enslavers remained in power and dictated the living conditions of African descendants in the present. She refused to tolerate their attempts to leave African-descended women in the era of slavery. Céspedes declared that Black women were prepared to defend their full worth: "You invite us to fight? Well then we will fight." She asserted that Black women's value as mothers was equal to that of white women. "Woman only asks for justice," she proclaimed, "but justice in every latitude of the word." She asserted that individuals like Benjamin de Céspedes would not hinder women's ability to "enter into a period of real moral progress."[89]

If whites were responsible for maintaining Blacks' degradation in the past, African descendants held responsibility for the future of the race. A *Minerva* contributor known only by the pen name ORP determined, "If the colored race wishes to cordially dignify itself and hold public office . . . , [it should] begin to form the family within the dictated precepts by morality and required by the law."[90] ORP asserted that enslaved women who entered into sexual relationships with their white enslavers, whether willingly or by force, had lived in a state of "degradation." She argued that, given this history of sexual subjugation, marriage represented an act of "self-respect" and "self-love" that brought the "love and esteem of the other individuals of one's own race." Matrimony served as the only way a woman could conserve "a clean name that one can pass on to her children." Moreover, children should form the moral families that their mothers had been denied.[91]

Calls for matrimony appear to have had limited influence on the broader community of African descent. Statistics suggest that the majority of the population focused little on forming married households. Blacks were more likely to live in domestic unions and in census reports identified as single. Almost half of all children of African descent were born to unmarried parents and thus considered by many elites to be "illegitimate," in comparison to 12 percent of white children. Children of these unions lacked access not only to virtue but also to the names of patriarchs and legal rights such as the right to inherit property.[92] Formal marriages between whites and African descendants remained rare, especially those between white women and Black men. Meanwhile, white men and African-descended women formed domestic partnerships that some Black women viewed as a favorable option for the advancement of themselves and their children. Non-elite Blacks' low marriage rates suggest at least two possibilities: that poor families of African descent could not afford the ceremonial fees or that they forged popular-class notions of respectability that affirmed concubinage or serial monogamy. The decision to forgo standards of civilization suggests poor Blacks' rejection of Catholic marriage as the only way to maintain respectability.[93]

Certainly, elite persons of African descent recognized that many in the Black population entered consensual unions without the formality of marriage. Some writers lamented the lack of married households as a carryover from slavery. One wrote that slavery had "hardly produced wives, but instead concubines."[94] Others addressed the moral progress of the race. A writer in *La Fraternidad* wrote in 1889, "The numerous marriages that have been verified some time ago among people of color evidently prove the moralizing tendency of this much-maligned race."[95] Discussions regarding the formation of married households illuminated the chasm between elite and upwardly mobile African descendants and the laboring poor. Elites attempted to close this gap by policing the sexuality of young men and women, setting an example for the broader community and defending the virtue of those who adhered to codes of respectability.

"The True Helpmate of the Civilized Man"

"One of the things that today we lack," the *Minerva* contributor V. Kop y Torres explained in 1889, "is women's [education], because they are called to contribute the great part of the moral perfection of our families."[96] Kop y Torres linked education to the modernization of the domestic sphere. Her emphasis on moral reform mirrored perspectives articulated in the national Cuban press. Indeed, she argued that the state of female education constituted Cuba's greatest impediments to modernization, an impediment at the intersection of patriarchy and anti-Black racism that undermined Black women's advancement.

Racial regeneration advocates routinely emphasized women's illustration as a strategy for proving their fitness for citizenship. Carlota T. of Santiago de Cuba instructed her "sisters of the race" to "look to the *mirada* culture with little regard for women's instruction, today, with a pat on the forehead, recognize man's selfish egoism and see that the true helpmate of the civilized man is the educated woman."[97] On one level, being "illustrated," refined, signified that an individual had obtained the formal training necessary to obtain skilled employment. On another level, elite persons of African descent called for poor Blacks to learn proper social etiquette that fell in line with bourgeois values. From this perspective, illustrated individuals engaged in practices like playing musical instruments, wearing contemporary fashions, writing poetry, and learning the *danzón*.

Elite and upwardly mobile Blacks' emphasis on racial regeneration through schooling reflected shifting ideas of women's education in Cuba. Most elite Cubans determined that women's education should focus on their domestic training as moral gatekeepers of the home. By the 1880s, many asserted that formal schooling should prepare women to maintain their own and their families' financial stability. During a lecture in Key West, Florida, of the society El Progreso, the *mulato* intellectual Martín Morúa Delgado emphasized the connections between women's education, social progress, and economic survival. He affirmed women's domestic role as man's "complement" but said they should continue to grow throughout their lives in order to best benefit society. Furthermore, he said, education helped protect "the vast number of women who had no one to depend upon" and had individuals "who depended upon them."[98] Morúa posited that an education should not train women to work in the tobacco factories, where their wages were inferior to those earned by men, or in linen shops or cafes. Rather, education should be an ongoing process, in a girl's socialization as a child by her parents, a young adult's preparation for college, and a woman's instruction for her chosen career. *Minerva* and other Black newspapers printed his speech as a series, thus circulating gendered ideas about labor, illustration, and regeneration.[99]

María Storni recognized the material benefits of an education for formerly enslaved women like herself. She saw herself as a successful example of learning. She had attained an education while living in Havana and pleaded with women to embrace schooling as a strategy for personal advancement. Storni was well aware of the challenges women would confront in pursuing these goals. Even those who had the privilege of studying rather than working long, laborious hours encountered racial and gender discrimination. Persons of African descent often found themselves turned away from religious schools that provided most of Cuba's educational opportunities. Storni observed, "It is well known how neglected [women's education] is, if indeed the woman of our race has ever received the attention she deserves. . . . [F]or many people educating females is a question of ornamentation, and thus not entirely essential."[100] She remained steadfast in her belief that women needed to "exist for more than the pleasure of dances," and she asked that an association be founded in Cuba for the instruction of Black women.[101] Certainly, balls provided important opportunities for being socialized according to elite expectations. Yet emphasizing dance detracted from women's intellectual development.

Other Black newspapers documented the establishment of institutions by African-descended women to fill gaps in educational access. In 1888, the recent graduate Mercedes Cova established a school for girls in Havana.[102] Six years later, the *directorio* announced its members' intentions to establish a boarding school for girls from the provinces to study in Havana.[103] Many of these institutions remained in a precarious position for financial reasons. In Cienfuegos, the director of the Colegio Santa Ana approached the town council to request a monthly fund of seventeen pesos to cover a teacher's salary for training fifty poor girls of African descent. The council denied her request.[104] When Black children gained access to public schools, many confronted discrimination within the classroom. The Black newspaper *El Hijo del Pueblo* reported that a Sancti Spíritus school director allowed teachers to discriminate against "girls of the Black race"; the writer asked authorities to "impose any sanction on said teacher for that attitude."[105]

In March 1892, the *directorio* published a call for all *sociedades* to meet in July in Havana. Attendees from sixty-five organizations met and reflected on the state of education in their respective areas. Residents of Santiago de Cuba said that the city's schools admitted children of African descent. Members from other cities complained that their local governments had failed to establish schools for Black children, thus hindering racial advancement opportunities. This occurred, in part, because of the cost to build schools for Black boys and girls. At the same time, the municipalities restricted Black children's admission to existing schools, creating a caste system that undermined social harmony. The *directorio* launched a campaign for the integration of all public schools. Its campaign reinforced the work of Black women who approached city councils for government funding for their schools. When *directorio* leaders turned to the courts to challenge segregation on constitutional grounds, the government ruled in their favor and established a small fine for municipalities that failed to admit Blacks to their public schools. However, these limited provisions did little to integrate the public education system.[106]

The campaign for racial equality in education tested the state's commitment to enforcing the rights of its most marginalized populations. Ultimately, the failure of the colonial government to ensure Black civil rights buttressed Black activists' commitment to independence. Notably, men headed the campaign for educational access. Women may have been teachers and students, and many women submitted petitions for the state to intervene, but men spoke on behalf of Black associations. Men wrote most of the articles addressing discriminatory incidents. This dynamic reinforced the patriarchal leadership of African-descended men while further marginalizing Black women within the public realm.

• • •

The racial dynamics that shaped the post-Zanjón public sphere presented a paradox for African-descended women who pursued social integration. Elite and upwardly mobile Black women took advantage of the late colonial reforms that opened new opportunities for their self-expression. They affirmed the dominant model of civilization as they asserted their morality and intellectual capabilities in the pages of the Black press. Women carried out their responsibilities to uplift the broader population of African descent through associations. Their public activities figured prominently in the formation of a Black public sphere. Yet, in asserting their ability to adhere to dominant, Eurocentric standards of womanhood, women who embraced racial regeneration sustained the very tenets of anti-Blackness used to marginalize them in their endeavors.

The women who entered into the Black public sphere troubled dominant constructions of Cuban identity as they claimed honor. Their ideas about women's public roles grew from personal desires to reconcile the tensions between racism and antiracism. Women helped build a vibrant public sphere through newspapers and magazines, associational life, and civil rights campaigns that forged pathways for racial integration. Their activities occurred largely independent of white women's social and political spaces, though they often promoted similar ideas of patriarchal gender roles. At the same time, an analysis of African-descended women's public activities during the late colonial period demonstrates how whites and Blacks formulated different expectations of women's public behavior.

During the US Occupation of 1898–1902, US officials sought to Americanize the island under the guise of progress and modernity. They suggested that all Cubans were unfit for self-rule because of their racial heritage.[107] Racial regeneration activists continued to reinterpret these same discourses to affirm their merits for citizenship. Elite and upwardly mobile women of African descent navigated the national and Black public spheres in support of dominant agendas to civilize the emergent nation. They drew upon a tradition of political activism established during the post-abolition period, and their engagement with racial politics would continue to evolve following the establishment of the republic.

2

Writing Black Political Networks during the Early Republic

Following the establishment of the republic, hundreds of literate and semi-literate African-descended women penned letters to Black male politicians. Most requested access to pensions as the family members of veterans who served in the wars for independence; others sought aid in challenging racial discrimination. Their letters addressed exclusion from educational and professional opportunities, the limits of nationalist discourses that proclaimed racial equality, assumptions that African descendants lacked civil virtue, and the failure of the government to support Black veterans. They used letter writing, in other words, to shape an evolving political system in which they lacked formal power.

A close reading of Black women's letters reveals how their approaches evolved throughout the early republican period. During the initial years of the twentieth century, most women of African descent who wrote letters to politicians sought the material resources to which they felt entitled as citizens. By 1908, they increasingly critiqued inequities within Cuba's political system. That year, a group of Black veterans broke from mainstream political parties when they formed the Partido Independiente de Color (PIC, Independent Colored Party). Leaders asserted that the established parties had failed African descendants; they demanded institutional reforms on behalf of Black citizens. A broad segment of the population of African descent championed the PIC's cause. Yet Black and white politicians from the Liberal and Conservative Parties called for its end on the grounds that it undermined racial unity. Among them, the Black activist Juan Gualberto Gómez advocated for men of African descent to penetrate existing political institutions.[1] He leveraged his influence over the Black electorate to advocate for their access to resources. Letters published in the PIC newspaper, *Previsión*, as well as those submitted privately to Gómez demonstrate Black women's endeavors to achieve racial equality within this context.

Transformations in Cuba's political system compelled Black women of diverse backgrounds to stake citizenship claims through letters in particular. The Platt Amendment formally ended the US Occupation in 1902 but allowed for future interventions to protect US economic interests in Cuba.[2] The 1901 Constitution granted suffrage rights to all men regardless of race. Partido Conservador Nacional (National Conservative Party) leaders and US officials, however, argued that African descendants remained incapable of meeting the supposed standards of civilization necessary for citizenship and were thus a hindrance to national progress.[3] Elite whites projected a white male citizenry that reluctantly incorporated Black men into the political sphere while marginalizing men and women of African descent socially and economically. They mocked the service of Black veterans, who confronted high rates of unemployment or found themselves relegated to menial positions while their white counterparts received high-ranking public posts. They invoked a rhetoric of racelessness, that Cuba existed as a society without racial distinctions, to imply that race no longer hindered citizens from achieving socioeconomic advancement. Racial inequities, elite whites insisted, resulted from Blacks' inability to uplift themselves following the abolition of slavery.[4]

Historians have demonstrated that discourses of racelessness limited the extent to which US government officials and white elites could exclude men of African descent from political life.[5] Universal male suffrage ensured African-descended men's importance in upholding political networks; Black men became an important voting bloc, ran for office, and supported candidates of major parties.[6] In turn, they leveraged their influence for access to state resources and employment.

African-descended women who were concerned by instances of racial exclusion thus confronted a challenge: Black male politicians were best positioned to address their individual and collective concerns, yet publicly contesting their daily experiences of racial discrimination might lead to accusations of undermining national unity. Letters elucidate the creative strategies Black women from diverse class backgrounds adopted in a political climate of racial silence. Elite Black women ceased to publicly protest racist incidents and instead addressed racial discrimination though private exchanges. Unlike Black men, the women rarely wrote for publications or held political forums, choosing instead to present themselves as nonthreatening public figures. Women of the PIC, on the other hand, openly endorsed the party's vision of racial justice. These women wrote as members of a largely working-class community and characterized race-based organizing as patriotic.

The political approach of the PIC, with its predominantly working-class membership, conflicted with the interests of Black civic club leaders from more privileged backgrounds. This divergence has led many scholars to place the PIC in opposition to elite Black leaders like Gómez. However, PIC leaders and Gómez relied on patronage networks to advance their political goals as well as addressing the material concerns of their supporters. Letter writing served as a strategy that cut across ideological boundaries. Black women who penned letters, whether elite or upwardly mobile, helped sustain patronage networks that bridged the two political communities.

A gendered analysis of the discourses put forth through women's letters reveals a common, patriarchal vision of racial citizenship. Each political community embraced the patriarchal tenets of racial regeneration put forth by activists of the late nineteenth century. Many letter writers self-identified as Black women or as members of the *raza de color* (colored race); they voiced their support for racial advancement through thrift, hard work, education, patriotism, cultural refinement, and sexual virtue. They emphasized their standing as the daughters, mothers, and wives of patriotic men. These approaches reflect a strategy that would continue to evolve throughout the republican era. Indeed, PIC leaders anticipated the critiques of a future generation of Black activists who would enter the political sphere during the 1920s. They claimed state protection against racial discrimination and articulated a broad agenda for social reform. Collectively, African-descended women who wrote letters did so to navigate expanding labor and educational opportunities as Cubans forged a modern nation.

Men of Political Foresight

As Cubans called for the consolidation of political power through social unity, demands for racial silence reached their peak, shaping the context in which men of African descent practiced politics. Gómez emerged as a prominent figure in the establishment of the island's political system during the US Occupation. He and other Black activists, having participated in the thirty-year movement for national independence (1868–1898), endeavored to fully integrate African descendants into republican institutions.[7]

Gómez's approach to race-based activism reflects the tenuous nature of racial dynamics during the transition from US territory to independent nation. He rose to prominence as a leader in the struggle for civil rights among African descendants during the 1890s.[8] His anticolonial sentiments eventually placed him at odds with the established order and led to his imprisonment.[9] Gómez served as a delegate during the 1901 Constitutional Assembly. However, following accusations that his efforts to organize veterans of Oriente Province demonstrated his desire to create another Haitian Revolution, he refrained from promoting any causes that may have been specific to the experiences of Black Cubans.[10] Instead, he began to establish organizations that aimed to unify whites and persons of African descent. He cofounded the Partido Independiente (Independent Party), later renamed the Partido Republicano Independiente (Independent Republican Party), and he joined the Partido Liberal (Liberal Party) in 1905. Gómez's strategy proved successful; Cubans elected him to Congress for numerous terms throughout the 1910s and 1920s.[11]

Women of African descent appealed to Gómez as an arbiter of state power. The Fondo Adquisiciones at the Archivo Nacional de Cuba holds thousands of letters submitted from citizens across the island to Gómez throughout most of his political career. The letters offer insights into his work on behalf of racial equality beyond the public view. The Cuban historian Oilda Hevia Lanier contends that Gómez intentionally focused on providing individual assistance to persons of African descent. This approach allowed him to circumvent race-based organizing. It also, as Hevia Lanier explains, enabled him to attend to "the regional differences that conditioned the ways in which Blacks and *mulatos* were treated."[12] In this sense, Gómez might be considered a caudillo, as he sustained a following of loyal supporters by providing Blacks with access to schools, employment, and pensions.[13] Gómez remained a well-known figure within Black civic circles; he attended society functions, serving as the *padrino* (godfather) of younger members, and wrote articles for the Black press.

Beyond seeking vital resources, women of African descent who wrote Gómez venerated him as a model of patriarchal authority. Most addressed him as a politician. Some women wrote Gómez to offer condolences to his family following the death of his wife, to send words of kindness, or to foster relations that might benefit them. Numerous letter writers recognized his commitment to the advancement of *la raza de color*.[14] Most women who wrote Gómez chose not to include any reference to race. Certainly, many letter writers may not have identified as persons of African descent, and the rhetoric of racelessness discouraged race-based discussions. That Black-identified women were likely among those who wrote letters without identifying their race reinforces the historian Melina Pappademos's argument that race consciousness was one of many factors that shaped Black civic activism.[15] Some women venerated Gómez as a Black political figure in particular; others articulated separate identities through which they staked claims as citizens.

Most prominent Black male leaders focused on penetrating government structures rather than leading campaigns for racial justice.[16] Gómez's political power lay in his ability to marshal Black activists in support of Liberal Party candidates. Politicians of all races attended Black civic club events to enhance their social standing among the population of African descent. Civic club members and affiliates gained access to resources that included schools and job opportunities. Black men were especially likely to seek favors during political elections. African-descended men who benefited from patronage networks became supporters of particular political parties.

Obtaining the resources Black women sought from Gómez often depended on the support of white politicians. Gómez advocated for his supporters through letters to prominent figures. In 1909, Gómez sent a letter to President José Miguel Gómez to follow up on a request to obtain positions for six women who worked as typists. Recalling their recent conversation, Gómez reminded the president that "various youth of the colored race" who had attended the secondary school of Havana "complained of having studied in vain, for the title did not serve them, as they failed to achieve an influential career." Gómez further opined that "people who did not meet the [same qualifications as] these young people" occupied public administrative positions.[17] President Gómez, apparently, told him to forward their names. Yet seven months later, only two of the eight individuals whose names he put forth had obtained positions. Gómez followed up with President Gómez to again advocate for the six remaining young people. Public administration was one of the few sectors that provided financial security to Cubans of any race, as foreign businessmen dominated private property and manufacturing.[18]

Perhaps it was this issue that fueled Rafael Serra y Montalvo's skepticism of the major political parties. The Black patriot-intellectual and tobacco worker contributed to independence while in exile; he helped raise funds and formulate a nationalist agenda for racial fraternity through the press. Serra quickly grew wary of the political dynamics following the early establishment of the republic. "Our political parties," he wrote in 1903, "do not seem interested in the creation of a unified, vigorous national conscience."[19] Just as President Gómez was slow to address the concerns of Gómez, most party leaders failed to follow through on their promises to their constituents.[20]

Figures like Gómez and Rafael Serra y Montalvo promoted a model of empowerment in which African descendants coupled racial regeneration strategies with formal political engagement. Their publications directly confronted racial inequities while affirming the need for Black civic associations. They asserted that all Blacks should obtain the schooling necessary to obtain new labor opportunities in a modern society. Elite Black activists also appealed to the major political parties to advocate for racial justice through formal representation as well as racial integration in social venues and state institutions. In 1908, Serra was elected to Congress as a representative of the Conservative Party, alongside the African-descended intellectual Lino D'Ou of the same party.[21] In this way, elite Black activists bridged the Black public sphere and national political system.

Unsurprisingly, the approaches utilized by both Gómez and Serra proved limited in quelling racial tensions. The August Revolution of 1906, during which independence veterans led an armed revolt against President Estrada Palma, prompted several Black activists to form the Agrupación Independiente de Color.[22] Later renamed the Partido Independiente de Color (PIC), the organization supported Black veterans marginalized within the military and labor sectors. Members included individuals from across the island in urban and rural areas and varied kinds of work: day laborers, peasants, artisans, and more.[23] During the PIC's brief existence, from 1908 to 1912, its leaders Evaristo Estenoz and Pedro Ivonnet created one of the most radical platforms of any political party of their time. They established the party not as a personal dispute with white Cubans but "for the compelling reason that we love the independence and the democratic institutions that have been granted by Cuba's revolutionary heroes, in virtue of those by which [Cuba] is now a free and sovereign nation."[24]

Certain constants informed the political philosophy of the PIC as its leaders pursued racial equality. At its founding, the party primarily focused on championing the right of veterans and their families to receive pensions by calling attention to the sacrifices made by soldiers of African descent to ensure the independence of Cuba. Some PIC members asserted that Cuban independence would have been inconceivable without the large, voluntary participation of Black soldiers in the liberation army. Estenoz and Ivonnet also challenged racist practices within the military when white soldiers were routinely promoted over their equally qualified peers. Party members generally recognized that the marginalization of Black veterans mirrored the lack of government interest in empowering the broader community of African descent. Thus, by advocating on behalf of Black veterans, the PIC helped establish a large base of support throughout the island. The historian Serafin Portuondo Linares explains that the PIC later expanded its agenda to promote representation in government, justice before the law, free and obligatory education, universal instruction, labor reform including eight-hour workdays, open immigration to all races, and "as a moral issue," the "revision and fiscalization of all of the expedients made effective during the first American intervention conceived to date."[25]

This understanding of political activism addressed the very real crisis affecting Cubans of all races and African descendants in particular. Black male leaders confronted stereotypes of Black biological and cultural inferiority through their activism.[26] They challenged the rhetoric that positioned persons of African descent as unfit for participation in modern life. Indeed, Estenoz declared in 1908, "The *independientes* wish to show the world the culture and civility of the Cuban colored race."[27] In many ways, Estenoz's declaration echoed the aspirations of elite Black civic activists like Gómez and Serra, who upheld patronage networks. Yet PIC leaders departed from such leaders by responding to the material concerns of the broader population of African descent.

"To See the Light of Truth and Justice"

Racial regeneration advocates remained cognizant of how education allowed for personal advancement within the labor sector, and they understood that the odds were stacked against them. Black men and women faced exclusion in education as well as in the burgeoning nursing and clerical sectors. Economic cycles of prosperity and crisis further complicated racial dynamics and left most Black families in a precarious position.

For most individuals of African descent, the vision of racial regeneration articulated by elite Black activists was likely more an aspiration than a reality. The majority of Black families lived in poverty, unqualified for high-paying positions due to low levels of education. While 51 percent of all whites were literate at the turn of the twentieth century, only 28 percent of Cubans of color could read or write. This profoundly affected male suffrage, as only 24 percent of Black males met the literacy requirements in comparison to 58.5 percent of white males. Seventy percent of Black women were illiterate, in comparison to 52 percent of white women. Inequalities in literacy persisted throughout the early decades of the republic. By 1919, 51 percent of Blacks over the age of ten were literate, and 63 percent of their white counterparts were able to read. Santiago de Cuba was an exception to this trend, as the majority of African-descended women in that city were literate.[28]

Low literacy levels became both cause and effect of Black women's marginalization in the labor market, and education provided a route for improving one's socioeconomic status.[29] Yet access to schools stood as a major obstacle for many families. Many institutions required tuition fees that the majority of Cubans were unable to afford. Acceptance to primary and secondary programs required social connections that most families of African descent did not possess, and entrance exams to high school and university programs required fees and reading, writing, and math skills that limited women of African descent and their children in obtaining advanced education. And for those children who were accepted, Black families complained of racism in private religious schools.[30]

Women of African descent comprised the majority of female workers, but practices of discrimination in schools and the broader workforce constrained their opportunities for socioeconomic mobility. According to the 1907 census, 65 percent of the 73,520 females over fourteen years of age and with gainful employment were of African descent.[31] White women were more likely to come from homes in which a father or husband was the sole financial provider. Although most white women were without gainful employment, those who did work labored predominantly as professionals, often as teachers.[32] Thus, only 6 percent of white women worked outside of the home, and 20 percent of women of color depended upon their own labor to support themselves and their families.[33] Racial divides in female employment increased by 1919, when nearly three-quarters of all female wage earners were women of color.[34] Black women who worked did so primarily in agriculture or as domestics in the urban sphere. They made up a mere 2 percent of laborers in the trade and transportation sector.[35]

In 1906 the Cuban government passed an immigration law as part of its strategy to whiten the population. The law allocated one million dollars to Spanish colonization programs. It reserved 80 percent of the funds to relocate European and Canary Island families to Cuba.[36] Such policies had limited success. From 1902 to 1907, an estimated 128,000 Spaniards immigrated to Cuba; almost 800,000 entered Cuba from 1902 to 1931. Yet, only 70,000 settled permanently.[37]

The sheer number of Spaniards working in Cuba influenced shifts in the racial composition of several labor sectors. The historian Alejandro de la Fuente links the drop in overall Black women's employment from 1899 to 1907 to their displacement by younger Spanish women immigrants. During those years, Spanish women's participation in the labor force increased from 21 percent to 32 percent.[38] Employers preferred white Cuban and Spanish women as workers in the developing areas of nursing, secretarial work, and retail.[39] De la Fuente determines that as white employers came to prefer Spanish women as domestic workers, Black women in urban centers were pushed toward factory work. Many women of African descent turned to the informal sector as street vendors and sex workers.[40] Therefore, the displacement of Black women within commercial and domestic sectors exacerbated their marginalization in employment.

The displacement of laboring Black women by Spanish immigrants exacerbated an already tenuous situation. US and Spanish businessmen dominated the nation's economy. Foreign businessmen bought up land

and displaced rural Cuban workers.[41] They imported Caribbean migrant laborers to work on sugar plantations.[42] Many Cuban laborers migrated from rural areas to cities in search of economic opportunities. Low wages led many to reside in impoverished neighborhoods. Throughout the republican era, most managerial positions in the private sector were held by foreign workers. As a result, public administration became the principal industry through which Cubans of all races competed for access to well-paying employment.

Men and women of African descent struggled to secure positions in public administration. A 1904 article in *El Nuevo Criollo* protested the lack of posts held by people of color.[43] The writer complained that "the precedent was set that for another individual of color [to obtain a post], one had to be vacated by another of his own race." The article noted that many Black men and women had been displaced without cause, as some Black teachers had experienced when they were suddenly fired. At the same time, white teachers openly opposed having children of color in their classrooms. *El Nuevo Criollo* also cited a lack of politicians and police officers of African descent.

Even as Black women confronted racism and sexism in their daily lives, they did make strides. Cuba's literacy rates in general and the community of African descent in particular increased steadily throughout the early republican period. Only 30 percent of Blacks were literate in 1899. Literacy among Cubans of African descent more than doubled by 1907 to nearly 67 percent, nearly eliminating the racial literacy gap.[44] The number of women of color professionals also increased. From 1899 to 1924 the number of teachers of color in public education grew from 3.4 percent to 15.8 percent.[45]

Many Black women who obtained an education realized that their training did not ensure access to employment. Carmela López Garrido requested Gómez's assistance in securing a position. A certified typist, López tried diligently to find employment in Havana. She saw Gómez as her last hope. Though she primarily wrote the letter in Spanish, she explained in English that she hoped he would pay attention to her solicitude, writing, "because I think it is very hard to be not working perfectly knowing my trade." She wrote in both English and Spanish to demonstrate her skills as a bilingual typist.[46]

In February 1912 the educator María Amparo Callara boarded a train in her hometown, Pinar del Río, to go to Havana to raise concerns with the secretary of public works about recent issues at her school. In a later letter to Gómez, she explained that the director of the school in which she worked "established inequalities" between them "for the fact that I am of the opposite race of her and in her judgment inferior in every way."[47] Frustrated, Callara turned to the school superintendent for support. The superintendent, rather than address her concerns, opted to maintain his distance from the incident. Callara concluded in her letter to Gómez, "This is without a doubt the aspect that has led me to realize that I am still not seen; in this situation, it may not be possible to see the light of truth and justice."[48] While Callara did not state if she ever met with the secretary of public works, she sought Gómez's assistance in addressing her discriminatory treatment as a Black educator.

The grievances Callara cited in her letter to Gómez point to the ongoing struggle for racial regeneration among elite and upwardly mobile African descendants. The challenges Black women faced while navigating the labor market might have felt familiar to those who came of age during the late colonial period. Spanish immigration policies and exclusion from prestigious positions were old tactics used by elite whites to maintain their dominance and tactics whites used to restrict Black women's entry into new fields of employment. The ways in which race dictated African-descended women's access to labor and educational opportunities was not limited to Cuba. Indeed, men and women of African descent experienced similar forms of exclusion from new labor sectors throughout the Americas.[49] In Cuba, however, the rhetoric of racelessness informed the forms of action Black women might take. African descendants risked backlash when they publicly confronted racism, and many who took such risks turned to the Partido Independiente de Color to demand racial justice.

"If Only to Maintain Their Dignity"

In 1908 a woman of African descent from Holguín submitted a letter to *Previsión* in defense of the Partido Independiente de Color.[50] She determined that the Moderate Party of President Tomás Estrada Palma had failed to adequately address the routine acts of racial discrimination in the government and labor force. The "cubana holguinera," as she signed her letter, asserted that "men of color should separate themselves from the [Liberal and Conservative] political parties if only to maintain their dignity."[51] Her views were neither unusual nor extreme among African descendants who supported the PIC. As the daughter of parents who worked "for the betterment of themselves," she saw her successes and the successes of others as key to the progression of the race. Yet institutional racism stymied her progression on at least two occasions, she wrote. Her husband received numerous medals following his involvement as a soldier in the wars of 1868 and 1895. However, decades later, he remained a captain while less-accomplished whites were promoted to the status of colonel. The writer studied to become a teacher, but she was unable to attain a position to practice her profession. Meanwhile, though she lost two brothers in the independence movement, she witnessed the sisters of white veterans secure employment in that vocation. Angered and disconcerted, the *holguinera* proclaimed her hopes for a "complete triumph" of the *independientes*.[52]

PIC press editors regularly published letters from female supporters like the *holguinera* throughout the island and abroad as a strategy for crafting party rhetoric. The PIC press buttressed the party's platform for racial equality.[53] Editors supplemented pamphlets and party leaders' speeches with news editorials to mobilize Blacks and other supporters. They used Black women's letters in particular to illustrate the perspectives of supporters who joined the movement. In turn, women who supported the PIC staked claims as citizens who framed their patriotic commitment to racial justice. In limited instances, women writers joined men in openly critiquing racism during the early years of the republic.

Black women's published letters reflected a broader commitment to ensuring the party's success. Though no statistical data identify the number of women involved with the PIC, women supported party politics through *comités de damas* (ladies committees) known as the Damas Protectoras de los Independientes de Color (Women Protectors of the Colored Independents). Each committee regularly elected officials, and many posted the election results in *Previsión*. Women held secondary leadership positions. They organized social events and helped raise funds. Moreover, they recruited men and other women into the organization. Their efforts helped the PIC grow quickly. By 1910, chapters existed throughout the island and abroad in communities such as Key West and Tampa, Florida. Numerous issues of *Previsión* featured lists of Black civic clubs throughout the island whose members supported the PIC.

Women who submitted letters to *Previsión* engaged in a patriotic dialogue that reified the national independence narratives. Julia Argüelles de García of central Cuba, who received *Previsión* from her godparents, Juliana García de Castañeda and Fernando Castañeda, proclaimed the newspaper "the triumph of rights, peace, and reason." She resided in the district of José Martí and grew up in the town of Manacas, where "with great pleasure that athlete, that bronze titan they call [African-descended independence leader] Antonio Maceo made use of the word of honor."[54] Maceo served as a general in the Liberation Army and died during the Cuban War of Independence; he became recognized as a national hero during the early twentieth century. Argüelles de García invoked the legacy of Cuban heroes like Martí and Maceo to define herself as a supporter of the PIC engaged in national discourses.

Carmen Piedra asserted that men of color possessed "the high honor of being men." Historically, their sex obligated them to serve when needed by their homeland, as their country called them to abandon the duty of their homes and shed blood. Piedra pondered why, despite making such contributions, so many men of color retreated from the "beautiful walk of exalting our race and liberating us from the moral slavery in which we live sinking?"[55] She determined that Black men, ordained by God with "the title of 'man,'" should challenge white men to recognize their civic responsibilities to protect their families and nation as well as valuing men of color. "If I possessed such a beautiful title of 'man,'" she wrote, "I assure you all that I would be one of the most fervent fighters for conquering the rights of our race." The time had arisen to "lift the veil" that shielded men from their duties.[56] Manuela Labrado y Garcias of the town of Cruces echoed similar sentiments: "Ah! If I represented by myself the 'Black' race and if I wore trousers instead of a skirt, I would not hesitate a single instant to cast my vote for you [PIC leader Evaristo Estenoz]. Proceed serenely in your endeavor, and perhaps at the end we will raise our victorious heads and we will see our efforts accomplished. This is all I desire for the future of our race."[57] Hence, the women cited the lack of political power afforded to them as they implored Black men to valiantly step up and fulfill their natural duty as leaders. Such expressions compelled men of African descent to action in service of the PIC by simultaneously invoking shame and venerating Black male political authority.

Women frequently exalted the PIC leader Evaristo Estenoz as an exemplar of valiant manhood: patriotic, unrelenting, and deeply committed to defending the interests of the Black race. Cecilia Lara submitted a letter to *Previsión* to express her excitement over the latest issue. "I am very glad," she stated, "that this newspaper came into my hands, because I have always felt Black, absolutely Black. It seems that heaven put it in my hands to tell me: Here you have a Christ, General Estenoz, champion of your race, it is time you show what you are: a Black and Cuban woman."[58] Comparing him to the messianic figure of Jesus suggests that she and other Blacks viewed Estenoz as a figure destined to deliver the race from oppression. Carmelina Bequer of Palmira urged Blacks, "by instinct of conservation," to follow the teachings of Estenoz, whom she called "the Great Redeemer of our time."[59] Bequer valued his mission to have Cuban society recognize the civilization of the Black population. Even more, Estenoz's message stood in line with personal goals. Bequer thus proclaimed Estenoz the most important figure of the period to defend the "rights of our heroic and suffered race."[60]

Women's veneration of Black male political authority took on particular significance as many politicians worked to legally ban the organization. The party came under attack by political leaders who asserted that the group undermined Cuba's national unity. Political elites circulated rumors of a "Black conspiracy," asserting that the PIC was racist and aimed to create a Black republic similar to that of Haiti, in order to undermine the party's influence.[61] In September 1908, Liberal and Conservative Party members joined forces by bringing two hundred supporters to disrupt an *independientes* meeting in Havana. This incident only fueled tensions between the PIC and government. In January 1910, *Previsión* printed an open protest of the discrimination against Blacks at a Havana hotel owned by North Americans. The government responded by seizing *Previsión* and arresting Estenoz.[62] A jury sentenced Estenoz to six months' imprisonment. As protesters demanded his release, the *mulato* Senator Martín Morúa Delgado proposed a bill that would outlaw the PIC and prohibit the organization of any political group on the basis of race. Widespread protests resulted in Estenoz's pardon by President José Miguel Gómez within a month. However, Morúa's campaign to ban the organization by appealing to the rhetoric of racial equality succeeded. Following the passage of the 1910 Morúa legislation that outlawed the party, PIC members found themselves subject to increased harassment and even prosecution. As men faced government persecution, women deemed men's commitment to the organization patriotic and essential to the progress of the race. Carmelina Bequer thus encouraged Estenoz, "Do not falter in your endeavors, as you will soon be remunerated."[63]

Women's letters affirmed their complementary role in supporting the patriarchal leadership structure of the PIC through feminine sacrifice. The reader Eulalia Morales praised the intellectual labor of *Previsión*'s male and female writers for bringing about "a glorious stage for our race" through the newspaper's publication, from which would come the birth of "our well-being in the future."[64] Morales recognized women for encouraging the men of the PIC "from the columns of *Previsión*." She celebrated women for their "self-denial," faith, and enthusiasm as they exalted the work of the race.[65] She emphasized writing as a political strategy through which women might carry out their feminine duties.[66] In particular, she commended individuals such as Rosa Brioso as a PIC leader from Oriente, who confronted "all of the impossibilities of the difficult work that has been entrusted to us."[67]

Rosa Brioso became one of the most prominent activists to mobilize African descendants in support of the PIC. Brioso's leadership began in Santiago de Cuba, and by 1910 she had become the national leader of the Damas Protectoras del Partido Independiente de Color.[68] Brioso ardently defended Black patriotic manhood. She lauded Estenoz alongside Antonio Maceo Grajales as African-descended champions of "equality within the homeland."[69] She viewed Estenoz as one of the great political leaders who risked jail in pursuit of democracy and racial egalitarianism. Brioso drew from the patriotic rhetoric of Maceo and the work of Estenoz to critique contradictions within Cuba's political system. Activists such as Estenoz, she claimed, worked not solely on behalf of the Black population but for the development of a just republic. Brioso depicted PIC members as allies of the nation rather than its adversaries. This was most apparent in Black support of the president, one of many elected officials who "owed Blacks his high position."[70] She disregarded attacks on the work of Estenoz and maintained that the movement's triumph would make up for his hardships.[71]

Brioso took care to legitimize the PIC as a political party by aligning herself with the racial rhetoric of the nation. She asserted that Estenoz's protests against racial discrimination and government corruption exemplified the definitive act of patriotism carried out by a man of color. One of her many articles published in *Previsión* relayed the humiliation inflicted upon Blacks "who have felt their dignity trampled upon."[72] Many had been deterred when silenced within politics, denied from obtaining professional positions, or jeered at for their assumed cultural inferiority. She insisted that one must not feel dejected, as such sentiments undermined "the great work of *Previsión*."[73] More importantly, she claimed, conceding when faced with discrimination strengthened the work of the opposition and further reinforced Blacks' ability to be disregarded as citizens. Brioso promoted the unification of the community of color so that "all men [of color] achieve the respect and consideration to which all men are entitled." She accentuated the *independientes*' goal of obtaining equality, explaining that "all [men] are equal and the only thing that should distinguish them is one's talent and virtue."[74] Brioso affirmed the nationalist rhetoric of racelessness as she announced her support for Estenoz's protests on behalf of Blacks who confronted racism in employment and politics.

The Cuban government's ban on race-based political parties continued to infuriate the PIC members who felt that their rights had been denied. From May 20 to May 30, Estenoz helped organize a public protest in the eastern part of the island. Historians have asserted that the demonstrators aimed to provoke another US intervention that would achieve foreign support for their political platform.[75] Yet what began as a peaceful demonstration quickly turned into a massacre. Over the course of several months, the Cuban army killed thousands of Black Cubans, including the PIC's leaders, some of its official members, and others believed to be affiliated with the party.[76] Hundreds more were arrested and placed on trial for their association with known members or due to rumors of having supported what became known as the racist rebellion.[77]

Brioso's promotion of PIC leaders in the face of increasing government repression elucidates the risks Black women took when publicly challenging the nationalist tenets of racelessness. Brioso helped mobilize women in support of the party's male leadership. Her willingness to undermine the government ban on race-based political organizing may have been prompted by the gendered nature of national politics, in which women possessed little to no political power. Elite politicians determined that only men had the capacity to change the electoral system. Still, the activism of women such as Brioso helped disrupt the dominance of the

Liberal and Conservative Parties, and women's involvement made them persons of suspicion during the May 1912 protest by PIC members and the government's violent repression of its members. Here, women's efforts to exhibit their patriotism and respectability through letter writing was undermined by their experiences during the 1912 massacre. Incidents of racial violence demonstrate the delicate balancing act women of African descent took on as public actors who directly confronted anti-Black racism.

For Every Black Who "Believes Himself Equal to the White"

Although the law positioned men as full citizens with political power, fears of a Black uprising also made women of African descent suspect as threats to national stability.[78] A prominent example is the government response to Black women during the 1912 massacre. For women of the PIC, letter writing supplemented their efforts to circulate party literature, raise funds, organize events, and defend men facing persecution. These activities reflected their efforts to have the state intervene on behalf of marginalized Blacks, even as they violated the tenets of racelessness. African-descended women experienced backlash from government officials and the mainstream press during this period. Historians acknowledge that militias that formed out of fear of an impending race war occasionally confronted Black women, including women who were not affiliated with the PIC.[79] Many women faced harassment, police searches, and arrest. Women were among those injured and killed by armed civilians, and thousands lost family members.

It is difficult to ascertain the extent of Black women's involvement in the protests. Eyewitness accounts from government officials as well as everyday citizens suggest that men comprised the majority of the protesters in Oriente during May 1912.[80] However, studies of the PIC and Cuban nationalism provide glimpses of African-descended women's agency during and following the protests. For example, the historian Lillian Guerra references the Black women's club Missionaries of Progress, established in Pinar del Río following the August Revolution of 1906. On the surface, the organization appeared to function in a manner similar to elite civic clubs that promoted racial advancement. Yet when officers arrested a group of rebels in 1912, they discovered on the women in the group proclamations issued by the Missionaries of Progress. One proclamation read, "I invite you [in the name of General Estenoz] never again to feel weak in order to pursue the grand and noble labor he has begun, for his is seconded by many Blacks with dignity and *vergüenza* [humility] . . . because they understand that [the PIC] has been born in a brilliant hour for every Black who, with reason, believes himself equal to the white."[81] Guerra contends that the women's words reveal their belief that by supporting men of the PIC they would bolster their own social status. Certainly, their emphasis on Estenoz's male leadership resembled the strategies of women who submitted letters to *Previsión*. Moreover, the existence of Missionaries of Progress raises the possibility that other women's organizations may have served the PIC's initiatives.

Court registries and mainstream newspapers reveal that government officials targeted women of African descent for their perceived connection to the PIC. In Banes, police detained Margarita Planas for her role as a "propagandist." The town's mayor, Ricardo Rizo, accused Planas of circulating party literature to persuade "those of her class to join the rebels." As evidence of her guilt, he noted that Planas's home had been spared during a recent fire in the region; furthermore, he claimed that her home functioned as a meeting place for rebels to "conspire" against the government. Rizo blamed Planas for supporting the rebels in their illicit activities, in addition to serving as "a great proponent of racist ideas."[82] Accusations that Black women conspired against the nation-state were made repeatedly.

Women of African descent were implicated in a variety of crimes as well. The *mestiza* Isabel Caballero of Santiago de Cuba faced imprisonment for looting local stores, taking clothing and fabrics, rum, and food.[83] While Caballero's motives remain unknown, other women claimed to act on behalf of the PIC to supply the rebels or meet the needs of their own families. In other cases, police questioned and occasionally arrested women who might surrender information about the activities of their male family members, especially their domestic partners. The historian María de los Ángeles Meriño Fuentes proposes that the police may not have arrested many of these women but instead used them to obtain information being withheld by men. Officers who searched the homes of PIC members' wives and girlfriends found rosters with names of associates, receipt stubs for memberships, and copies of the party's newspapers.[84] In that sense, government officials did not take African-descended women seriously as political actors; rather, they targeted Black women to curtail the authority of Black men who stepped outside the bounds of appropriate political behavior.

Racial anxieties fueled the reactions of government officials and white civilians to Black women; they generated the perception that all persons of African descent were potential conspirators against the nation. The Havana-based newspaper *Diario de la Marina* charged that the *independientes* sought to launch a rebellion, "without rhyme or reason," against "the Cuban people and public peace." The paper called upon "all who love the nation" to recognize the threat at hand and "to prepare themselves to defend order and institutions with true resolution."[85] The editors of the *Diario de la Marina* thus dismissed the political concerns of the PIC and instead portrayed the protests as an act of war. Though initially targeting party associates, accusations against PIC affiliates escalated with time. Newspaper editors and contributors called for the protection of "Cuban" citizens, a term used to refer to whites, from persons of African descent. In Santiago de Cuba, Manuel Domingo Hernández and Julio Hernández, leaders of the elite civic club Luz de Oriente, wrote to Gómez, "Here the situation is difficult for us the people of color who are not with the *independientes* [but] are treated as though we are and with suspicion by whites."[86] Whites suspected that Blacks traveling for work and leisure served as spies for the PIC. They stopped and questioned many, sometimes jailing or even killing African descendants. Even in regions that had little to no PIC activity, residents feared a potential attack. Many Black families grew concerned for their safety and fled their homes to nearby towns and cities.[87]

The culture of fear that targeted Black men and women as enemies of the nation emboldened acts of racialized violence throughout the island. By depicting Black men and women as threats, the government and mainstream press rendered invalid the social causes promoted by the PIC, including its patriotic emphasis. Fears of a race war took on a sexual dimension as white men called for the defense of white womanhood against Black violence. Many whites repeatedly asserted that the *independientes* sought to rape white women. White fathers and husbands required the women of their households to remain indoors to protect their safety and virtue. Rumors began to circulate that Black men had assaulted white women, inflaming such concerns. These rumors resuscitated colonial-era tropes that tied white male honor to the sexual virtue of their wives and daughters. Rumors invoked the image of a white civilization that needed defense against African barbarism, a metaphor for the development of the nation and the role of Blacks in its future. Therefore, white men played out their apprehensions surrounding Black men's political power by stressing their need to guard white women's sexual virtue.[88]

Ultimately, white anxieties surrounding the sexuality of Black men helped reify the racialized boundaries of respectability through which white elites devalued Black womanhood. While the mainstream press asserted the vulnerability of virtuous white women, it depicted women of African descent as uncivilized *brujas* and immoral individuals.[89] Press representations undermined the humanity of Black women and helped substantiate violence against Black women and children. They presented women of African descent as social threats who needed regulation and if necessary, repression. One of the most extreme cases of government-sanctioned violence was the massacre at La Maya. On May 31, 1912, the Cuban general Carlos Mendieta gathered his troops outside of the community in Oriente Province. Mendieta, who had grown tired of waiting to go into battle, sought an opportunity to test his new machine guns. He invited journalists to witness the military power of the Cuban army and ordered his troops to fire rounds into group of individuals he claimed to be PIC rebels. Entire households were among the 150 persons of African descent who were injured or killed. Days after the massacre, a fire damaged several properties in La Maya. Military officials spread rumors that the PIC protesters had set the fire and damaged the entire town, fueling the perception that the *independientes* were savages.[90]

The 1912 massacre greatly altered the context in which Black men and women asserted their merit for citizenship. The historian Aline Helg argues that the event "unmasked" deep-seated racism among white elites and popular classes.[91] Within local communities, white Cubans attempted to enforce racial segregation within public spaces including parks, hotels, and restaurants.[92] Anti-Black sentiments led many to declare that African descendants should go "back to Africa" or at least "out of Cuba."[93] Rumors of Black conspiracies succeeded in undermining the political influence of African-descended men, as Black representation fell in Congress. However, both the Liberal and Conservative Parties continued to seek the support of

Black voters; they endorsed Black political candidates and accommodated elite men of African descent by appointing them to government administrative posts.[94]

Without "Good Fortune nor Father, Son, or Husband"

The enduring significance of Black male political authority is illustrated by the letters African-descended women penned to figures like Gómez. Many Black women and their families used letters to tap into patronage networks as they pursued socioeconomic mobility. In June 1912, during the violent government backlash against PIC protesters, Cristina Ayala wrote Gómez with an urgent request, to help her navigate upcoming exams as "the only teacher of color" in the Güines school district. She made no mention of the current political events. Ayala sought to wield Gómez's "recognized talent, reputable *ilustración* and incontrovertible influence" for her professional advancement as well as the "honor of our race." She explained that most who sat for the exams did not know who would evaluate them and thus could not advocate for themselves. That Ayala referenced the absence of other educators of color indicates the precarious existence of Black women in the field of teaching, a growing sector in which US officials and political elites aimed to modernize the island through literacy and professional training.

Although Ayala's appeal to Gómez reflected the methods Black women privately employed to circumvent discriminatory practices, her approach should not be interpreted as contrary to the strategy of PIC supporters. Ayala appealed to Gómez in the absence of male family members, as she was unable to depend on "good fortune nor father, son, or husband." The Havana resident explained that her sick brother, a member of the Partido Independiente, "contributed much towards the placement of the members of said party on the Board of Education, which would support me." She cited her brother's contributions to the Partido Independiente in anticipation of the professional benefits it previously provided for its members. Like women who endorsed the PIC, Ayala also staked citizenship claims by aligning herself with a Black male voter.

It is difficult to determine how many women who wrote to Gómez supported the PIC, yet one theme distinguished private letters from those published in *Previsión*: how the writers framed their vulnerability as Black women. In August 1915 Ana María Álvarez Martínez wrote to Gómez asking for assistance in furthering her education. The twenty-one-year-old woman had struggled to support herself and her nineteen-year-old brother since they were orphaned eleven years earlier. She lived in the town of Florida, where the rent was cheap. She supported the local societies of Santa Clara, La Bella Unión, and El Gran Maceo, noting that she preferred La Bella Unión. In 1914, during a chance encounter with a local Black civic club member, Eulojio Montenegro, Álvarez learned of the universities for African Americans in the United States. Alvarez eventually learned to write so that she might contact Booker T. Washington and enroll in one of his universities. She wrote to Gómez, "I have not been able to facilitate the trip [to the United States] due to a lack of resources."[95] She sought his help in furthering her education, she explained, "for the well-being myself and my class" because she "greatly desired to progress."[96]

For some women, demonstrating their commitment to racial progress justified their requests. Such individuals cited their aspirations as members of "the colored race"; they drew connections between their individual concerns and collective improvement. Other women sought to leverage Gómez's political power to seek justice in cases of discriminatory employers.

Most commonly, Black women emphasized their positions as the widows, sisters, and daughters of veterans who desperately needed pensions as caretakers of children and elderly family members. In 1919 Rita Baldoquín, niece of a Liberation Army general, from Manzanillo, wrote Gómez after the state stopped her uncle's pension without explanation. She described her uncle as "a man who is incapable of reclaiming anything" due to his poor health.[97] She explained, "Seeing that he is old and infirm, I have wanted to handle some business for him, as there are many who have done patriotic work—maybe less [than him]—and yet enjoy more than him."[98] Baldoquín implied that the allocation of pensions did not always match contributions to the nation. Her contention that Gómez was "the only person who can do something for the colored race" suggests that she perceived race to be a determining factor in one's financial circumstances.[99]

Gómez received hundreds of letters regarding pensions between 1920 and 1923. This likely occurred due to the reinvigorated veterans movement, which gained momentum in the early 1920s.[100] Many women solicited pensions from the state on behalf of their lost husbands and on occasion, emphasized the men's military service during the nineteenth-century independence movement. Gabriela Oliva Viuda de Sausa, a widow from Cienfuegos, sought state support for her family. Almost a year had passed since she had last received a payment from her late husband's pension. As she lived far from her family, Oliva struggled to care for her two daughters and her mother. Gómez was a friend of her late father, Domingo L. Oliva, and her brother, Rafael, and one of the few connections Oliva had to President Alfredo Zayas. She badly needed his assistance. She wrote Gómez "to see if you can resolve such a terrible situation as soon as possible."[101] She hoped he could convince Zayas to issue a government decree that would continue to dispense pensions to veterans who had fought for national independence and their families. By convincing the government to expand the pension program, Oliva sought a specific political action that would remedy the grave situation of women whose families lived in poverty. She reflected on the status of her community when she lamented, "Today there are so many families that have lost their *jefe*."[102]

The reality that women of African descent had disproportionately lost their husbands fighting for national sovereignty during the wars for independence complicated Black women's aspirations for social mobility. Louis Pérez estimates that in 1899 as many as three in every five wives of color were widowed. Havana had the greatest number of widowed women of color: nearly four of every five wives were widowed.[103] The absence of male breadwinners made even more difficult the already unstable financial situations of families struggling to survive in depressed communities.[104] In her memoir, *Reyita*, María de los Reyes Castillo Bueno, a Black woman reflecting on her life experiences, recalled how her widowed grandmother Emiliana "Mamacita" Duharte struggled financially. The wife of a free Black bricklayer, Mamacita lost her husband during the Ten Years' War. Soon after his death, Mamacita and her seven children returned to Santiago de Cuba, where the family fell into poverty. She recounts in *Reyita*, "[Mamacita] had to struggle to survive, to feed and shelter herself and her children."[105] Mamacita made and sold candy in the streets to earn money. She also put out a table on festival days. Left without financial support, widowed women became the sole providers for their children and often their parents as well.

The economic turmoil of the 1920s exacerbated the precarious position of struggling families. The collapse of sugar prices and a banking crisis led to rising unemployment. President Alfredo Zayas responded to pressures from US Ambassador Enoch Crowder by cutting the national budget in half, eliminating government positions and public works funding.[106] He implemented reforms to commerce, finance, elections, and even the lottery system. *Colecturías*, discounted sets of lottery tickets for retail sale, became critical to the financial welfare of many families.[107] The widow María Smith of Itabo, Matanzas Province, asked for a "*colecturía* to be able to cover my needs and to have my daughter near doctors." Her daughter suffered from illness. "But at the cost of a lot of sacrifice I have bought three lots in [the town of] Columbia, and I have not been able to finish payments for the same reason," Smith explained.[108] Ana Sánchez Viuda de Martínez of Santiago de Cuba wrote to contest her late husband's forced retirement, which she called an injustice. Sánchez stated, "Aside from the moral part that represents, it is also material; I wish that my children might receive their father's retainer because it is modeled so that it will be greater than the pension he receives as a veteran."[109]

Inocencia Silveira of Guanajay had asked in January 1924 for assistance in securing a *colecturía* for her father, the veteran and poet Vicente Silveira, to have extra income. She added, "All of my family are veterans of Zayas."[110] Silveira referenced her family's support for the revolts of 1906 and 1917, during which the politician Alfredo Zayas helped lead Liberal Party supporters against the corruption of the Moderate Party.[111] She continued, "Thus, my old friend, it would be an act of justice, as both my father and my brother find [themselves] with few resources and a large family, that you might provide a *colecturía* since they are forever Zayistas." Her husband, Julian Pérez, was a twenty-year veteran. Silveira wrote, "His work within the Liberal Party has always been ample and fruitful, and those twenty years of consecration and of work have only obtained promises."[112] Silveira was persistent. Four months later, she wrote to remind Gómez of their recent conversation at Artemisa as well as the struggles of her male family members to secure employment despite their loyalty to Zayas. Later that year, she wrote to thank him on behalf of her family for his "goodness."[113]

Silveira's critique of the unfulfilled promises made by the Zayas administration points to growing popular dissent. In 1923, the Veterans and Patriots Association emerged in protest of failed economic policies.[114] Association members challenged corruption in the electoral system and Zayas's use of his presidency to amass wealth at the expense of working citizens. Calls for his resignation evolved into a potent national force. Members of the Veterans and Patriots Association met government repression with calls for revolution. Though unsuccessful, the movement propelled a wave of popular resistance that had the potential to bring more women into national political life.

• • •

Anti-Black racism continued to undermine the aspirations of Black women who pursued socioeconomic mobility. At the same time, racelessness discourses compelled many women of African descent to abandon public protests in favor of new strategies for intervening in the political system. Certainly, tapping into patronage networks was not the only way Black women entered the political area. Pedro Padrón notes that tobacco stemmers went on strike throughout the early decades of the twentieth century. Women of African descent also participated in the 1915 labor and communist congresses.[115] A comparison of the public appeals of women of the PIC, no doubt aware of *Previsión* editors' interest in using such letters to advance the party's agenda, with those submitted in letters to Gómez elucidates overlapping yet distinct approaches for challenging anti-Black racism in particular. Submitting letters to Black male politicians like Gómez enabled women of African descent to tap into patronage networks. Those who submitted letters to *Previsión* helped shape the patriarchal rhetoric of the PIC that emphasized Black male political authority, race pride, and Cuban nationalism. The publication of such letters became a radical act through which women challenged the racial silence. Both groups of women employed a patriarchal understanding of racial citizenship that venerated Black male political authority. They used letters to disrupt notions of a woman's place solely in the domestic sphere while affirming their familial ties as wives, daughters, and mothers.

The brutal repression of PIC activists greatly affected how Black activists addressed racial discrimination. It revealed the great lengths the state would go to limit race-based organizing. Prominent Black politicians and civic club leaders denounced the PIC and its mission. No doubt their allegiance to major parties influenced their response, as they also affirmed these groups. Adhering to elite gender conventions became even more important for affirming Blacks' image as nonthreatening citizens within this context. Indeed, beyond *Previsión*, most women whose writings were published in the early twentieth-century Black press rarely discussed the discriminatory acts they experienced in their daily lives.

3

Leadership of Recognized Character

Comportment and the Politics of Elite Black Social Life

As Cuba transitioned from Spanish colony to US-occupied territory in January 1899, the everyday activities of men and women living across the island became "laden with political meaning."[1] Linguistic practices, public celebrations, monuments, and clothing choices, the Cuban historian Marial Iglesias Utset has argued, reflected conflicting ideas regarding the present and future of the island. Foreign and elite Cuban businessmen and government officials oversaw broad changes that shaped national institutions. Individuals from all social classes joined debates over Cuban nationalism, Spanish cultural heritage, and the incorporation of North American traditions. This dynamic continued to unfold following the establishment of the republic in 1902, when Cubans sought to exert control over the nation's progress through seemingly mundane decisions about their personal lives.[2]

Cuba experienced rapid economic and social changes that shaped national culture during the early twentieth century. US officials modernized the island's infrastructure; their investments in its transportation system and technological capabilities transformed neighborhoods.[3] Foreign investments in the sugar industry led to an economic boom that benefited a growing Cuban wealthy class. White Cubans comprised the majority of this expanding social group. Elite and middle-class whites moved into newly erected luxury apartment buildings. They frequented exclusive restaurants, theaters, and sporting and civic club events. Privileged men and women defined their social status also when they purchased elegant consumer goods advertised in magazines like *Bohemia* and *Carteles*.[4]

As much as the everyday behaviors of this privileged social class indicated an embrace of modern cultural values, they also reflected old racial attitudes. In 1905, President Tomás Estrada Palma planned a reception for liberation army veterans without inviting the wives of Senator Martín Morúa Delgado, the only senator of African descent, and of Black Representatives Antonio Poveda Ferrer and Generoso Campos Marquetti. The president apologized and insisted that he did not intentionally fail to invite the women. Elite African descendants believed otherwise. Editors at the Black newspaper *La Antorcha* pondered, "If this is what takes place in the capital, what will happen in the provinces?"[5] The editors likely recognized how grand events like a presidential reception conveyed the refinement of elected officials and by extension, the elite classes who asserted their political authority. Estrada Palma's failure to invite the wives of prominent Black politicians served as an affront to the respectability of Black women. Indeed, elite whites reluctantly incorporated African-descended men into formal politics but determined that most Blacks lacked the qualities necessary for entry into spaces they deemed exclusive.

The exclusion of Black wives from the presidential ball exemplifies the practices through which many elite whites promoted racial superiority in an ostensibly raceless nation. It calls attention to the circumstances that led privileged Blacks to emphasize comportment as a political strategy. The omission of Black wives from the presidential reception mirrored African descendants' social marginalization more broadly. Black men and women complained of being prohibited from entering restaurants and hotels as well as being harassed by police throughout the island.[6] Whites required African descendants to walk on the outskirts of public squares in cities; transgressing these boundaries resulted in violence on numerous occasions.[7] Press reports of Black criminality among African-based religious practitioners reinforced assumptions that Blacks were an imminent threat to the security of white elite society.[8] Ongoing discrimination in employment compounded such frustrations.

Public comportment was a political strategy during the early years of the republic. Iglesias Utset's framework is useful in showing how elite African descendants negotiated gendered understandings of racial citizenship through their public behaviors.[9] As elite Black civic activists navigated electoral politics, they promoted gendered forms of bodily comportment in all realms of elite social life.[10] Elite persons of African descent, in addition to venerating a patriarchal leadership of recognized character, continued to emphasize the formation of nuclear households. Women enacted bourgeois femininity through their attire, mannerisms, and domestic activities.

Well-dressed socialites attended events that demonstrated their refinement to the broader society; they created exclusive spaces for affirming elite Black women's virtue while distancing themselves from poor individuals of African descendant. They circulated photographic portraits of accomplished subjects to convey the respectability of women who gave lectures, became educated professionals, and formed civic organizations. Elite and upwardly mobile women of African descent negotiated the terms of patriarchy through their public roles, which reflected modernizing expectations of feminine behavior. Public comportment, in this sense, became a way for Cuban women of African descent to forge a modern image that contradicted disparaging racial stereotypes.

Like the women who contributed to the development of the Black public sphere during the final decades of the colonial period, the individuals who shaped elite social life during the early twentieth century responded to patriarchal expectations. Historians such as Alejandro de la Fuente, Frank Guridy, and Melina Pappademos assert that dominant standards of morality led elite Black men and women to emphasize patriarchal norms of domesticity in their civic club activities.[11] Women rarely served as official members of Black associations led by men. They took on complementary roles to men as an extension of their caretaker responsibilities. In many ways, this pattern resembled the social structure promoted by racial regeneration advocates during the late colonial period. Yet elite women of African descent who protested racism in the late nineteenth-century press became silent on issues of anti-Blackness following the establishment of the republic. Adhering to patriarchal standards that compelled women to racial silence became *the* approach for contesting racism. Everyday practices of comportment enabled elite Black women to challenge assumptions of racial inferiority in lieu of public protests.

An emphasis on patriarchal standards of comportment only partly explains the political actions of elite Black women. Many Cuban women, regardless of race, imagined their identities in ways that extended beyond the male gaze. Although the 1901 Constitution disenfranchised all women, a younger generation of activists challenged colonial-era gender norms as they sought personal autonomy within and beyond the domestic realm. Some took advantage of the expanding school system, which they viewed as preparation for their nationalist roles as mothers of future leaders.[12] Many women gained professional employment as nurses, pharmacists, educators, and typists. Women of African descent who encountered discrimination in the labor force challenged stereotypes of inferiority by performing femininity in ways that reflected traditional and modernizing expectations. On one hand, elite Black women demonstrated their civility at religious events like weddings, baptisms, and onomastic day celebrations. At the same time, they negotiated women's civic engagement through public discussions of feminism as well as the establishment of associations. By taking on leadership roles at the local level, elite women of African descent staked claims to community progress. Finally, consumer practices and sociopolitical activities buttressed a cosmopolitan image of elite femininity that privileged, African-descended women engaged. Elite Black social networks, in this regard, responded to and shaped dominant ideas of Cuban womanhood more broadly.

Sitting for a Portrait

The connections between gendered comportment and elite Black political aspirations are visible in the photographic portraits created during the early twentieth century. However, the historiography of Black photographic portraiture has focused largely on the efforts of African Americans to construct counternarratives to offensive racial stereotypes.[13] More recently, scholars have theorized Black photographic portraiture within an Afro-diasporic perspective.[14] Such studies demonstrate how privileged African descendants living throughout the Atlantic world sought to forge modern identities through visual culture. Elite and upwardly mobile Blacks living in post-abolition societies of Latin American and the Caribbean used photography to imagine freedom, and those who resided in Europe documented their aspirations as migrants. Both groups utilized the camera to bolster their political aims. African Americans, Black Caribbean and Latin American populations, and Afro-Europeans employed similar representational strategies, from the composition of photographic portraits to contemporary fashions, to communicate ideas of gender and racial citizenship. Populations of African descent also circulated their images through publications that informed individual strategies for racial representation.[15]

Elite and upwardly mobile Cubans of African descent employed photographic portraiture as a strategy to radically reimagine their place in a modernizing nation. Photographers captured family members, entertainers, political leaders, and affiliates of local community groups who chose to document key moments of their lives. Photographic images highlighted the relational ties through which men and women presented themselves as dignified citizens. The circulation of photographic portraits through the Black press enabled elite African descendants to challenge stereotypes without violating the terms of racelessness. Women played a role in developing the narratives as part of a Black political agenda. Indeed, most photographs that I consulted were individual portraits of women.

In my analysis of Black Cuban photographic portraiture, a salient point I have observed is how persons of African descent acted as agents in shaping visual representations in Latin America and the Caribbean. In a study of South American highlands cultures, the anthropologist Deborah Poole argues for the role of a "modern visual economy" in shaping discourses of race that entails "the intricate and sometimes contradictory layering of relationships, attitudes, sentiments, and ambitions through which Europeans and Andeans have invested images with meaning and value."[16] The visual culture scholar Beatriz González-Stephan has theorized how, within the visual economy of nineteenth-century Brazil and Venezuela, the *carte de visite* portrait "constituted a trivial replacement of an older archive of aristocratic visual codes by new technologies that adroitly promoted mechanisms of identity."[17] Both scholars demonstrate the ways colonial racial hierarchies figured into photographic traditions of the modern era. At the same time, they privilege photographs in which marginalized Native American and African-descended sitters had little control over their images.[18] Many of the images cited in the studies of Poole and González-Stephan originated as ethnographic works produced by social scientists engaged in the study of racial difference; others were created by enslavers to document their property. The photographs I examine, instead, were created for the personal enjoyment of Black Cuban sitters in order to center their perspectives on race making, family life, and nationhood.

Months after President Palma Estrada excluded the wives of Black politicians from his presidential reception, *El Nuevo Criollo* editor Rafael Serra circulated two photographic portraits of his daughter Consuelo on the occasion of her college graduation. The June 1905 edition featured Consuelo on its cover, and she appears in her graduation gown in a portrait on an inside page of the same issue (figure 3.1).[19] An accompanying article celebrated Consuelo as a young *triunfadora* (victor). Heralded as the "kind

Figure 3.1. The educator Consuelo Serra y Heredia in her graduation regalia. From Rafael Serra, *Para blancos y negros: Ensayos políticos, sociales y económicos*, vol. 4 (Havana: El Score, 1907). Courtesy of Manuscripts, Archives, and Rare Books Division, Schomburg Center for Research in Black Culture, New York Public Library, Astor, Lenox, and Tilden Foundation, http://digitalcollections.nypl.org/items/510d47da-70cf-a3d9-e040-e00a18064a99. Also published in *El Nuevo Criollo*, June 18, 1905.

and intelligent" daughter of the independence war veteran, an unnamed contributor examined Consuelo's character in great detail. The writer regarded Consuelo as a distinguished leader of her community who had pushed herself "to her ultimate limit," which was one of her many traits to be admired. Consuelo Serra had recently graduated from the New York Normal Institute. The author commended her for making a name for herself as she maintained her "mission to defend and exalt Cuba in a foreign school." After she graduated with "the highest and most dignified marks," her father celebrated the occasion with "a deserved tribute" to Consuelo; he chose to "express physically *through a portrait*" his pride.[20]

The profile that accompanied Consuelo Serra's images conveys the affective role of photographic portraiture.[21] As the author revered the younger Serra for her commitment to uplifting herself and the nation through education, the photographic portrait was identified as a visual marker of feminine attainment. The writer hoped that the photograph would serve as "satisfaction, encouragement and consolidation" for other Cubans. The author suggested that readers "take pride" in the ability of individuals to prove their intellectual capability, a triumph "conquered in foreign countries."[22] By demonstrating Consuelo's attainments, the image signaled the honor of her father as a politician and as his family's patriarch. Consuelo's accomplishments evidenced the progress of Cubans in the United States as well as Blacks living on the island.

Early twentieth-century studio portraits like those of Consuelo Serra mirrored images captured during the late nineteenth century. But few Black publications from the colonial period possessed the financial means to print photographs. Magazines like *Ecos Juveniles* (1909–1910), *Minerva: Revista Universal Ilustrada* (1910–1915), and *Labor Nueva* (1915–1916) joined *El Nuevo Criollo* in affirming Blacks' civility through photography.[23] Each publication featured photographic portraits of its contributors and readers, most often women, on its covers and throughout its pages as the sole subjects of the portraits. Editors also published images of male socialites and politicians as well as entertainment groups and children on occasion. However, no Black periodical that I consulted featured a photographic portrait of a nuclear family.[24] Editors like Rafael Serra used photographic portraits to reinforce the textual conversations regarding racial equality and the role of Black men within nuclear families, and they did so by visualizing women of African descent at the center of a modernizing society.[25]

Black periodicals enabled elite women like Consuelo Serra to circulate their images among a dynamic sociopolitical network. They affirmed women of African descent who successfully modeled domestic femininity for Black Cuban readers across the island and in the United States. They offered a feminine counterpoint to the masculinist image of African-descended civic leaders that editors sought to project. Elite Black women sitters also conveyed to elite whites the refinement of elite persons of African descent. It is likely that the published photographs were voluntarily submitted by those closely linked to the editorial board, as the editors did not publish official calls for photographs.

Photographic portraits published in the early twentieth-century Black press repeatedly depicted women sitters in domestic settings that projected a sense of moral leadership. The placement of Consuelo Serra seated in a chair in a domestic interior framed her femininity in a particular light, as a cultured woman with the composure and social attainments of a respectable woman. Her clothing and proper pose illustrated her modesty. As much as wearing contemporary fashions reflected a level of material attainment, the props in the photographic image also served as "dream objects" through which the sitter and photographer created a visual narrative of bourgeois femininity to be ascertained by the viewer.[26] Each carefully selected prop—flowers, table, columns, and decorated backdrop—replicated a decorous sitting room where elite women greeted and entertained their guests. *El Nuevo Criollo* readers recognized in the young woman's portraits material objects that they may have possessed or aspired to own.

While the portraits of Consuelo Serra illustrate her class standing for the readers of *El Nuevo Criollo*, it is likely that the photographs were originally created for private use rather than publication in a periodical. As such, the images may have been taken to distribute to a close circle of friends and family. The portraits served as artifacts that captured the graduate at a pivotal moment in her life as a young, educated woman; such a portrait was to be hung on the wall of a living room, framed and placed on a table, or sent as a postcard to a family member in another city. Whether viewed privately or circulated publicly, the images made use of visual markers to convey success. Each element of a photographic image illustrated the attainments and aspirations of the sitter, creating a "visual vocabulary of womanhood" that reflected dominant standards of women's public behavior.[27]

Consuelo Serra's photographic portraits resembled those of white elite and middle-class women published during the period. Contemporary magazines like *Cuba y América*, *Bohemia*, and *Mariposa* featured photographs of individual female sitters wearing simple, tailored clothing. Most subjects appeared in domestic settings rather than in outdoor settings. Those featuring white women also incorporated props such as clothing, jewelry, and flowers to imply dominant standards of bourgeois femininity to the largely elite and middle-class readership. Mainstream magazines and newspapers rarely featured women of African descent. The exclusion of photographic portraits of Black women enabled editors to shape a particular image of Cuba. They affirmed elite white civility while largely ignoring the attainments of Black elite populations. Photographs in the early feminist publications *Aspiraciones* and *Revista de la Asociación Femenina de Camagüey* featured only white women from established families.

Photographic portraits thus served as a visual technology through which elite white Cubans reproduced gendered ideas of racial superiority. Between the late nineteenth and early twentieth centuries, a global community of eugenicists linked human fitness and assumptions of racial difference to national progress.[28] To transmit these ideas into Cuban culture, the government initiated several projects intended to facilitate larger discussions on the state of the nation. In 1915, the Ministry of Hygiene and Welfare established "beautiful baby" contests. With photographic portraits of young, white children, beautiful-baby contests emphasized the idea that environmental conditions could bring about racial progress, that Cuba could build a strong population through moral, hygienic, and physiological improvements.[29] Organizers widely advertised the contests and received support from businesses throughout the island. Through such practices, government officials projected the moral health and environmental conditions of Cuban citizens along racial lines.

Images of elite white men and women published in the mainstream press projected modern refinement, and those that featured Black men and women between the 1840s and 1910s helped cement stereotypes of Black racial inferiority. During the 1860s, the French anthropologist Henri Dumont sought to distinguish African ethnic groups by creating daguerreotypes of the enslaved. He claimed to differentiate social behaviors as well as disease along racial lines. In 1915 and 1916, the Cuban anthropologist Israel Castellanos used Dumont's images to theorize connections between Blackness and criminality.[30] Fernando Ortiz's *Hampa afro-cubana: Los negros brujos;*

apuntes para un estudio de etnología criminal (1906) and Rafael Roche y Monteagudo's *La policía y sus misterios en Cuba* (1908) claim connections between Afro-Cuban religions and criminality. Each text incorporates visual images to illustrate the authors' theories. Ortiz's book features sketches of Orisha statues, musical instruments, and Blacks dressed for religious ceremonies; Monteagudo's work presents drawings of Abakuá figures and religious signs as well as photographs of altars. Because social scientists and politicians equated whiteness with national progress, they asserted that Blacks' supposedly immoral character and superstitious behaviors threatened the modernization of society.

Degrading portrayals of African-descended women buttressed racial hierarchies that privileged white male patriarchy. They undermined the legitimacy of Black male political agency; within a patriarchal society, if Black men proved incapable of controlling the sexual behavior of Black women, their ability to navigate the political realm as civic leaders could be questioned. Poor images of women of African descent not only negated their contributions to society but also situated them as impediments to national progress.

Photographic portraits that illustrated African-descended womanhood within a framework of domesticity presented a counternarrative to such images. In this sense, Consuelo Serra's appearance in a domestic interior setting demonstrates the utility of Jasmine Nichole Cobb's framework of the "transatlantic parlor" that "provided a place wherein viewers could contemplate the impact of Black emancipation."[31] More than a representation of intimate interior spaces, posing in a setting removed from urban streets or rural fields broke with stereotypical images that associated Blackness with slavery and menial labor.[32] It removed Black women sitters from sites of labor deemed masculine, such as agricultural or factory work, or immoral, such as sex work. The setting also affirmed the female sitter's position as the lady of the house rather than as a domestic servant.

As elite Black women challenged stereotypes in their construction of a public image, portraits of individuals such as Consuelo Serra's in her father's magazine claimed Black women as models of physical beauty. Serra appears clean, with meticulously coiffed hair and tailored clothing. Similar images portray elite Black women in erect poses, wearing accessories such as jewelry and hats. A photographer's or sitter's projection of the attractiveness of African-descended women featured persons of African descent in control of their own images. Editors reinforced the subject's femininity by labeling the woman as *bella* (pretty) or *simpática* (kind). As photographers, portrait sitters, and editors articulated a highly politicized alternative narrative of Black female identity, they aimed to "produce beauty" by drawing from an image of physical attractiveness that did not appear within visual representations of white dominant culture.[33]

For People of Taste

Eleven years after the publication of Consuelo Serra's photographic portraits in *El Nuevo Criollo*, the weekly magazine *Labor Nueva* featured the socialite Antonia Hernández in its May 14, 1916, issue (figure 3.2). Summaries of recent elite Black social events surrounded her image. Editors heralded Hernández as a "distinguished lady" who represented, "with the approval of our subscribers" and "a good number of supporters," the town of Coliseo; *Labor Nueva* circulated her image throughout the island.[34] Certainly, the appearance of the photographic portrait gave the young woman cause for celebration, as it promoted her honorable reputation before a wide audience. The image put forth a recognizable model of elegant femininity for the magazine's readership. Hernández's clothing called attention to her virtue as a sophisticated socialite. Her light-colored shoes and the dress that draped her entire body illustrated her extravagant femininity characteristic of the Edwardian period.

Similar to the portrait of Consuelo Serra, Hernández's position in an elegant domestic interior setting projects her command over the home as an accomplished, cultured woman. She appears seated in a short folding chair. An elaborately designed carpet or tiled floor creates an ambience of affluence. The curved base and sides of the chair suggest a regal seat. In addition to the design of the parlor space, Hernández's pose projects social refinement. She confidently tilts to her right, crossing one ankle over the other, and seems to look past the viewer as though absorbed in contemplation.

As a commodity accessible mainly to elite and upwardly mobile populations, Black publications placed women like Antonia Hernández on the cover of almost every issue. This reflected a common practice through which editors sought to attract buyers, as they used covers to present visual icons of femininity.[35] Viewers would have immediately recognized the hairstyles and clothing as modern trends, the seated positions as popular

justo tributo de admiración, simpatía y gratitud a los que, en momentos terribles concibieron la idea de fundar un Centro en el que la enseñanza elemental no le fuera negada a los que no tuvieron la fortuna de nacer de la unión de padres europeos.

Parece que la Directiva de ese Centro o había pensado de acuerdo con nosotros, o ha querido atender las indicaciones que hubimos de hacerle en nuestro número anterior, al reseñar la hermosa velada recientemente celebrada en los salones de la recién constituida sociedad "Casino Musical", en conmemoración de la muerte de Raimundo Valenzuela: lo cierto es que el programa de la Velada de este año, ha sido distinto al que estábamos acostumbrados.

Helo aquí:

Primera parte

1.—Sinfonía por la Orquesta del Profesor Sr. Pablo Valenzuela.
2.—Discurso por el Sr. Primitivo R. Ros.
3.—Poesía por la Srta. Melanea Acosta.
4.—Trot de Cavaliere de Anton Rubinsteins, ejecutado al piano por la Srta. Josefina Sterling y Malagamba.
5.—Concierto VIII-Bleriot; por la niña Dolores Quesada y el Sr. Erasmo Gómez.
6.—Discurso por el Sr. Saturnino E. Carrión.

Segunda parte

1.—Lily of the Valley, por Sidney Smith, ejecutado al piano por la Srta. Liduvina Valdés.
2.—Discurso por el Sr. Sergio Cuevas Zequeira.
3.—Poesía por la Srta. María Ignacia Matehu.
4.—Gran selección de "Bohemia" de Puccini, para trío de violín, violoncello y piano por los señores Julián Barreto, Antonio Mompó y Gonzalo Roig.
5.—Discurso resumen por el Sr. Juan Gualberto Gómez.
6.—Baile por la orquesta del profesor señor Pablo Valenzuela.

A las dos menos diez minutos de la madrugada, descendió de la tribuna nuestro querido amigo el señor Juan Gualberto Gómez, e inmediatamente, (después de obsequiada finamente la concurrencia) dió comienzo la parte bailable, en la cual la orquesta merecidamente reputada del señor Pablo Valenzuela, dió comienzo a la ejecución de los más bonitos bailables de su inagotable repertorio.

Y ahora, reproduzcamos algunas de las muchas buenas cosas recientemente publicadas por nuestro amable compañero Enrique Ortiz en la sección "Vida Social", de nuestro estimado colega "Heraldo de Cuba":

Nota de amor.—

¿Quieres saber, bella lectora, de quién se trata?

Pon en acción tu fina suspicacia, y a un cuerpo flexible y airoso, siempre elegantemente vestido, agrega un andar lleno de gracia, y supón leve sonrisilla en una boca pequeña y espiritual, y de seguro que las iniciales que corresponden a su nombre y primer apellido te re ultarán: V....... S....., coloca después, a su lado, a un joven que sabe de leyes, de conversación fácil y rápida, tan rápida co-

SRTA. ANTONIA HERNANDEZ

Dama distinguida del pueblo de Coliseo, donde representa, con beneplácito de nuestros suscriptores, a "Labor Nueva", que cuenta en esa culta localidad un buen número de favorecedores.

mo sus movimientos y voluntad; y alcanzarás adivinar que se trata de A. M., que canta a V. su dulce amor, en estrofas rebosantes de amor y de pasión...

¿Qué más puede agregarse a todo esto para una ligera compresión?

Nada hay en firme aún; pero... el cronista no está autorizado para decir.. ni lo que ha dicho.

Alfredo Rodríguez.—

Mejorada completamente de las dolencias que hasta antes de ayer lo retuvieron en cama, se encuentra ya el joven Alfredo Rodríguez.

Matinée.—

Varias damitas en unión de los señores N. Zamora y Gerardo Herrera, están organizando una alegre matinée que tendrá efecto en Junio próximo en los amplios salones de la Sociedad "La Mariposa", en el Cerro.

"Minerva Club".—

A partir del lunes 15 de los corrientes, comenzará su serie de Ensayos y Recepciones el "Club Minerva".

Figure 3.2. The socialite Antonia Hernández of Coliseo. From *Labor Nueva*, May 14, 1916, 11.

poses for women in photographs, and the domestic settings as markers of elite social standing, whether women worked as professionals or remained in the house as homemakers. An analysis of self-fashioning through photographic portraiture, therefore, must consider the common features that linked photographs published in the Black press.[36] Beyond documenting personal moments, photographs reveal how minute details communicated the relation between consumption and gendered comportment.

Elite Black women strove to invoke a vision of womanhood that implied progress, largely conveyed through their attire, as they ventured beyond the domestic sphere. Some promoted these values as seamstresses who outfitted their clients in the latest fashion trends. Vicenta García de Estenoz, wife of the Partido Independiente de Color (PIC) leader Evaristo Estenoz, operated a French fashion boutique. A writer of the PIC periodical, *Previsión*, explained, "An elegant woman should always have the tact to dress herself, and carry in each circumstance a dress that flatters her."[37] The writer pointedly suggested that an individual's clothing emphasized her feminine status within a modernizing Cuban society. Moreover, the author recommended that a woman be conscious of how she represented herself throughout her daily activities, as her activities and appearance reflected upon both her family and race. As the 1910 *Previsión* article illustrated, the strong connection between "an elegant woman," clothing, and public representation often informed contemporary discourses of racial uplift.

Notions that women's attire was inexorably linked to racial regeneration proliferated in Black publications. In 1893, a writer for *La Igualdad* described fashion as "a perpetual renewal of the precedent."[38] Fashion column writers with pen names that included "María Antoineta" and "Varona" identified seasonal trends or linked controversial garments to changing definitions of womanhood. The columnists regularly featured details of the appropriate fashion trends that arrived in Cuba from London and Paris. They paid great attention to the changing fabrics, colors, and design of contemporary clothing, noting, for example, when skirts became more fitted or blouses more intricate in detail. They noted how fashion consistently evolved in relation to changing political contexts that produced new understandings of femininity. In a 1910 edition of *Minerva*, a writer focused on the individual style options available to women: "At this time, fashion is undergoing a state of transition. Therefore, there is no fixed style that all of society follows."[39] The writer implied that women had a variety of trends to choose from when assembling an outfit. Though the columnists did not publish reader responses, the stylish outfits worn by women in photographs in the same issues suggested that wearing modish clothing was a means of asserting elite social standing. Fashion columns depict how Black women's understandings of femininity vacillated between the Victorian ideals of pious women relegated to the private sphere and the modern, bourgeois roles in which women demanded access to public politics.

Hernandez's decision to wear her particular dress followed stylistic norms from the era.[40] Hernandez wears a typical afternoon lawn dress from the period.[41] Afternoon dresses created for intimate gatherings at home or outdoor sporting events tended to be white, detailed with handmade embroidery, and lined with fine, white silk net. The craftsmanship of Hernandez's dress reflected her social status, as it was likely tailormade to fit her body. Tailor-made clothes were unavailable to most Cubans. Therefore, as fashion marked Hernandez's gender and class status in society, it also drew boundaries between the privileged classes and laboring poor.[42]

In addition to clothing, accessories such as flowers accentuated the femininity of portrait sitters. Hernandez holds a bouquet of flowers on her lap. Similarly, in a photographic portrait in *Labor Nueva* of June 18, 1916, the schoolteacher Isolira Sabión touches a basket of flowers with one hand and holds a fan in the other (figure 3.3). She sits coolly on a bench, her left arm resting on its back. Though she appears in a studio, the bench and backdrop place her in a park setting. The basket creates a scenario in which Sabión might have picked or purchased the flowers for her home. The floral arrangements suggest a well-maintained home; they signal the domestic virtue of both sitters.

Fans likewise enhanced the gendered images of women sitters. One *Labor Nueva* cover features María Luisa Hernández and María de Jesús Gómez on the cover of *Labor Nueva* (figure 3.4). The cover image is one of the few photographs to feature two women who were not family members. The seated woman holds a fan in her hands. The fan clearly served as a practical accessory that women used to cool themselves on a hot day. But fans also became popular fashion and home décor statements for bourgeois women in the 1860s into the 1930s. Fans bridged the realm of fine art and the mass consumer market; they communicated sexuality and style.[43] Women carried fans to local soirees, the opera, and other leisure events.

Figure 3.3. The professor of public instruction Isolira Sabión of Santo Domingo. From *Labor Nueva*, June 18, 1916, 1.

Figure 3.4. María Luisa Hernández and María de Jesús Gómez of Colón. From *Labor Nueva*, April 23, 1916, 1.

As women were increasingly entering the public sphere as students and working professionals, and some established political organizations, items such as fans and flowers reinforced traditional ideas of femininity. They signified beauty, innocence, and fragility. Strategically placed accessories, in other words, enabled photographers and female sitters to negotiate traditional gender norms with new expectations of women's social roles.

As Black magazines promoted consumer practices to portray the modern refinement of elite women, they presented readers with goods that offered to modify the readers' physical appearance. Commercial advertisers of the early 1900s were cognizant that hair could represent progress and beauty, and hair-straightening products that targeted Black consumers established clear differences between African-descended and white women's hair. Advertisements for the hair-straightening cream Pomada Mora regularly appeared in *Minerva* from 1910 to 1915. The product sold for forty cents in salons such as the Bazar Inglés of Havana or by agents throughout the island. The Pomada Mora advertisements frequently featured images of Cubans of African descent using the product, thereby affirming the practice of hair-straightening. In April 1913, a full-page advertisement depicts a hair stylist applying the pomade to a Black woman's hair. An April 1914 ad features a drawing of "dark-skinned" couples dancing in a ballroom, the women in the latest fashions of dress, with feathered headbands and fans. The female and male dancers have sleek, shiny, dark hair. The image is accompanied by text noting, "At a soiree, one can see the advantages of Pomade 'Mora.'" The manufacturer advertised the "safe procedure to soften the more rebellious hair."[44] The company claims imply that coarse hair was the antithesis of normative models of beauty. Straightening one's hair thus became a way to comply with societal norms.

The Pomada Mora advertisement that appeared most frequently in *Minerva* features before-and-after drawings (figure 3.5). The "before" image shows the profile of a woman with a head of very curly, coarse hair pulled back into a bun. The "after" sketch faces the "before," showing the woman's profile with her now gently wavy hair pulled back into a similar hairstyle. The accompanying text states, "Safe procedure to soften the more rebellious hair, *so as to make it straight and silky like the purest Caucasian*" (emphasis mine). Thus the advertisement used the image of whites' "straight and silky" hair to establish an ideal model of beauty to which Blacks should aspire. The manufacturer also advertised, "In this house there is a diverse

Figure 3.5. Pomada Mora advertisement. From *Minerva*, July 1912, 20.

and select range of braids and curls for women of color."[45] While the text acknowledges a range of hair types and styles, the juxtaposition of the images implies that purchasers of Pomada Mora could improve their image by chemically altering their hair texture.

It is unclear whether the women who appeared in *Minerva* used hair-straightening products, and most women appeared with puffy hair rather than the slick styles portrayed in the advertisements. Still, the Pomada Mora advertisements in the magazine complicate the understandings of Black womanhood and progress in relation to beauty standards. Despite the regular appearance of such ads, the writers of *Minerva* did not specifically discuss hairstyles in their columns. Certainly, some Black women straightened their hair by using products like the Pomada Mora. The publication of advertisements that encouraged women of African descent to change their hair may have resulted from a necessary financial decision by editors. Their publication also reinforced an image of Black beauty that conformed to Eurocentric standards and placed women of color outside the boundaries of ideal beauty due to their kinky hair. As signifiers of modernity and progress, advertisements for cosmetic products such as hair pomade implied that coarse hair was an imperfection that needed to be fixed.[46]

The Best of the Colored Race

In their photographic portraits, elite persons of African descent flaunted their modern cultural behaviors as evidence of their refinement. Published coverage of social events reinforced visual images through detailed accounts of the exclusive groups of attendees who gathered in elegant locations. The Black press announced university graduations, annual soirees, weddings, baptisms, and religious celebrations. By heralding the activities of consummate women and men of African descent, Black publications promoted race pride. Published coverage demonstrates how elite civic club members enacted bourgeois patriarchal standards through their sociopolitical networks. An examination of Black associational life reveals that concerns over comportment spilled into the social lives of elite persons of African descent.

A prominent example is the "sumptuous wedding" of the Santa Clara residents Margarita Guerra y Guerra and Hermenegildo Ponvert D'Lisle.[47] Described as "a true event in our social world," the *Minerva* columnist López Silvero went to great lengths to document the extravagance of the occasion.[48] He noted the beauty of the Plaza de Chao chapel, which was almost too small to hold the "huge crowd" of well-known society members that gathered. Among the more than one hundred guests in attendance were African-descended luminaries including Juan Gualberto Gómez, Generals Agustín Cebreco and Generoso Campos, Representatives Saturino Escoto and Primitivo Ramírez, the mayor of San Fernando de Camarones, Fire Chief Gumersindo Carrera, and Chief of Police José Cabrera, and the presidents of the local Black civic clubs El Gran Maceo and La Bella Unión. Attendees enjoyed musical selections such as the Italian composer Pietro Mascagni's "Ave Maria" and German composer Wilhelm Richard Wagner's march "Logengrin." Guests were "handsomely presented with fine pastries and famous liquors served in silvery cups with bell rims."[49] Following the reception, they enjoyed a buffet pasta dinner at the "reputable" Hotel Telégrafo. The young bride received a variety of gifts with which to begin her new life as a wife, including a silver compact from Gómez, a vanity case from Campos Marquetti, and a diamond and emerald pin from the groom's father. The groom purchased Guerra y Guerra's bridal gown, bouquet, and "travel suit." Women gave the bride china and religious relics, among them a basin for holy water and an ivory crucifix. The couple also received a "multitude of expressive and heartfelt telegrams from different people of Las Villas [Province] and the republic capital."[50] Silvero concluded the article by stating that the night of the wedding, the couple left for Havana "in an elegant railroad parlor car."[51]

The coverage of the wedding of Guerra y Guerra and Ponvert D'Lisle reflects how major social events enabled elite African descendants to display their material attainment. Social announcements were merely a part of an interrelated narrative. The men and women who attended such events used Black publications to buttress their political standing. For African-descended civic activists, the formation of nuclear households demonstrated that the race had made substantial progress since the end of slavery. Moreover, the young Santa Clara couple organized their nuptials during an era when material status assumed new salience among Cubans of all races. They exchanged rings at a time when Black women and men made a connection between material consumption and their impending entrance into adulthood as elite socialites.

In citing the presence of prominent politicians, Silvero illustrated how elite African descendants maintained selective social spaces.[52] Many of the attendees played prominent roles in forging Black political networks sustained by civic clubs. Some Black associations founded during the postabolition period such as the Centro de Cocheros, later renamed Our Lady of Charity, remained active into the twentieth century.[53] Others were established after the fall of colonialism. In Havana alone, more than half of the sixty Black civic clubs registered with the Cuban government in 1928 had been formed after 1902.[54] Organizational records suggest a professionally diverse group of male members. Luz de Oriente, one of Santiago de Cuba's most prominent Black organizations, had members who were tobacco workers and urban artisans such as carpenters, blacksmiths, painters, barbers, and tailors as well as businessmen, doctors, lawyers, and pharmacists.[55] In Havana, Club Atenas maintained its elite status by accepting only professionals, while the Unión Fraternal accepted both professionals and artisans as members.[56] Most groups used dues to ensure that only individuals with the proper means could seek membership.

Black civic associations occasionally distinguished themselves by color, especially in the eastern region of Cuba, where the proportion of the population of African descent was larger.[57] In Guantánamo, Club Moncada and Nueva Era provided exclusive social spaces for *mulatos*, while Blacks joined the society Siglo XX. Notably, society men and women seemed to establish these color boundaries through social practice rather than official policy; no society document that I consulted defined itself as an organization solely for Blacks or *mulatos*. Given the prevailing nationalist discourses of race-lessness, most Black associations made no mention of race in their bylaws. City guides and oral testimonies support the probability that distinct *mulato* societies did exist, although occasions did arise in which social boundaries became more fluid. Yanira Mesa Jiménez argues that "deep links and relationships" existed between Santa Clara's Black society El Gran Maceo and *mulato* society La Bella Unión.[58] Women attended society events based on their affiliation with male society members, and their affiliations may have changed as they married.

Maintaining color boundaries, however, did not occur without occasional criticism. Eladio Garzón Carrión, a Black resident of Santiago de Cuba, wrote an opinion piece published in the regional newspaper *Oriente* in which he lamented the status of the Black community. Garzón wrote in reaction to an exposé published in the newly created newsletter *La Invasión de Maceo*, whose name referred to the African-descended general Antonio Maceo.[59] Garzón complained that "Blacks invalidate themselves due to egocentrism and lack of unity." He observed that Club Aponte represented Blacks, while Luz de Oriente and El Casino Cubano served the social interests of *mulatos*. Garzón declared the "necessity for social reform" among African descendants and posited that Club Aponte "must change the direction" or "the direction must change the system." He asserted that Blacks' ability to unify across class and color lines would be crucial for ensuring the development of society. It is possible that Garzón was himself a member of Club Aponte, as he called upon the members of that organization alone to promote "social brotherhood among Blacks in their various classes, family organization, economic solvency, and intellectual significance and representation in public life."[60]

Some associations enforced boundaries of exclusion along color lines, but most functioned as spaces into which women could enter only as the wives, daughters, mothers, or board-approved *socias* of its most respectable male members. Associates emphasized that their members came from *gente decente* (good families). Men and women who sought access to civic club activities had to meet various requirements, among them "having good customs and a good reputation."[61] Each association established guidelines that outlined the process through which individuals could become members, who qualified for membership, the rights and duties of each member, and the penalties for violating organizational codes.[62] Occasionally, however, clubs such as the Unión Fraternal continued the tradition of allowing women to participate indirectly through *comités de damas*. Though seldom documented in official records, auxiliary group members elected formal leaders, held fundraisers, and organized parties as well as other social and educational activities.

Displays of cultural refinement at association events connected club members to processes of social ascent, helping to further delineate social boundaries. Dances, similar to weddings, became particularly important venues for such exhibitions. In Santa Clara, the annual Baile de las Flores (Floral Dance), which was held each May to celebrate the beginning of the spring, was one of the region's most anticipated events. The ball called for specific attire for men and women; men wore white or light-colored suits, and women wore gowns of similar shades. Young women carried bouquets of white or pastel flowers, and many women held ornate fans as they danced the *danzón* with their husbands or male escorts. Alferio Noriega recalled that everyone purchased elegant new attire for the annual ball, noting, "No one dressed in older clothing."[63] The Floral Dance is also featured as an important event in the novel by the Santa Clara native Pedro Pérez Sarduy, *Las criadas de la Habana* (The maids of Havana), which he based on the stories of his mother, Marta. Narrating Marta's experiences as a young Black woman during the republican era, Sarduy writes, "The Floral Dance was the one all the young people, especially newly-weds, looked forward to each year."[64] The event marked a rare occasion when working-class Santa Clara residents would flaunt their earnings. Marta recalls, "It was unforgettable, especially when you knew that what you had was worth a year's work, because sometimes the gowns could cost up to 100 pesos and the dances took place three or four times a year, and, like I said before, you wouldn't for the life of you go to two dances wearing the same outfit."[65] *Las criadas de la Habana* also provides insight into the racial boundaries that separated Santa Clara's numerous clubs, in Marta's words:

> [My friends] liked to party and to spend wildly on occasions such as the great Floral Dance of the Bella Union Society, which was for colored people. That day there were festivities throughout Santa Clara: at the Grand Maceo Society, for mulattoes and certain wealthy Blacks; at the Spanish Casino, the Vedado Tennis Club and at the Lyceum, facing Vidal Park, where the wealthy whites held their celebrations. But we weren't bothered with those festivities because the members of the Bella Union did everything possible so that ours would be the best organized and with the best bands.[66]

Here, Marta's character demonstrates an acceptance of racial and class distinctions. Sarduy's account of his mother's life provides a more complex picture of associational life in which the laboring poor attended civic club events.

Social events between elite and laboring poor Blacks did not take place without issue. The historian Frank Guridy details how, during the 1920s, several members of El Gran Maceo filed a complaint with the provincial government in Santa Clara for having been expelled from the society for bringing an uninvited female guest to a dance. Board members of the club had become concerned about the decision of its members and *señoritas* to attend parties sponsored by organizations other than El Gran Maceo. Fearing that the association of some members with clubs that board members viewed as less respectable would diminish their own club's reputation, El Gran Maceo affiliates sought to distance themselves from women of the laboring classes. They carefully regulated who could or could not attend their events. Months after the complaint was filed, leaders of the society held an emergency board meeting to establish formal regulations and guidelines dictating the public comportment of El Gran Maceo's affiliates. The male leadership stipulated that "no young lady can be considered an invited guest if she works as a cook or maid in any establishment or private home."[67]

Elites like those of El Gran Maceo enacted bourgeois patriarchal norms through the policing of Black men's and women's behaviors. In turn, those who gained entry to civic club events created spaces that validated their manhood and womanhood according to dominant standards. They hoped to contest anti-Black racism among whites by crafting their own exclusive spaces. Crafting exclusive social spaces along the lines of class, color, and gender led Black elites to distance themselves from the laboring poor. Displays of material wealth demonstrated these boundaries as well. At the same time, patriarchal standards of public behavior that emphasized bourgeois morality also enabled working-class Blacks to project individual respectability and refinement.

"Involving Women in All Facets of Collective Life"

During the 1910s and 1920s, as the burgeoning feminist movement and family law reforms presented Cuban women with greater autonomy beyond the domestic realm, many elite Black men affirmed their patriarchal honor by reasserting traditional gender roles. They uplifted the beauty and intellectual achievements of those they considered exemplary African-descended women, and they scorned others who engaged in behaviors deemed indecent. They defined the ideal woman as patriotic, culturally refined, sexually virtuous, and altruistic. In 1905 the patriot-intellectual Rafael Serra venerated the educational accomplishments of his daughter Consuelo on the pages of *El Nuevo Criollo*. In 1920 the Club Atenas member and intellectual Miguel Ángel Céspedes asserted,

> Our women . . . must be self-sacrificing and long-suffering. As girls, they must be the angels of our happiness, as young ladies, the source of our sweetest dreams, as mothers, loving and protective of our collective health and education, as wives, finally, faithful to sacrifice, and, similar to the pure virgins of pagan Rome, always careful to keep burning in our chests, with their praise and caresses, the lamp of their love's holy flame.[68]

In his discussion of women in society, Céspedes limits women's authority and instead emphasizes their unconditional commitment to the family. He emphasizes women's roles as daughters, wives, and mothers, positions carried out with love for the well-being of their communities. His language resembles the rhetoric of patriotic womanhood that celebrated *mambisas* (women of the independence movement) while limiting suffrage to men. For elite Black leaders, the integrity of Black masculinity and the success of racial regeneration were contingent upon women's ability to conform to dominant behaviors of femininity. And yet, an acknowledgment of how the Black press documented the public activities of elite women raises a question regarding comportment as a political strategy: How did elite Black activists reconcile patriarchal expectations with modernizing perspectives on women's civic engagement during the early years of the republic?

Women's options for navigating patriarchal expectations through civic participation remained an issue for negotiation. Black writers like Juan Gualberto Gómez advocated for women's expanded civic responsibilities. "One of the characteristics of our century," he declares to *Minerva* readers, "will be the efforts that have been achieved and will continue to be achieved in involving women in all facets of collective life."[69] Gómez became a vocal proponent of women's edification. He deemed women "man's sweet and irreplaceable companion." Moreover, to fulfill their mission in society and the home, he contended that women of the twentieth century should learn to "think and feel like men." Gómez proposed that publications such as *Minerva* serve as "an experimental camp" in which the youth of both sexes contribute to "the advancement of their race in the fields of literature and the arts."[70]

Though elite Blacks argued that women should think and feel like men, they did not promote gender parity. The *Labor Nueva* contributor Julián González affirmed gender binaries when he asserted that women's "natural nobility" or spiritual nature rendered them superior to men.[71] In November 1910, the *Minerva* writer María Risquet de Márquez suggested that women had begun to overcome the traditional expectations that limited them to lives of submission and ignorance. "The woman who yesteryear only served to perform routine chores or to live among frivolities today rises . . . lifting [herself] to the level of man," she observes with satisfaction. No longer, Risquet asserts, would a woman's duties be reduced to chores. Yet while she expressed her excitement for women's opportunities in the young republic, she did not seek to break the mold altogether. She seemed skeptical of formal political participation: "I do not admire the woman who wants to invade reckless spheres of government and politics; penetrating as it burned in a field where feeling dies, hardens the heart, and evil reigns from undermining virtue." She viewed the political sphere as a space that corrupted women's "pure morality." Risquet declared her admiration for women "who, without deserting the sacred precinct of the home—nor abdicating the sanctified title of wife and mother—studies, and triumphantly tears a leafy branch of science or adorns her face with the precise diamond of the immortal crown of fine arts."[72] She determined that racial advancement required women to maintain their virtue as enlightened caretakers.

Not all elite African descendants agreed with Risquet. While most Black club leaders restricted women from formal membership, instances did arise in which women held primary leadership positions. In April 1902, the "meritorious patriots" Mercedes Águila Ambiles and her husband, Valeriano Garbey, established the Centro Cultural Martín Morúa Delgado at their home in Santiago de Cuba. Present at the opening event were the children of the couple, María Patrocinado Garbey Águila, Alejandrina Garbey Águila, and Juan Francisco Garbey, as well as Alberto Castellanos and José Tablada Fuentes. The founders drew inspiration from Morúa; they set out to do "the work of routing the progress of our heroic eastern province [and] our country in general" through "constant dedication to learning and patriotic and civic virtues, in all of its manifestations." [73] The center joined a network of elite *sociedades* on the island such as Club Atenas of Havana and Club Aponte, Casino Cubano, and Luz de Oriente of Santiago de Cuba. The organization remained active throughout the duration of the republic. Its female members uplifted women's social roles by proposing events including El Día del Hogar y de la Familia (Day of the Home and Family). They also fought for the recognition of Blacks' contributions to the nation's formation. During the 1950s, María P. Garbey Águila, who then presided over the organization, advocated for the construction of a public statue to honor Martín Morúa Delgado in Santiago de Cuba. This later instance in which women and men organized across gender differences shows that women held key leadership positions in certain clubs.

Though seldom documented, some Black Cuban women created their own spaces for activism by establishing organizations solely for women. In 1910 a group of elite women founded the feminist club Minerva in Havana to foster their feminist principles and uplift the broader community of color. The club had a regular column in *Minerva* to promote women's duties in achieving national progress. The following decade, a group of African-descended women established the Asociación Patriótica de Damas Amiradoras de Moncada (Patriotic Association of Lady Admirers of Moncada) to memorialize the revolutionary leader Guillermo Moncada. Women of the Oriente Province organization held a yearly procession to commemorate Moncada's contributions to national independence.[74] These are the first known Black women's clubs to be established during the republican era, and it is likely that others existed but were never formally registered with the provincial governments. For each organization, women's connections to male family members, fathers, brothers, and husbands who were professionals and politicians, helped enable the women access to the press and the income necessary to write. Yet the existence of such organizations demonstrates that women of African descent continued to form autonomous groups in order to promote a particular Black women's agenda.

That elite Black men and women enthusiastically supported certain organizations while dismissing others points to the gendered, cultural, and class-based approach to determining which public practices were appropriate for women. Such instances of exclusion and inclusion routinely defined the exchanges between men and women of African descent. Elite Blacks viewed the Centro Cultural Martín Morúa Delgado, the feminist club Minerva, and Damas de Moncada as respectable because of the nature of each organization: respectively, to promote intellectual development, memorialize fallen heroes, and uplift male leadership. Women of these associations participated in the social life of the Black community in a variety of capacities, yet they consistently embraced the dominant model of respectability. Elite Black women embraced modern gender norms through feminist discussions. Still, social norms dictated that they uphold rather than challenge patriarchal gender conventions as they navigated the public sphere. Such actions were an extension of their work to challenge anti-Black racism by demonstrating their progress as virtuous, enlightened figures.

• • •

Black associational life involved elite women of African descent navigating patriarchal discourses by employing sociocultural mechanisms during the early years of the republic. Black publications and civic clubs sustained their public activities as white political elites enacted practices of racial exclusion. Yet, more than a belief system that maintained women's subordinate position, adhering to patriarchal standards of public comportment enabled Black women to defend their womanhood without violating the tenets of racelessness. Elite African-descended women's investment in sexual morality, exclusivity, and civic leadership that complemented men shaped their engagement in all aspects of Black associational life.

This approach had its limitations. Black club members' investment in dominant racial ideals sustained elitist practices through which they asserted their superiority over poor African descendants. And despite their commitment to building a modern society, most held ambiguous perspectives regarding women's public roles. They affirmed women's expanded roles in public life. But the terms of their involvement remained unclear.

These dynamics would continue to evolve as a younger generation of Black activists came of age. Though elite persons of African descent rarely debated this issue in the press, private letters reveal the obstacles they confronted in securing employment in the sectors for which they had trained due to their race. The economic crisis of the late 1920s and the 1930s exacerbated citizenship struggles across social groups. Economic frustrations led a younger generation of Black activists to question the limits of racelessness and patriarchal discourses over the next several decades. Subsequently, elite women of African descent reformulated their expectations for citizenship.

4

Feminism and the Transformation of Black Women's Social Thought

Although feminism entered into Cuban literary circles by the dawn of the twentieth century, it was slow to take root as a political movement.[1] Women remained disenfranchised under the 1901 Constitution. Few women held positions as journalists and professionals who might leverage influence among male politicians. Most elite women's associations instead dedicated themselves to performing charity.[2] This would begin to change by the 1910s, as legal reforms and an economic boom fueled the emergence of feminism as a framework for interrogating patriarchal dynamics within Cuban political life.

Elite Black women's literary activism reflects this trend.[3] Writing for the Black press, women of African descent theorized their role in building a modern nation following the establishment of the republic. "It is undeniable," declared Salie Derome in 1904, "that woman has helped man conquer all of the terrains on which he has fought for the betterment of his rights, but it is also true that she has been rewarded with the most punitive ingratitude." Derome expressed the discontentment of African-descended women who had quickly grown weary of their prescribed positions. Derome placed herself in accord with elite white feminists when she lamented that despite their efforts, the Cuban woman continued to live "weakened as a child."[4] The following decade, a group of elite African-descended women asserted their roles as members of a growing professional class through their column, "Páginas feministas" (Feminist Pages), in the Black magazine *Minerva: Revista Universal Ilustrada* (1910–1915). These intellectuals, who formulated perspectives that differed from those of Derome, articulated their rights and obligations in relation to ideas of domesticity rather than challenge patriarchy. They determined that their education and moral superiority equipped them to prepare their largely illiterate and impoverished communities to meet the expectations for republican citizenship.

A small but influential group of elite Black women employed feminist thought as a citizenship practice from the 1910s into the 1930s. The women who wrote for publications like *Minerva* represented an island-wide network that bridged movements for women's rights and racial equality. They shared a goal of integrating women of all races into public life as contributors to nationalist projects. The African-descended feminists writing during the 1910s empowered a new generation of elite Blacks who, during the economic crises and political turmoil of the 1920s and 1930s, began to recognize women as formal leaders of Black institutions. The civic engagement of feminists of African descent extended beyond the Black public sphere to women's associations and political parties. Like prominent Black male civic activists such as Juan Gualberto Gómez, Rafael Serra, and Gustavo Urrutia, many feminist writers emerged as Black brokers who connected their local communities with state resources.[5]

Black feminists forged a dynamic political tradition that evolved throughout the republican era. Those writing during the early twentieth century adapted racial regeneration goals to fit expectations of racial silence. Rather than publicly addressing racial discrimination as many Black women writers had done in the late nineteenth century, later elite women of African descent challenged perceptions of racial inferiority through the act of writing. In this sense, writing served as a comportment strategy. Those who wrote poetry and articles did so, in part, to demonstrate their intellectual refinement.[6] Among them, Úrsula Coimbra de Valverde wrote for the Black publications *El Nuevo Criollo* and *Minerva*.[7] She penned essays on the literary achievements of women of African descent from the eighteenth century onward, championing their intellectual capabilities. Similarly, María G. Sánchez asserted the importance of Black women's literary production to "honor our own prestige for our improvement."[8] Black feminists writing for *Minerva* exemplified these perspectives as they pondered the extent to which women should take advantage of legal reforms regarding the family. They sought to reconcile modernizing gender norms in which women might expand their public roles with the traditional standards of domesticity that underpinned racial regeneration platforms.

By the 1920s, ideas of the "modern woman" that affirmed women's public engagement apart from a patriarchal head prompted new Black feminist strategies. Women of all races claimed their right to public pursuits as consumers and professionals. They leveraged their expertise as educators, doctors, and community activists to demand greater political authority. Cuban women joined an international wave of women's activism that shaped social welfare reforms. Scholars of Latin America and the Caribbean have demonstrated that women's social welfare activism entailed creating public health services for poor families, promoting hygiene and proper parenting, and expanding access to education, initiatives that shaped state formation.[9] In Cuba, women's participation in popular class struggles of the late 1920s and the 1930s accelerated their entry into formal politics. Cuban women achieved suffrage with the ratification of the 1934 Constitution. Feminists of African descent navigated this context by focusing on the particular experiences of Black women. Writing for the *Diario de la Marina* column "Ideales de una raza" as well as the Black magazines *Boletín Oficial del Club Atenas*, *Adelante*, and *Renacimiento*, they theorized how race intersected with gender discrimination to maintain the impoverishment of African-descended women.[10] Black feminists thus rejected racelessness discourses as they reinterpreted patriarchal norms to fit the ideal of modern womanhood.

As was the case with models of domesticity prevalent at the turn of the twentieth century, Cuban racial ideologies shaped understandings of the modern woman. By the 1920s, state officials recognized that the attempts to whiten the national population through Spanish immigration had failed, as Blacks remained a sizable proportion of the population.[11] Cuban scientists shifted from asserting inherent racial inferiority of African descendants to emphasizing how material conditions, particularly low wages and high unemployment rates that led to poverty, affected mortality and the moral and cultural breakdown of Black communities.[12] Both transformations prompted a new rationale for addressing the African presence in Cuba.[13] Nationalist intellectuals used scientific studies to argue that all races were created equal.[14] Similar to Brazilian and Mexican nationalist narratives that claimed racial democracy, Cuban intellectuals highlighted the influence of racial miscegenation in the formation of a modern nation.[15] Writers and artists celebrated the melding of European and African traditions to produce a distinct *mulato* culture.[16]

Black women encountered narratives of modern Cuba that underscored their ambiguous position in society. Literature, magazine covers, and popular music helped refashion stereotypical imagery to fit modernizing gender norms along racial lines. Representations of young white socialites replicated the image of glamour found in Hollywood films. The same venues portrayed women of African descent as rumba performers, witchcraft practitioners, street vendors, and sex workers.[17] Women of African descent thus stood at the intersection of shifting gender and racial discourses in both antagonistic and complementary ways.

Black feminist activism also illuminates the persistence of social tensions in a period of political democratization. The historian Robert Whitney has demonstrated how the mobilization of the middle and working classes led to the collapse of Cuba's oligarchic rule between 1920 and 1940.[18] Established Black civic leaders were scorned for their close association with President Gerardo Machado, whom Cubans ousted during the Revolution of 1933.[19] A younger generation of Black activists, women as well as men, criticized the elitism of those leaders. In their writings they affirmed the dignity of poor Blacks. African-descended women of various class backgrounds collaborated with white feminists but had few opportunities to have their writings published in white-oriented national magazines. Black feminists also complained of marginalization within political parties. Practices of racial and gender exclusion thus continued to affect the ways women of African descent navigated the political sphere.

"The Future of the Fatherland"

Historians have examined how democratic reform movements of the early twentieth century enabled women's political participation in Cuba and Latin America more broadly. Lynn Stoner has argued that Cuban reformists promoted women's education and new family legislation in an attempt to exclude the Catholic Church from politics. [20] Women gained the right to file for divorce, receive alimony, and maintain authority over their children. More women attended universities and pursued professional careers. Some men and women called for women's right to participate in the electoral system. Guiding these discussions was the belief that women's prescribed role as morally superior caretakers of the household qualified them to participate in national politics.[21] Asunción Lavrin contends that increasing political activity among the working and urban middle classes prompted important changes in Latin American democratic societies during the 1910s and 1920s. In her study of Chile, Uruguay, and Argentina, she explains that the rise of national feminist movements entailed shifting policies and understandings of womanhood addressed women's rights. These understandings required that both men and women develop "new concepts of gender relations and gender roles."[22] Still, most elite women who sought to influence national policy articulated their rights and duties in relation to domesticity rather than challenge patriarchy.

And yet the established scholarship, while important for understanding the role patriarchy played in women's activism, has been limited in its analysis of racial dynamics within Latin American feminist movements.[23] Mainstream feminist movements first emerged among elite and middle-class white women whose social connections enabled their access to presses, professional opportunities, and the attention of politicians. In Cuba, while this community of privileged white urbane women held varying perspectives on how to enact legal reform, they adhered to the nationalist tenets of racelessness by adopting a race-neutral discourse regarding women's issues. In practice, most white feminists maintained a sense of racial superiority to their Black counterparts. The Black press does not feature activities that African-descended women attended. No evidence indicates that white feminists reached out to Black women during this period, nor are they mentioned in the rosters of their organizations. Evidence thus suggests that most white feminists excluded Black women from their publications and organizations prior to the 1920s.

In 1910, the year Congress passed the Morúa Amendment banning race-based political organizations, a group of elite Black women launched the feminist column "Páginas feministas." The column appeared in the second run of *Minerva*. Edited by the progressive political leaders Oscar G. Edreira and Ildefonso Morúa Contreras, the magazine documented the economic, political, and cultural activities of privileged Blacks rather than Black women in particular.[24] Editors took care to assert that *Minerva* was "not a magazine of parties or races."[25] "Páginas feministas" columnists contributed to this mission as they formulated what might be considered the first of two waves of Black Cuban feminist thought of the early twentieth century.[26] The first wave includes writings published in the "Páginas feministas" column of *Minerva*, 1910–1913; the second wave includes feminists' writings published primarily in Black columns and magazines of 1928–1938 such as *Diario de la Marina*, *Revista Atenas*, and *Adelante*. Their poetry and articles exhibited the moral and intellectual capabilities of elite African descendants for a broader public.

The discussions facilitated by "Páginas feministas" editors reflected the perspectives of the writers' white counterparts. Contributors articulated ideas about Cuban womanhood within a patriarchal framework while remaining silent on instances of racial discrimination. African-descended women outlined their civic duties as enlightened caretakers whose social roles complemented those of men. In this sense, elite Black women formulated a political agenda that often found agreement with white feminists' concerns regarding legal reforms while responding to elite Black goals of regenerating the population of color. Consuelo David Calvet declared, "*Minerva* is proud of its people; prestige of the unfortunate Ethiopian race: symbol of progress and civilization."[27] David's declaration marks a rare instance of a columnist publicly linking herself to a global Black diasporic population.

Minerva is the only magazine known to have published Black women's feminist perspectives during this early period. The column editor Prisca Acosta de Gualba's feminist collaborators included the intellectuals Gloria Alonso, Mercedes Zayas, Nieve Prieto, and Tecla Castillo de Escoto. Most column contributors came from prominent families of African descent. Acosta de Gualba worked alongside her husband, the journalist Miguel Gualba, in reestablishing *Minerva*.[28] Angelina Edreira joined *Minerva* through her familial ties to her husband, the editor Oscar Edreira. Vestalina and Arabella Morúa Delgado, both column editors and music teachers, were the daughters of Senator Martin Morúa Delgado and sisters of the coeditor Ildefonso Morúa Contreras. These women participated in the first iteration, *Minerva: Revista Quincenal Dedicada a la Mujer de Color*, which circulated in 1888–1889, after abolition. Those who contributed to its second phase from 1910 to 1915 supported its apolitical stance.[29] Women of *Minerva* thus departed from those of the Partido Independiente de Color by emphasizing women's issues.

In 1911, Acosta de Gualba founded the Feminist Club Minerva as an organization through which to sustain the community. She and her co-organizers envisioned an association committed to "the progress of the arts, literature, and sports" that would rise to the level of existing feminist groups in cities such as London, New York, Paris, Berlin, and San Francisco.[30] That the women aligned with international groups reflects their cosmopolitan vision of womanhood that connected Black Cuban political values with those of boundary-pushing activists from nations most Cubans viewed as socially advanced. The women likely became aware of feminist activities that took place abroad through the Cuban mainstream and Black presses, which featured social, political, and cultural developments throughout the Americas and Europe, as well as international travel.[31] *Minerva* provided no other details regarding the activities of the feminist club. It is possible that organization members were more intent on formulating a collective feminist identity through the column.

Feminism provided a philosophy through which elite Black women drew from international women's movements as they negotiated their roles in republican political life. Curiously, the women did not define feminism for themselves. In the February 1912 issue of *Minerva*, an excerpt appears by the Spanish feminist La Infanta Eulalia, who was on tour for her book *Au fil de la vie* (Throughout life). The author challenged assumptions of biological differences between men and women that were used to defend patriarchal dynamics, and instead she suggested that only social differences existed.[32] In a 1913 column, the Black intellectual Jasón Miseret contended that the codification of marriage customs naturalized sexual inequalities. He determined that women suffered not only physically but also intellectually by being condemned to the home. Over time, he predicted, feminism would lead to the eradication of racial and sexual prejudices by undermining "religious and centrist impulses."[33] La Infanta Eulalia's and Miseret's articles were among the most radical perspectives published in *Minerva*. Their inclusion suggests that the feminist editors debated and many likely embraced progressive gender roles.

Minerva's feminists emphasized education, motherhood, patriotism, and the arts within the framework of bourgeois domesticity. Carmelina Serracent argued in 1910 that from women derived "the future of the fatherland."[34] Serracent contended that Christian-educated women possessed the spiritual knowledge necessary to cultivate the hearts of young men who might become soldiers, politicians, magistrates, or governors. She wrote the *Minerva* column "Mundo religioso" (Religious world), in which she encouraged Catholic religious beliefs and practices. Serracent graduated from a school run by the US-based Oblate Sisters of Providence, a Catholic order founded by women of African descent.[35] The schools emphasized religious morality in addition to traditional education that would prepare young women to attend universities.

"Páginas feministas" articles on education elucidate how class values shaped early Black feminist thought. Lucrecia Loret de Mola described uneducated individuals as social disappointments who failed to contribute "to the betterment of the country and to join the enlightened citizens on the glorious pages of the history books."[36] True intellectual development, she wrote, required rigorous study that spanned years. Loret concluded that one's decision to walk away from an educational opportunity was justifiable only if they lost a parent or had to take care of a child. Such claims overlooked the privileges required to pursue schooling full time, rather than work to support one's family, and gain entry to a university. Such perceptions enabled elites to buttress their own sense of moral authority by distancing themselves from the laboring poor.

If "Páginas feministas" provided a platform for elite women of African descent to fashion a modern image of virtuous enlightenment, aspects of the mainstream feminist debates threatened to undermine that image. In particular, as male politicians initiated property, marriage, and divorce reforms to protect the holdings and privileges of the propertied classes, Cuban feminists used debates on women's legal rights to insert themselves into the male-dominated political world. A 1917 property law granted women authority over their family assets, even after they married, in addition to the right to sue and maintain control over their children from previous marriages. Proposed divorce bills aimed to shift power over marriage as well as birth and death registration from the Church to the secular courts. When the divorce law was finally passed in 1918, both men and women gained the option of filing for divorce, and women gained the right to alimony and authority over their children. Many women avoided public discussions of divorce, which still were considered a threat to Catholic principles and domestic security.

The proposed marriage laws created a paradox for *Minerva*'s male and female writers. On one hand, embracing the right to divorce might help elite Blacks portray their modern refinement as enlightened citizens. On the other hand, the magazine's contributors could appear to be furthering the image of Black immorality. Divorce challenged the model of the moral and legal family that had become crucial to controlling public comportment. Elite whites presupposed the lack of nuclear families within the Black community as "as an inherent trait of blackness" that reflected their "congenital inferiority."[37] Privileged African descendants, to challenge misconceptions of their health and civility, presented matrimony as a strategy for regenerating the Black community. Thus, even as marriage reforms made divorce more accessible, statistics suggest that Blacks did not avail themselves of this opportunity as much as might be expected. In fact, the national rate of marriage among nonwhites doubled between 1899 and 1943.[38] African descendants of various class backgrounds appear to have given more attention to advancing the social standing of their families than on taking advantage of divorce legislation.[39]

These factors led many Black feminist writers to formulate conservative responses to marriage debates. Of the hundreds of articles published in *Minerva* from 1910 to 1915, only two directly addressed divorce. The first, in March 1911, appeared in the feminist pages. Titled "El divorcio," Serracent identified divorce as a sociological issue: "In my opinion, one should not approve the divorce law, at least for now. Given our intellectual and economic conditions, character, and customs, its establishment would engender disastrous results."[40] Serracent suggested that Cuban women in general lacked the "intellectual preparation" necessary to enjoy liberties such as divorce.

Serracent juxtaposed Cuban women's progress with that of women in the United States. She described Cuban character as excessively passionate and lustful, leaving women without rational control over their behavior. Moreover, in the case of divorce, women from the United States had enough education to survive without husbands. In contrast, Cuban women had less formal training and thus often found themselves in a lower economic status as divorcees. Serracent linked divorce to the potential danger of descending into "lower" lifestyles as domestic workers or prostitutes, and she equated poverty with dishonor and illegitimate children.[41] For Serracent, matrimony ensured sexual morality and provided economic stability under a patriarchal guardian.

More than a year after the feminist column came to an end, a 1914 article in *Minerva* revealed a different perspective regarding womanhood and national progress. In "¡Divorciémonos!" (Let's divorce!), an anonymous writer presented divorce not as a threat to happy marriages but as a shield for women in violent relationships. Married women lacked legal protection against spousal abuse that in some cases became so severe that husbands murdered their wives. Reflecting on this reality, the writer presented marriage as a dictatorial space in which men dominated women with free reign. The author suggested that the divorce laws would help dignify the Cuban woman by "remedying her from matrimonial tyranny."[42]

Above all, the writer noted the benefit of divorce reforms for transforming women's social opportunities. Politicians and social reformists alike had failed to support a woman's right to choose her husband or contribute to making major household decisions. Divorce, at least in theory, presented women with the opportunity to protect themselves and their children. The author concluded that divorce should be more easily accessible for women. The divergent perspectives on divorce presented by Serracent and the anonymous writer represent distinct visions of how legal reforms could affect women's social roles and opportunities. That *Minerva* published only two articles on the subject indicates a national trend in which few women opted to take a stand publicly. Marital reforms created anxieties for most Cubans concerned with Catholic virtue and women's economic security; they especially concerned elite Blacks dedicated to projecting an image of collective morality.

"The Greatest Obstacle in the Regeneration of Blacks"

With the issue of divorce unresolved, debates over patriarchal dynamics continued to evolve after *Minerva* ended its feminist column. Certainly, not all Black women writing during the period identified as feminists. But critiques of men's social roles demonstrate how women used intraracial dialogues to challenge patriarchy, thus signaling shifts in how women publicly asserted themselves. By the mid-1910s, a younger generation of Cubans of African descent attained elite and middle-class status; many of them had grown frustrated with the declining political influence of civic clubs. They observed how, despite the commitment of elite African descendants to the Liberal and Conservative Parties, the number of high-ranking Black officials had declined.[43] This emerging class heavily criticized established civic clubs for their lack of decency and modern sensibilities as well. Decency discussions were not new; late nineteenth-century writers as well as *El Nuevo Criollo* contributors in 1904–1906 addressed acts of immorality, but the manner in which elite African descendants articulated gender roles within their publications reflects a shift. Male association leaders established a unification platform that entailed two strategies for socioeconomic advancement: forming an umbrella organization to advocate for political influence, though not as a distinct party, and building a selective, modern constituency of respectable men and women to represent the highest potential of the race.[44] They sought appointments to public posts, elected positions within established parties, and funds for civic organizations. Both strategies promoted an exclusive patriarchal leadership that elites deemed superior to the laboring poor.

Black civic activists remained fearful of their extinction as a race in response to social science studies of the period.[45] Published reports asserted that the population of African descent had entered a state of physical and moral decline. In a study published in 1915, Jorge Le-Roy y Cassá argued that Black female mortality was higher than white female mortality and "the 'colored' race was slowly disappearing from the national territory." His contemporary Gustavo Mustelier asserted that this process occurred largely because of Blacks' lower natural growth rate, the large number of African-descended women who served as sex workers, and the number of Black men in prison.[46] Backed by statistical data, scientists and politicians assumed that cultural inferiority and immoral behaviors threatened the vitality of the Black population.

The journalist Ramón Vasconcelos responded to these discussions in his column, "Palpitaciones de la raza de color" (Palpitations of the colored race). Published almost weekly in the national newspaper *La Prensa* in 1915 and 1916, "Palpitaciones" contributors appealed for Black men to assume their rightful positions as leaders of their communities. In August 1915, Vasconcelos, under the pen name Tristán, faulted women as "the greatest obstacle in the regeneration of Blacks." He characterized women of African descent as morally deficient in comparison to their white counterparts. He asserted that Black, *mulata*, and *mestiza* women possessed varying levels of virtue. Vasconcelos implored respectable members of the Black population to "prepare women for the fight against the evil limitations" of the lower classes through education. He called upon men to restore women to the home, as their "great mission" to uplifting the race lay within the household.[47]

Caridad Chacón de Guillén, a reader from Havana, responded to Vasconcelos in a letter entitled "Mi opinión" (My opinion). She shared his concern regarding "the carelessness with which many women of our race see marriage, and how they are easily delivered to the brothel."[48] The former ladies committee president for Divina Caridad suggested that "Palpitaciones" readers "need not be alarmed" that a man of color would criticize the sexual indiscretions of Black and *mulata* women, for these critiques "should be said." It was important that "one understand the difference between being the wife of a poor immaculate man who lived honestly, versus being an unnamed concubine."[49] Troubled by the large proportion of unmarried couples that included women of African descent, Chacón enthusiastically advocated for reform through "moral education." She proposed that Black civic clubs hold conferences to remedy the widespread matter.

Not all writers supported the generalization about women debasing the community of color. In an especially charged letter in 1915, a reader identified only as Indiana reprimanded Vasconcelos for arguing that Black women lacked virtue. She countered that the real problem lay not in women's sexual behaviors but in the relations between husbands and wives. Many men were abusive and therefore undermined the institution of marriage. This dynamic, she asserted, was the real reason many women decided to live with rather than marry partners. Only when men complied with their duties as husbands and gentlemen would more women choose to marry.[50]

Indiana and others endorsed a bourgeois model of womanhood while protesting the wrongdoings of men. In a second letter, Indiana pondered, "[If] the Black man marries his wife only to submit her to ill treatment and not to love her and make her a queen of the home, how can a woman in such circumstances obey her husband or try to inculcate her most high duties to family and society?"[51] She also complained that male leaders of Black civic organizations placed too much emphasis on dances and as a result brought virtuous women into contact with women of questionable character. Parents who had "educated their daughters in the sacred principles of morality and decency" often kept their daughters away from the associations. Her observations reflect how elite Black women distinguished themselves from those they viewed as women of questionable conduct. For Indiana, men needed to reform themselves as well as the associations they led in order to be worthy of the company of virtuous women.

Despite such calls for virtuous male leaders, many women were no longer satisfied with having patriarchs serve as the only authoritative figures. In August 1915, a woman identified as N. Lesnar declared, "The unification of the *sociedades de color* is not a problem that concerns only men, but also the women who follow them step by step and even contribute their part."[52] She asserted that both sexes needed to play a role in the process of community regeneration.

Increasingly, women considered their individual improvement to be a crucial step toward collective progress, a perspective that would evolve during the early years of the republic. Thus, by the mid-1910s, individuals like the journalist Ana Hidalgo Vidal of Cienfuegos demanded new civic responsibilities for women. She proclaimed, "Only when we have loyally interpreted our rights and duties . . . when we fix our attention on our own advancement and the advancement of the rest, only then will we have accomplished the first step of progress."[53] In a similar vein, María G. Sánchez resolved that women were more apt than men to overcome the difficulties necessary to achieve progress. Sánchez brazenly stated that a woman was entitled to feel that she was "the owner of herself."[54] As Sánchez called Black women to action, she placed herself in accord with others who questioned the terms of patriarchy.

"Legitimate Pride Being Cuban and Being Black"

By the late 1920s, elite African descendants acknowledged the limitations of racial regeneration strategies that emphasized racial silence. Despite declaring their moral virtue and cultural superiority over poor Blacks, they continued to confront prejudice in restaurants and hotels as well as housing. In 1928 the journalist Gustavo Urrutia lamented that decent families were not allowed to lease units in skyscrapers and modern apartment buildings of Havana.[55] Black families who possessed the financial means to socialize and live in the most fashionable establishments and neighborhoods frequently found themselves restricted from entry.

Elite Blacks were not alone in their struggle with racial discrimination. Poor families of African descent faced an additional set of challenges due to their socioeconomic status. Blacks' control of farmland as both renters and owners decreased 50 percent between 1899 and 1931 as foreign investors took over the sugar industry.[56] African descendants who worked in factories and agriculture were usually excluded from the most skilled positions. They were underrepresented in the expanding employment in civil service, transportation, and the telephone industry. The decline of Cuba's economy during the late 1920s exacerbated these circumstances, as falling wages and rising unemployment left persons of African descent and Cubans in general in precarious financial situations. High unemployment led many poor Black women to turn to work in the informal sector as laundresses, domestic servants, street vendors, and sex workers.[57]

Younger African descendants developed divergent views of political activism that reflected generational perspectives; having grappled with higher rates of unemployment than older elites, they were more attuned to socioeconomic inequities. This generation of intellectuals insisted that Black elites abandon outmoded gender norms in favor of new and modern expectations of women's civic engagement. Subsequently, women joined men in defending their right to protest racism. In 1929 Inocencia Silveira proclaimed, "We are not racists; we are an entity aware of its duties and its rights as free citizens."[58] The Guanajay resident asserted that Blacks wanted only to be able to enjoy the same "moral and material benefits" as white Cubans. The Havana educator Consuelo Serra de G. Veranes invoked the intellectual José Martí's vision of racial equality and reminded readers that the goal of all Cubans should be to finally create a nation "with and for all." She declared, "We feel dignity and legitimate pride being Cuban and being Black, because Black Cubans have done so many good and worthy things, in all phases of Cuban life, that are distinguished and salient."[59] For her, the actions of previous generations demonstrated the worth of African descendants as citizens. Serra's rise to prominence in Havana was enabled by her distinction as the daughter of the revolutionary leaders Rafael Serra and Gertrudis Heredia.

Consuelo Serra's professional career served as a testament to the value of Black men and women as Cuban citizens. She devoted her life to building institutions that would help uplift the population of African descent in Havana. For her, establishing schools was a strategy for connecting poor African descendants with elite Black resources. She graduated from college in New York City (figure 3.1); six years after returning to Havana she founded El Sagrado Corazón de Jesús school, later renamed the Escuela Hogar Consuelo Serra.[60] The boarding school had seventy girl students ages six to fifteen. Serra employed ten teachers who educated students through the elementary level; she ran a separate department for high school pupils. Serra later became an English professor at the Normal School of Havana. She received two doctorates, one in pedagogy in 1920 and a second in philosophy in 1934, both from the University of Havana. Beyond her work in the classroom, she "delivered lectures over radio and for societies in Havana."[61] The Black magazine *Adelante* reported that she "masterfully exhausted the suggestive theme 'The Race Problem in Cuba'" during an event for the alumna association of the Oblate Sisters of Providence.[62]

In the press as well as academia, Serra theorized racism from the standpoint of Black women and children. In a 1929 interview she recounted a childhood conversation with her mother. Serra would ask her mother, "Is it true that ebony [skin] is an impediment to triumphing in life?" Her mother repeatedly assured her that anything was possible, as she "sought to vanish a false concept that existed during those times."[63] In a later article, Serra adamantly denied that her Blackness had created an obstacle for her to succeed. She noted that she had "white and blonde friends" with whom she had fought for women's rights, and she promoted solidarity among Cuban women of all races. Although Serra affirmed instances of racial unity, she also stressed that Blacks faced a "double duty" in achieving "democratization."[64]

Established elites like Consuelo Serra maintained prominent social positions during the 1930s, as Black civic clubs of Havana opened their doors to upwardly mobile women like Ana Echegoyen de Cañizares. Echegoyen grew up in a "forgotten *pueblecito*" (small town) outside of Havana. She moved to the capital city to pursue an education and graduated from Havana Normal School. She was the first Black woman professor of methodology in the Department of Education at the University of Havana. Echegoyen moved quickly up the social ladder in Havana. Heralded as the "prototypical Cuban woman," she worked on behalf of the "Cuban woman in general and the Black woman, in particular."[65] She organized conferences that centered youth and women in Black political discourses.

Black feminists remained committed to the principles of domesticity even as they took on greater public roles. Through *Adelante*, Echegoyen joined the ranks of progressive elite Black circles that affirmed women's leadership, yet she articulated a traditional understanding of women's social roles through the monthly column "Para la mujer." For her, women possessed the "sacred mission" of directing and guiding others toward human improvement. She viewed mothering as a woman's most important role in society.[66] By affirming the role of mothers, she challenged racial stereotypes regarding the failures of Black mothers. Echegoyen joined Consuelo Serra and other Black feminist writers of the period who argued for social welfare reforms that would benefit families of African descent.[67] Such reforms encompassed educating Black women in child-rearing and hygiene in addition to building skills necessary to obtain skilled employment.

In 1935 Echegoyen and Consuelo Serra cofounded the Black women's civic organization the Asociación Cultural Femenina (ACF, Women's Cultural Association) for "the civic and cultural betterment of women."[68] The founders conceived the organization broadly around supporting "any patriotic activity that serves to consolidate the ideological principles of the republic."[69] Perhaps to recognize the range of political affiliations held by its members, they distanced the association from electoral politics. Its membership consisted of a highly selective and privileged group of women, many of whom identified as feminists. Serra served as the association's inaugural president. Its leaders also included the suffragist Catalina Pozo Gato and the educators Adela García de Falcon and Juana Oliva Bulnes. Association members connected with Havana's educated Black population through the events of elite civic clubs such as Club Atenas. That ACF membership consisted of Black women suggests that the members continued to experience exclusion from most elite white women's organizations and male-headed Black associations or at least saw the importance of spaces exclusively for elite women of African descent.[70]

The association's objective of attending to disadvantaged women and children demonstrates that its members did not abandon racial regeneration strategies altogether. They provided nursery schools for working mothers, offered typing classes for poor girls, and sought to establish a library. They led literacy campaigns as "a firm step toward a better future for Cuban women," at times partnering with the elite white women's association the Lyceum and Lawn Tennis Club.[71] Women of the ACF also organized dances as well as fine arts and fashion expositions. Although they were concerned with problems affecting all Black women, they continued to distinguish themselves from poor women of African descent through cultural events and their affiliations with other elite associations.

The association's activities reflect changes in elite Black women's political organizing during a period of political democratization. Popular protests that emerged in resistance to President Gerardo Machado y Morales (1925–1933) opened a space for new actors in the public sphere. Black women formed allies across racial, socioeconomic, and even national boundaries. ACF members built relations with African American women as part of their internationalist approach to achieving reform. They cohosted elite Black socialites from the United States through Club Atenas events, and they examined racial inequities in both nations through the Cuban and

US Black press.[72] At the same time, by collaborating with such groups as the Lyceum and Lawn Tennis Club, association members expanded their public presence beyond the Black public sphere. Elite women of African descent joined popular movements through affiliation with various women's groups. Mary Ignacia Matehu, a well-known doctor and member of the ACF, served on the central committee of the Unión Nacional de Mujeres (National Women's Union), a group established "to fight for the national liberation of Cuba and organize women to obtain their just social valorization."[73] Her leadership reflected the rise of prominent women who traveled between women's associations, Black civic clubs, and labor parties to promote a broad platform for democratic reform. These women hailed from different class backgrounds. The domestic worker Elvira Rodríguez became a vocal leader of the Union of Domestic Workers, and the tobacco stemmer Teresa García contributed newspaper articles as an executive committee member of the Cigar Workers Union. They established ties with radical activists such as Felicita Ortiz and Consuelo Silveira who entered the communist movement through labor unions. Perhaps the most prominent communist leader was Esperanza Sánchez, a pharmacist in Oriente Province who served as the only Black woman elected as a delegate to the 1940 Constitutional Assembly. Collaborations between elite and laboring poor women of African descent furthered Black feminists' agenda for addressing structural inequities.

Black feminists' attention to social disparities occasionally led them to critique the elitism of African-descended Cubans. In *Diario de la Marina* in November 1930, the intellectual Gerardo del Valle engaged in a written debate with the feminist writer Catalina Pozo Gato over the nature of Black women's oppression. The column editor Gustavo Urrutia likely arranged the exchange, as he employed such strategies throughout the duration of his column. In his essay del Valle echoed the conservative perspectives of racial regeneration advocates in which women's contributions to society lay in their duties as mothers. He characterized the ideal Black woman by two "transcendental qualities": a Black mother's "great love" for her children and her "passionate patriotism." Citing the example of the beloved patriot-mother Mariana Grajales, Del Valle declared, "The Black woman is proud of her Cuban nationality and proclaims it to the four winds. . . . Within her ignorance beats a rare instinct for social concern, rebellious and daring."[74]

Though del Valle praised certain women of African descent who adhered to standards of proper comportment as mothers, he identified the ways others became marginalized in impoverished communities. Although a high percentage of children of color were born into poverty, del Valle reported that statistically few African-descended women committed infanticide. He asserted that anyone who visited the *solares*, the poor urban housing communities, would find numerous women of color surrounded by four, six, or as many as ten children. These struggling Black mothers "fought heroically" to feed their families by washing or ironing clothes "without complaining about their cruel and selfish fathers." Importantly, he reminded readers that stores did not hire Black women, despite of the "pseudo-feminists" who did everything possible to ensure that Black girls would "clean the schools, learn a trade, or enter the normal schools," those that trained teachers, when they came of age.[75] Even as del Valle suggested that Black women were noble in sacrificing themselves for their families, he concluded that the majority of them were culturally backward.[76] Superstitious beliefs undermined the souls and pocketbooks of African-descended women and their families. True, he wrote, normal schools had produced some caring and conscientious teachers and professors of modern pedagogy able to "water the seed in the daughters of the people." He concluded that at the same time, their numbers lagged behind the majority of women who succumbed to "perverse occult ideals under the veil of mystery," that is, witchcraft, black magic, and ideas of false spirits.[77]

Catalina Pozo Gato penned a response to del Valle that she wrote "with indignation." She acknowledged that del Valle had accurately presented a segment of society and the "inhuman disappointing results" of its unfair prejudice. Pozo Gato affirmed his suggestion that poor Black Cubans should embrace bourgeois cultural expectations and oppose witchcraft. But she challenged "Ideales" column readers to focus on "the unwritten space" between the lines of his article that relegated Black women to "the fringes."[78] Specifically, she called attention to "the insurmountable, systematized and organized obstacles encountered by the educated Black woman, [who was] overwhelmed by the same reality of misery and defeat as the uneducated Black women."[79]

Pozo Gato's response to del Valle reflected how Black women writing during the 1930s shifted their discursive strategies from calls for moral respectability to critiques of systemic inequities. She adamantly declared that African-descended women had suffered from racial discrimination in employment, noting that a percentage of "culturally prepared and educated" Black women had received the same formal training as their white counterparts. Yet educated women of African descent rarely found opportunities to demonstrate the skills they had acquired. Many Black women who received training as dentists, pharmacists, lawyers, and doctors worked as dressmakers in stores controlled by "Poles" (Polish workers and business owners), earning a "vexing salary" that kept them poor. Even the most skillful and intelligent young woman of color had to accept jobs at minimum wage as operators rather than managers. Not even in private offices would Cuban or foreign employers hire "prepared girls" from the community of color. Pozo Gato identified the true problem: poor, Black women not having the same possibilities of employment as their "white sisters."[80]

Pozo Gato asked the column readers, "Is this humane? Is it just? Is it patriotic?"[81] She placed the blame on white Cubans for upholding racial inequalities in the labor force. She concluded that persons of African descent should seek justice by appealing to "good Cubans" and pursuing government action. This approach, she determined, should include enlisting organizations and writers who addressed social discrimination. Pozo Gato contended that Black Cubans should also seek legislation on behalf of every citizen whose parents and grandparents had shed their blood for independence.[82] Thus she framed Black women's marginalization as a limitation of Cuban democracy.

The "Ideales" editor Gustavo Urrutia used this published debate to illustrate the divergent perspectives through which Black intellectuals forged a modern racial discourse. Elite African descendants furthered the racial regeneration approach that emphasized moral respectability, such as in promoting marriage and denigrating African cultural practices, as key to addressing racism. They implied that poor Blacks were to blame for their social marginalization and impoverishment by failing to adhere to dominant standards of womanhood. Black feminists rejected this approach. Clearly, many remained invested in ideas of morality, as few of their articles denounced respectability. But they instead incorporated a class-based analysis of Black women's experiences to argue that social conditions perpetuated their marginalization.

A similar instance of conflicting views on poor Black families arose at the 1938 National Convention of Black Societies, one of several conventions organized periodically by Black civic club leaders to help coordinate their organizations' objectives and activities. The Havana lawyer Cloris Tejo attended the convention, which was dedicated to advancing racial equality. Several discussions left her infuriated with participants she labeled "Black aristocracy."[83] Delegates proposed the passage of law that would prohibit minors under the age of twelve from selling newspapers in the streets. Tejo explained that while she was "not in favor of children engaging in the sale of newspapers," she recognized that their work provided necessary income for their households. Thus, she could not allow their parents to be judged for allowing the children to work or for parents to feel forced to abandon their children out of financial necessity. She argued that doing so would only lead to the children populating the city streets "in search of the degrading alms that society throws them."[84]

Tejo challenged the delegates to look into structural issues rather than pass moral judgments. She stated that moral Black mothers did not have the fortune of attaining mobility through the political and social networks available to professionally established families of African descent. In addition, the activist passionately asserted, "The prisons need to be substituted with reform schools, because history has shown that prisons have not lessened the number of delinquents." Tejo suggested that the legal system should include a humanitarian perspective that recognized the experiences of the individual in "laws for constructive character-edifying."[85] By aligning herself with issues especially affecting women, Blacks, and the poor, Tejo situated African-descended mothers and children within the comprehensive agenda of the race. "The moral and economic liberation of poor Blacks must begin with the work of poor Blacks themselves," she insisted.[86] She affirmed her commitment to addressing the material circumstances of all women whose impoverishment led them to rely on their children's labor in the informal sector. Tejo acknowledged that this reliance included the work of poor children sent to sell newspapers and daughters whose mothers let them labor as sex workers. She thus suggested that the convention delegates address the economic conditions affecting poor families of African descent rather than denigrating their social behaviors.

At no time were all women of African descent of one mind about which political philosophy would best help them improve the social status of Black women. An increasing number of elite women analyzed how anti-Black racism intersected with sexism to leave most women of African descent in a precarious financial position. By the 1930s, a new cohort of women activists formulated a modern Black feminist discourse. As they put forth strategies for reforming society on behalf of Black women and children, they pondered their own roles as modern women.

Feminism and the Modern Woman

"The woman of today," explained the Black socialite María Teresa Ramírez in 1930, "is fundamentally equal to the woman of yesterday; only she has evolved, or maybe the new currents of progress and civilization have intoxicated her a bit, from the anxiety of revindicating 'rights,' like the bourgeoisie of the eighteenth century or the worker of the nineteenth century." Ramírez maintained that the woman of today remained "morally and psychologically" equal to her predecessors. She characterized the modern woman as intellectually greater and "her concept of life amplified." The modern woman aimed to realize one goal: "to become the dignified companion of the twentieth-century man who, apart from those who believe the contrary, still needs to see her as his 'sweet friend of heart and mind.'"[87] Ramírez joined a chorus of elite Cuban women, including those of African descent, who reinterpreted patriarchal expectations to fit modernizing gender norms in the 1930s.

Ramírez was not alone in emphasizing women's complementary role to men. The educator and feminist journalist Calixta María Hernández de Cervantes emphasized traditional gender expectations as she advocated for feminism in her article "Tópicos femeninos" (Women's topics). Hernández, responding to growing economic uncertainty, avowed women's right to fight as leaders for the triumph of Cuba and humanity. Yet, as she defended the feminist movement, she stressed that its ideology did not entail "the open fight of women against men to achieve the best posts."[88] Rather, feminists wanted women to fight alongside their male counterparts and asked only for "cooperation, justice and, above all, love."[89]

Elite Blacks' discussions of feminism reinvigorated debates over the moral image of the population of African descent. In August 1931, the Black feminist Tete Ramírez Medina argued, "Women's organic function does not constitute a burden that prevents them from fully realizing and fulfilling their sexual aspirations."[90] The *Adelante* contributor Gilberto Ante Jiménez critiqued those he perceived to be militant feminists: "The militant feminists, defending their theories of equal rights have deviated from the

truth—a fundamental biological principle in the study of sexuality." Jiménez acknowledged the ways men created laws that "capriciously limit the
ability of women," but he implored women to respect gender binaries in
order to avoid accusations of taking on masculine traits. "Woman should
be a mother above all," he insisted.[91] Such concerns were not limited to
male intellectuals. Ana Echegoyen cautioned that women should take care
to avoid adopting "masculine vices."[92]

The calls for traditional feminine behaviors issued by Jiménez and
Echegoyen reflected conversations taking place nationally. Legislators, intellectuals, and social scientists became preoccupied with the traditional
Cuban family in the 1930s through 1950s. As women took on greater roles
in the political sphere, critics reasserted the primacy of forming married
households in building a stable democracy. Legislators revised civil and
penal codes to change the regulation of marriage and divorce in accordance
with their ideas of sexual morality. Doctors contended that maintaining
nuclear households would improve the genetic traits of white citizens and
thus benefit the nation.[93] Indeed, many Cubans feared women would abandon their traditional duties as they gained new legal rights and social opportunities. Those who chose not to marry faced accusations of contributing to the disintegration of the nation through sexually immoral behaviors.

Yet while marriage remained critical to projecting Blacks' morality, it
was not elite African-descended women's only concern in a modern society. Hernández de Cervantes proposed that where marriage had confined
women to a life of servitude, opportunities to professionalize women's work
had created a path toward social liberation. Hernández explained, "The
modern woman can afford to pursue a man who satisfies the conditions of
creditworthiness, reliability, sensitivity, and sympathy that she likes." She
challenged the association between modern womanhood and immorality,
writing that the modern woman, rather than encourage promiscuity, retained control over her sexuality. But like Jiménez and Echegoyen, Hernández also insisted that women prioritize their domestic duties above their
individual independence. "Those of us who care about such matters," she
concluded, needed to forge a new understanding of marriage, as the institution was "intimately linked to the survival of the community."[94]

Black feminist activists of the 1930s, similar to previous generations, reinforced bourgeois standards of morality when they emphasized their civic
duties as feminine caretakers. Yet they promoted women's formal leader-

ship beyond auxiliary branches of male-headed civic clubs. Women of all races gained the right to vote in 1934. Hernández de Cervantes articulated a political vision in which women "were incorporated into the grooves of the electoral machine" as full citizens.[95] She argued that the Cuban woman, having participated in the fight for national independence, had "earned the right to penetrate the political arena in order to contribute with the support of her militancy to the resolution of the grave problems that presented themselves on the horizon of *cubanidad*."[96] She questioned whether women should "affiliate themselves with parties controlled by men or those that had been exclusively formed and run by women."[97] Hernández recognized that women took a risk in building political alliances with men when she reflected on the difficult union between the women's political organization Alianza Nacional Feminista (National Feminist Alliance) and the political party Conjunto Nacional Democrático (National Democratic Group, formerly the Partido Conservador). Conjunto leaders broke from their partnership with the feminist alliance to form a separate party and maintain the right to make their own decisions. Despite this political conflict, Hernández maintained that women should not isolate themselves from men.

Elite Black men and women cautioned that suffrage created a new and important challenge for Black women in electoral life. Hernández de Cervantes noted instances in which local politicians chauffeured African-descended women to the polls to vote for their candidates. The intellectual Manuel Machado suggested that women of African descent participate in electoral politics while remaining cautious of "pseudo representatives," especially given that "the vast majority of our women are domestics and that almost all of the 'haves' are bureaucrats." He criticized the failure by wealthy and middle-class white women to build "a radical and sincere work base, an apostolic identification between the 'lady' and the cook, a fraternal 'tete-a-tete' between the 'señorita' and the nubile family."[98] Machado stressed that Blacks must not allow exploitive employers to fire women for not casting votes in their favor, as many men already experienced.

As Machado anticipated, Black feminists' engagement with the national women's movement remained troubled by racial hierarchies. Few feminists of African descent had their writings published in national women's magazines edited by elite white women during the period. Women of African descent struggled to get their work published in national periodicals such as *Carteles* and *El Pueblo*. The Black columnist Gustavo Urrutia helped address this dilemma in 1933 when he announced that the white feminist magazine editors Berta Arozarena de Martínez Márquez and Renée Méndez Capote de Solís had reached out to him to recruit Black women to contribute to their magazine.[99] The editors sought to rectify divisions between white and Black feminists also by recruiting women of African descent for their recently formed writers' association. "We white women," Arozarena and Méndez explained in their announcement in Urrutia's column, "and you Black women work separated by the color line that ruins us both." They continued, "We recognize in you all of our strengths and weaknesses and call you to our side without requiring conditions."[100] No document that I found indicates whether any Black women did indeed become members of the writers association. That Arozarena and Méndez chose to reach out to elite Black women demonstrates that some white feminists were aware of the racial divisions within the women's movement and attempted to bridge such divisions.

Race complicated Black women's mission to fulfill modernizing standards of citizenship within national parties as well. In August 1939, Pozo Gato of the Partido Unión Nacionalista (Nationalist Union Party) lamented, "My name does not appear in any of the party assemblies hitherto constituted, despite having devoted all of my effort and energy and for whose rise and expansion I have fought so much."[101] Pozo Gato had a brief announcement published in *Noticias de Hoy* thanking those from "elements of all social classes" who led "demonstrations of affection and sympathies" in support of her contributions to the party. It appears that her marginalization led to divisions within the party. Pozo Gato declined any attempts to redress practices of discrimination proposed by her "friends, clients, and sympathizers." Rather, she encouraged members of the Havana branch of the party to work on its advancement in that city and consciously recognizing "the merits of the Cuban Black intellectual woman, helping her in an effective manner equal to that of the Cuban white woman intellectual, to [ensure her] best development and [to achieve racial] harmony."[102] While Pozo Gato did not cite specific incidents, her reference to Black women intellectuals is telling. She articulated a vision of democracy in which women of African descent were thinkers. Her approach created space for Black women to shape policy proposals and broader political discourses.

The image of the modern woman engendered a second phase of Black feminism that responded to national political reforms. Changing gender expectations presented elite women of African descent with new opportunities to engage in public life. While they confronted racial discrimination in their endeavors to have their works published nationally as well as to participate in political parties, they increasingly held formal positions beyond the Black public sphere.

• • •

The political circumstances that compelled Black Cuban feminists to racial silence ultimately buttressed their commitment to racial protest. Elite Black women writing during the 1910s formulated a feminist discourse that resembled that of their white counterparts. They adopted a race-neutral approach to debating women's duties in a modern nation. They affirmed patriarchal hierarchies in which women served as morally superior caretakers. Yet elite Black women also bridged feminist discourses with racial regeneration principles. In a context of racial silence, literary activism allowed feminists of African descent to challenge assumptions of racial inferiority while demonstrating their femininity.

By the 1920s and 1930s, economic grievances led feminists of African descent to critique the structural inequities that maintained their marginalization. Black women who formed part of a growing professional class complained of discrimination in employment. They, unlike their predecessors, publicly criticized how racism and sexism simultaneously ensured the impoverishment of African-descended families. As such, they centered Black women's particular experiences in debates over national progress. By the late 1930s, African-descended feminists turned to the electoral sphere to address their concerns. And while they asserted that the political participation of modern women would not compromise social morality, they recognized how social discrimination shaped their engagement with political movements beyond Black civic clubs.

Elite Black women's engagement with feminism also reveals their entry beyond the Black public sphere and into national political life. Many of the citizenship practices feminists of African descent employed to address systemic inequalities took place within the women's movement. Elite women of African descent drew from mainstream ideas of women's roles in their writings and their organizing strategies. They formulated distinct perspectives on national politics. In doing so, they bridged the mainstream feminist movement and Black politics. The issues raised by Black feminists manifested prominently as part of a national women's platform by the late 1930s, as they gained influential leadership positions across women's organizations. Such approaches enabled Black women to forge alliances as public citizens.

5

Racial Politics in the National Women's Movement

Before the 1920s, many feminists of African descent articulated a political agenda from the pages of the Black press. A few Black women joined mainstream organizations during the 1910s, though most faced exclusion due to their race. This would begin to change in the 1920s. Many African-descended women supported feminist campaigns for suffrage and social welfare reform during the 1923 and 1925 national women's congresses in Havana. Popular mobilizations of the period, which culminated with the Revolution of 1933, paralleled their entry into women's organizations across political leanings. Subsequently, the 1939 Third National Women's Congress boasted hundreds of African-descended women participants, many of whom served as organizers, representing organizations from across the island. The mid-1920s and 1930s thus witnessed the extension of both elite and working-class Black women's political engagement from the Black public sphere and labor organizations into national women's associations.

Black women's feminist activism calls attention to the role of race in the transformation of the women's movement. Though elite and middle-class white women initially excluded Black women of any class background from joining most of their organizations, they adhered to dominant expectations of racial silence. These women opened their doors to Black (and) laboring poor women as they sought to build a movement strong enough to achieve suffrage. White female leaders found themselves compelled to acknowledge issues of racial and class discrimination as they expanded their membership. By the 1930s, radical women activists of all races cited the particular experiences of oppression confronted by Black women. Their approach would continue to evolve throughout the decade as feminists incorporated solutions for addressing racial inequities into their national platforms.

Black and white activists who entered the women's movement forged strategic alliances that enabled them to advance causes they deemed important. This political contingent reflected a national, cross-organizational movement that democratized the public sphere. Economic crises prompted women, Blacks, and students as well as urban and rural workers to demand and win the resignation of the corrupt President Gerardo Machado in 1933. These political factions organized strikes and protests; they called for the formation of a government system that would finally realize the populist principles of the independence movement. The language that emerged as the result of such organizing emphasized the rights of all Cubans in a democratic nation.

The alliances forged by Black and white women activists led to their rise as an influential voting bloc. Women gained suffrage rights in 1934, and political parties approached women's organizations to seek votes for their candidates. Leaders of the national women's movement promoted an image of social unity that recognized the heterogeneity of women's experiences. They articulated a dynamic platform that addressed a range of issues but also emphasized women's roles as mothers and wives. Their approach proved successful. Male politicians attended the 1939 Third National Women's Congress to support women's demands, and several parties elected women as representatives during the 1940 Constitutional Assembly. Women of all races helped to build a coalition whose concerns would, in part, be formalized during that assembly.

Forging a National Women's Movement

During the early years of the republic, elite white women activists who sought to participate in the political sphere lacked the social power necessary to build a movement for profound reform. This resulted, to some extent, from a lack of cohesion among women's organizations. Groups like the Comité de Sufragio Femenino, Partido Popular Feminista, and Partido Nacional Feminista organized in 1912 to advocate for women's participation in electoral politics.[1] Five years later, women established the Club Femenino de Cuba to end prostitution and advocate for the establishment of women's prisons and juvenile courts in addition to political rights. Organizations such as the Asociación de Damas Isabelinas focused on charity endeavors, particularly public health care programs and policies affecting children. Women of these organizations established public works programs, became active in journalism, and approached male politicians to advance issues of importance. Elite white feminists thus separated themselves from Black (and) laboring poor women.

By the early 1920s, elite white feminists began to change their approach. Members of the Club Femenino, under the leadership of the white feminist journalist Pilar Morlon de Menéndez, invited women's organizations from across the island to attend the First National Women's Congress in 1923. They also invited male public officials. Delegates from thirty-one women's associations attended and represented diverse political viewpoints. Several Black women participated, though they did not serve as presenters or leaders. The women in attendance aimed to exert some influence over national policy as they addressed "the problems that affect the individual, family, home, and country."[2] Presenters discussed women's political participation, children's rights, abolition of the adultery law, labor rights, the white slave trade, public welfare, and women's education. The congress's final resolutions included obtaining suffrage rights and legal rights in addition to forging political campaigns to transform the court and prison system, establish social welfare programs at the national level, fight against vice, and educate laboring women. White feminist organizers thus promoted reformist approaches rather than revolutionary transformations; they spoke on behalf of poor women as self-appointed leaders regarding all women's issues. No evidence accounts for the responses of Black women who attended the event.

The political and economic turmoil of the 1920s led many white feminists to collaborate with poor and African-descended women. By 1924, white feminist leaders sought alliances with women of the popular classes as they debated legal reform. Organizers of the national women's congresses attended a board meeting of the Havana tobacco stemmers guild, and they found themselves "pleasantly surprised to see the degree of cultural advancement among laboring women."[3] The elite feminists, having observed interactions among women from different races, determined that working women were the future of national politics. The 1925 Second National Women's Congress included laboring women among its attendees who represented seventy-one organizations throughout the island. Two women of African descent presented: the tobacco stemmer Inocencia Valdés and the physician María Julia de Lara. The Black historian Angelina Edreira and the educator Rosa Pastora Leclerc attended as *vocales* (executive commit-tee members).[4] Delegates addressed themes similar to those of the first congress through a race-neutral analysis of Cuban womanhood. However, in the process of collaborating with laboring women, elite white leaders ex-panded their platform to emphasize material issues affecting poor families; among these were equal pay for men and women, health care centers for women, and affordable food options.

Inocencia Valdés's commitment to the rights of the working poor and women in particular brought her into contact with feminist activists. Valdés, like many female workers before her, joined labor organizations to fight poverty. She grew up in a politically involved family during the independence movement. She was the daughter of Juan Valdés, a tobacco worker who was forced to immigrate with his family to the United States after his revolutionary activities during the Ten Years' War. Inocencia Val-dés grew up in a household where revolutionaries regularly convened.[5] As a young worker, she served as secretary of the club Mariana Grajales and president of an organization called the Auxiliaries of the Revolution. From 1913 to 1917, Valdés migrated between Cuba and Key West for work before settling permanently in Havana. In 1918 she rose to prominence as a Havana activist after joining the tobacco stemmers guild; three years later, Valdés was elected president of the guild. In 1924 she was a delegate at the First Congress of the Worker's Federation of Havana, and she ar-dently fought for "equal work, equal pay, and for the vindication of the proletariat."[6]

The National Association of Women's Associations invited Valdés to speak on behalf of the Havana Tobacco Workers Union at the 1925 con-gress. She addressed the difficulties laborers faced because of the economic crisis. The crash of the economy during the 1920s led to the failure of the sugar and tobacco industries. Falling wages and unemployment forced the already poor workers to face starvation and struggle to pay rent. As Valdés presented the grim reality of tobacco laborers, she emphasized that the main problem lay in the limited employment opportunities available to women. Cuban women, she explained, had few choices beyond the tobacco industry and domestic service.

For many years, Cuban women had no doors open to them (except for, of course, domestic occupations), which [the tobacco industry] provided. Perhaps this has been the main motive or reason to explain the poor wages women have always earned for their work in the tobacco fields—forcing our sisters to find other sources to meet the specific needs of every proletarian home, as they become victims of their employers' greed. Later, when other industries were established in Cuba, that is, new fields opened to women's work, poor remuneration continued, despite what they naturally expected.[7]

Valdés called on delegates to help create educational opportunities for her colleagues. She suggested that association members establish schools to provide working women with the intellectual development necessary to obtain better-paying positions and "demonstrate that the Cuban woman is capable of doing the same as her sisters of other countries, countries where women shine at the same level as men."[8] Valdés's discussion of workers who fell victim to greedy employers exemplified the language through which labor activists criticized capitalism and class inequities. She emphasized sisterhood in race-neutral terms. Her speech helped sway elite feminists to take a stance on working-class women's issues. Upon concluding the congress, attendees announced in their official bulletin their support for women tobacco stemmers. Their final summary stated the need for laws to protect women workers "in all orders" and called for the establishment of night schools to prepare poor women for work.[9]

Though Valdés represented the Havana Tobacco Workers Union, including the tobacco stemmers sector, which was dominated by Black women, she did not mention race. Neither did the doctor María Julia de Lara in her speech on venereal diseases.[10] There are at least two possibilities for their omission of race in their presentations. First, in 1925, major labor organizations had only begun to address the ways racial discrimination affected Blacks. Critiques of racism had not yet become standard within discourses of the labor movement. Second, most white feminist associations did not incorporate race and the experiences of African descendants in their analyses of sociopolitical reform. Both women's speeches indicate that Black women activists sought to improve their rights and material conditions while affirming the nationalist rhetoric of racelessness.

Valdés's speech may have helped push the movement toward promoting workers' education. But elite white feminists remained reluctant to affirm a class critique that would challenge their social privileges, which they tied to moral respectability. Most attendees emphasized the traditional family structure as critical to ensuring national morality. They determined that poverty should be alleviated through education, social welfare, and formation of married households rather than challenging class hierarchies. The white lawyers Margot López of Havana and Ofelia Domínguez Navarro of Santa Clara disrupted this approach by calling for equal rights for children of unmarried parents on the grounds that the system unfairly punished such children. *El Mundo* reported that "an incident arose" when the white feminist Dulce Maria Borrero de Luján pushed delegates to act on behalf of those children. The newspaper writer explained, "[Borrero de Luján] asked for the just protection of maternity under any circumstance and later, a fierce discussion emerged in the Executive Committee of the Congress about certain comments that were aroused by the delegation of Camagüey."[11] When most of the delegates rejected proposals to grant equal rights to children regardless of their parents' marital status, radical white feminists who included López, Domínguez Navarro, and Borrero de Luján walked out of the congress.[12]

The contentious end to the 1925 congress left the feminist movement at a crossroads. Radical white women who called for the rights of children of unmarried parents challenged the social privileges held by elite white women who held conservative views on morality. Individuals like López and Domínguez Navarro contested traditional hierarchies as articulated within the framework of honor in order to demand a more inclusive political sphere. This ideological approach held the potential to radically reform the legal system on behalf of the poor. Radical activists, as such, sought to bridge class divides in their organizations.

Radical Feminist Activism and the 1933 Revolution

Valdés's speech at the Second National Women's Congress marked a turning point in which elite white feminists began to acknowledge the interrelation of gender discrimination with racism and class exploitation. Some sought solutions through their organizational platforms. Rather than speaking on behalf of laboring women, these elite white feminists pointed to Black women's perspectives as critical to achieving legal reforms.

Some white feminists who walked out of the congress later expanded their organizational platforms to recognize the particular experiences of

Black (and) laboring women. The radical feminist Alianza Nacional Feminista (National Feminist Alliance) recruited women of African descent of elite and laboring-class backgrounds as they sought to mobilize women in support of suffrage rights. Headed by Domínguez Navarro, the alliance in 1928 elucidated this strategy: "Companions of all races, of all social classes, you, white as Martí and Aragamonte, you, Black as Moncada and Maceo . . . What do we desire? That the right to suffrage is conceded to us plainly and without restrictions."[13] Alianza Nacional Feminista leaders, rather than uphold the rhetoric of racial equality, acknowledged racial distinctions. They likely did so to incorporate the critiques of African-descended women who addressed the intersections of race and women's labor issues. This broad conceptualization of womanhood appealed to many Black women, a large proportion of whom worked as tobacco stemmers; they were recruited into the mainstream feminist movement en masse.[14]

Black women professionals like Rosa Pastora Leclerc entered national politics through such organizations.[15] The Cárdenas educator attended the 1923 First National Women's Congress. She joined the Alianza Nacional Feminista shortly after its founding. Leclerc and Domínguez Navarro later became disillusioned when many wealthy members struggled to "grasp more advanced problems beyond charitable and social issues," which prohibited them from attacking matters that hurt working women.[16] The two women left the Alianza Nacional Feminista to form the Unión Laborista de Mujeres (Women's Labor Union) in 1931. They recruited a divergent contingent of feminists, among them Inocencia Valdés, denounced bourgeois capitalism, and advocated for a classless society. In 1933 they changed the organization's name to Unión Radical de Mujeres (Radical Women's Union).[17] They supported other groups that organized on behalf of working women, fought for the rights of children of unmarried parents, and "espoused socialist revolution."[18] Radical women thus built a multiracial cadre of activists who centered the rights of laboring women.

Women of the organization joined the anti-Machado movement that erupted in 1933. Despite the president's early successes, he incited protests across the island when, feeling confident in his support from political elites and the US embassy, he revoked his pledge to not run for reelection and amended the constitution so he could serve until 1934. The Unión Radical de Mujeres joined popular and middle-class youth organizations that considered his decision to serve a second term an indefensible violation of his earlier promise. Women spoke at strikes and provided legal defense for jailed activists; they proposed motions to have corrupt public officials dismissed from their positions. Machado actively and often brutally targeted threatening political factions. He ordered law enforcement to target the Unión Radical de Mujeres. Police stormed the group's offices and interrupted new-member orientations. Such actions did little to quell the women's activities. Leclerc helped mobilize a student branch and was among those jailed for supporting the guerrillas.[19]

Eventually, women of the Unión Radical de Mujeres came to oppose suffrage as an accommodation with the repressive Machado administration.[20] They broke from moderate feminist groups like the Partido Democrata Sufragista, Club Femenino, and Lyceum and Lawn Tennis Club that advocated for suffrage. Radical feminists held visions of reform that deviated from these groups. Rather than lobby for institutional reform, Unión Radical de Mujeres members rejected the corrupt political system and refused to work with its leaders.

Cuban women joined the opposition forces that lobbied for the resignation of Machado. In July 1933 activists met with US Ambassador Sumner Wells to negotiate an end to the anti-Machado protests. Among them, the white feminist Hortensia Lamar asserted that the president's leadership had lost its legitimacy and threatened Cuban democracy.[21] Radical activists including those of the Communist Party and National Committee of Campesinos and Workers led strikes to further undermine Machado's presidency. Machado attempted to negotiate with radical factions by agreeing to free political prisoners and to endorse their right to participate in electoral politics. Yet Wells disapproved of Machado's efforts to empower radical activists. He joined Cuban moderate factions in supporting a military coup that overthrew Machado in August 1933, leading to the interim presidency of Carlos Manuel de Céspedes.[22]

Pastora Leclerc continued to build a broad political career that translated her work as an educator into the formal arena. She helped found the Comité de Defensa de Sufragio Femenino (Women's Suffrage Committee), which "held interviews with prominent members of the assembly to publicize their positions on suffrage in the press."[23] In 1933 she cofounded the Frente Único de los Maestros, later renamed the Sindicato Nacional de Trabajadores de la Enseñanza. Four years later, she attended the third Conferencia Interamericana de Educación as a member of the Cuba delegation. She supported the Spanish Civil War and traveled to Spain with the Asociación de Auxilio al Niño del Pueblo Español to supply milk, clothing, and money for orphaned children at a school established by the association in Barcelona. Leclerc also represented that association in France and traveled to Belgium to escort fifty Spanish orphans back to Cuba.[24] Therefore, her commitment to the rights of children reinforced her participation in an international movement for democratic reform.

Black women activists' alliances with white labor and feminist leaders reflected a multiracial coalition that continued to evolve following the 1933 Revolution and Machado's overthrow that August.[25] Elite white women appealed to all women of African descent as they began preparations for the Third National Women's Congress. They hoped to build a sizable coalition of women who might influence reforms in "the new Cuba." In October 1933, the organizing committee issued a call to all Cuban women through the pages of the Black social column of *Ahora*. They explained the following: "It is necessary to begin, without delay, a work of reconstruction that is oriented in the sense of creating among ourselves a spirit of solidarity, and a clear understanding of our responsibility in the future. It is absolutely necessary that we be able to perform our civil and political rights effectively."[26] The committee expressed the members' particular interest in partnering with women of the prominent elite Black civic organizations Club Antilla, Unión Fraternal, Orientación, Atenas, Deportivo La Fe, Juventud Selecta del Cerro Jóvenes del Vals, and Club Maceo. Organizing members invited the female readers of the column to an upcoming meeting at the home of the activist Justina Sandó Tellez. The next congress would not meet for six years, but white and African-descended women of the elite classes continued to advocate for legal and social welfare reforms through a variety of organizations, especially after women gained the right to vote in 1934.

Organizing the 1939 Third National Women's Congress

Similar to the First and Second National Women's Congress of 1923 and 1925, the Third Congress operated under the assumption that Cuban women were responsible for ensuring national progress as mothers and wives. Yet articles published by Black women activists prior to and during the congress revealed philosophical transformations within the women's movement.[27] For one, the congress's platform incorporated a diverse mix of individuals and social perspectives. No longer solely comprised of and planned by white elite and middle-class members, the Third Congress brought together more than two thousand women delegates from all backgrounds: urban and rural, white and Black, the rich and the laboring poor, professional and nonprofessional including factory workers, domestic laborers, and *campesinas*, and those of various political and religious affiliations. Because of this diversity, dialogues during the event featured different perspectives on womanhood in relation to social equality. In addition, for the first time, congress organizers addressed the particular experiences of Black women; they emphasized racial unity, included racial discrimination on their list of social issues, and asserted the legal rights of African-descended women as workers. As participants committed to these efforts, Black feminists helped build a cross-racial alliance that would demand institutional reform during the 1940 Constitutional Assembly.[28]

Perhaps to prevent the clashes that took place during the 1925 congress, leaders established their inclusive intentions up front: "This women's movement will rise above all circumstantial religious or racial distinctions, constituting us as a force capable of guaranteeing the rights of women and children, the peace and progress of Cuban society."[29] If the women's movement was to be successful in obtaining social equality, race had to be acknowledged and discussed to address the multiplicity of women's concerns. Committee members and delegates circulated articles and interviews from a variety of national and regional newspapers and journals that appealed to women of all social backgrounds. They consistently stated their concern with what they felt was a failure of the government to protect women and children. Moreover, they insisted that all women be given the opportunity to advocate for themselves within public institutions as the equal of their male counterparts. As explained by the Black delegate Catalina Causse Viuda de Mercer of Oriente Province, "It is not a question of Blacks or whites, rather it is in the general interest of all conscious women, their duty and responsibility, to obtain a post in the collective movement for social betterment on behalf of our children."[30] Causse articulated her concerns within the framework of racelessness.

That Causse rejected the question of distinct Black or white interests is not surprising, considering that elite and working-class women of African descent played a significant role in the development of the congress. Black women's involvement disrupted the practice of elite white women organizing major congresses. Some white women may have resisted the changing social structure. The executive committee included prominent Black professionals and activists from throughout the island. Consuelo Silveira, a Black Havana labor leader, was the committee's vice secretary of finance. Ana Echegoyen de Cañizares was selected as the secretary of correspondence. The executive committee also included several women of African descent as *vocales*: Teresa García from the Havana Tobacco Workers Union, the educator and historian Angelina Edreira, the domestic worker and union leader Elvira Rodríguez, and the pharmacist Esperanza Sánchez Mastrapa from Gíbara in Oriente Province, as well as Catalina Pozo Gato and María Dámasa Jova Baró. Importantly, conference organizers aimed to create an atmosphere in which women would leave their political leanings behind in order to unify women of varying philosophical perspectives, yet many women represented the interests of social groups affiliated with labor unions and political organizations.

María Patrocinado Garbey Águila was at once uncharacteristic and representative of the Black women who attended the Third National Women's Congress. A prominent activist committed to social equality, Garbey held the rare position for a woman as the longtime president of the Centro Cultural Martín Morúa Delgado, a Black civic club in Santiago de Cuba.[31] In 1914 she had attended the National Labor Convention as a representative of "Cuban women from Oriente Province."[32] She brought her public leadership to the 1939 National Women's Congress to advocate for the betterment of all Cuban women. For Garbey, the realization of the National Women's Congress, to which she referred as the National Feminist Congress, marked "a significant step forward taken by the Cuban woman" in her evolution. Garbey predicted, "That which results will be helpful for women themselves and, as a consequence, for our country."[33]

Garbey's endorsement of the congress was certainly in sync with those of other Black civic clubwomen who expressly affirmed its mission. Indeed, elite and working-class women of African descent frequently organized other Black women on behalf of the feminist movement. Elite Black women of Havana associated with the Sociedad Antilla Sport Club held an assembly for Black women sponsored by the Federación de Sociedades Negras de la Provincia de la Habana to identify issues affecting Black women "to be brought to the Women's Congress."[34] Attendees represented the civic organizations La Unión de Bauta, El Progreso de Guanabacoa, and Vedado Social Club. Women of the civic club Luz de Oriente hosted a similar meeting to discuss the "main problems that affect the Black women of Oriente."[35] They aimed to compile a list of issues that concerned Black women and would interest "white women as much as women of color."[36] The clubwomen's suggestive evocation of both white and Black women claimed the possibility that Black women's equality would lead to "a better future for [all] Cuban women."[37]

Such directives, Black clubwomen asserted, supported a Cuban nationalist cause. In February 1939, women of the Federación de Sociedades Negras published the article "La mujer en general y la mujer negra en particular" (Women in general and Black women in particular) in the national communist newspaper *Noticias de Hoy*.[38] It was signed by members of the organizing committee of the Asamblea Provincial de Mujeres Negras and the elite clubwomen Mercedes Ruis de Andrade, Digna Ferrera González, and Francisca Romay Valdés, the feminist writer Cloris Tejo Hernández, and the committee secretary Esther Torriente Moncada. The brief yet loaded manifesto carved out a particular place for women of African descent in contemporary political debates as they addressed constitutional reform. Their language was straightforward and passionate. They asserted,

> [W]e cannot deny or ignore that sensitive developments—which have occurred in our Nation since before the foundation of the Republic—have created a painful situation in which one finds the highest percentage of exploited women, battered mothers, and lack of food to prepare and to educate men capable of conceiving a radiant future of justices and of laying the foundations for a society of brotherhood, peace, and love—where they find shelter from petty racial prejudice and economic inequalities that currently impede man's life. . . . That is why, despite our great ideological values, we hold in our minds a poor ethnic classification based on the absurdity of racial superiority or inferiority.[39]

The writers employed rhetorical strategies used by a variety of Black activists; they pointed out the discrepancies between racism and the nationalist rhetoric of racial equality as they addressed the contributions of Black women to state reform. They asserted that Cubans failed to achieve the principles of racelessness due to an investment in ideas of Black racial inferiority. Anti-Black racism emanated into all aspects of the daily lives of men and women of African descent.

Torriente Moncada and her peers spoke to Cuban women of all races. The women acknowledged that racial antagonism had historically separated white and Black women in the public sphere. Yet they maintained that such inconsistencies should not prevent women of African descent from joining the movement, as it was dangerous for them to "remain indifferent to the call to [all] Cuban women." Importantly, they spoke as "Cuban women, as conscientious mothers," committed to political redevelopment. Additionally, the clubwomen recalled the slave woman who, "in a gesture of humanity," offered "the fruits of her love" to the independence cause.[40] By denying ethnic differences among Cubans and reiterating Black women's role in the independence movement, the organizing committee members of the Asamblea Provincial de Mujeres Negras appealed to a vision of racelessness that remained an aspiration. To complete their "duty as women," they intended to fight "tenaciously so that the Black woman might take her place in the National Women's Congress as women."[41]

Perhaps the sight of so many women of African descent serving as organizing members and delegates alarmed some white women, or white women may have resented the prominent position that racial discrimination held in the congress agenda. A few weeks before the opening celebrations, *Oriente*, one of the major regional newspapers of the eastern province, printed a letter from the Black activist Pastora Causede de Atiés directed to other Black women of Santiago de Cuba. She responded to claims that "the development of assemblies with large numbers of Black women in attendance" resulted in racial prejudice within the women's movement. Causede emphasized the stake that women of African descent held in the movement: "We're struggling, we're applying the pressure that these key organizations need and appealing to women from the highest positions to the most humble." Causede put in plain words that Black women were "initiating a series of acts" to alleviate their own issues since their efforts had "not been matched" by their white counterparts.[42]

The author could have replicated the language of unification to appeal to those put off by the discussions of race at the National Women's Congress. Yet she purposefully pointed out the dilemmas confronted by Black women of the province in their daily lives. Causede astutely observed,

There is only one real thing that exists: the Black woman has responded to this clarion call because her problems have not been resolved; because it is difficult to enroll her children in some schools; because apart from making a physical, monetary, and intellectual effort it is difficult to achieve her desires; . . . because she does not have the right to hold public offices as more than a simple typist after many recommendations; because neither as a worker can she occupy a post in public establishments nor as a cook or nanny.[43]

Causede highlighted the limitations that she and her peers faced as mothers and workers, realities that illustrated the persistence of racial discrimination in Cuban society. Like activists and intellectuals who argued that capitalist exploitation perpetuated Black women's marginalization, Causede underscored the racialization of labor and how skin color determined one's access to employment. Racism, then, was more than an economic or social problem; it violated the individual freedoms to which every Cuban was entitled. Additionally, she determined that "the years of fighting" that Black men incurred during childhood were hardly rewarded as adult laborers, a compensation "always postponed." Not unlike Black women's marginalization in employment, a Black man might devote "the best years of his life to acquire a degree of proficiency," yet his training never seemed enough for "a post occupancy as judge or in our courts or Justice of the Diplomatic or Cuban consular."[44] If the Congress did not address these issues, Causede worried that the men and women of her community would be left behind in a developing society.[45]

The congress thus presented a moment to address these social inequities, outline a plan for legal reform, and galvanize white women in opposition to anti-Black racism. Analyses of Black women's experiences during the event demonstrated the intersection of racial, class, and gender oppression; they also called attention to broader issues such as access to health care and social services, equal pay and fair working conditions, and women's political representation. Women of African descent drew from these issues as they helped mobilize a large constituency of activists across the island.

The 1939 Third National Women's Congress

Noticias de Hoy estimated that two thousand women gathered in the Teatro Nacional in Havana for the opening presentations. A reporter observed that the venue "was completely full; even the hallways and spaces between seats were occupied by an indefinable number of women, who on this occasion, have been able to give full demonstrations of their collective desire for redemption and mutual cooperation for the achievement of their ends."[46] Notably, "women of all races and origins" could be observed throughout the theater.[47] Organizers of the 1939 congress thus succeeded in convening a socially diverse gathering centered on the empowerment of women as political actors.

Enacting unity proved more complicated, however. On the third day of the congress, executive committee president Berta Arocena resigned from her post, explaining, "Convinced of the apoliticism that work for the woman and child demands, I am deeply disappointed by the political tone that has predominated the opening and first plenary session of the Congress."[48] As congress organizers sought to unify women across political differences in support of a common agenda, many attendees booed speakers with whom they disagreed politically. Chaos erupted on multiple occasions as congress organizers struggled to reestablish tranquility. Arocena called out "the partisan division that discriminates against the women of the Assembly, taking it to the extreme to distribute the items of the Permanent Committee, with advantages and disadvantages for both, according to their political affiliations."[49] She lamented that groups of women sought to sabotage others based on their political affiliations. Others followed her lead. Representatives of the Club de Mujeres Auténticas and a Catholic women's association announced their resignations due to the political tone of the congress. The delegates Luisa Parra Téllez of the Asociación de la Prensa and the Partido Demócrata Republicano and Ana C. Rivas Rocores of the Partido Demócrata Republicano de Guantánamo left the congress as well.

Delegates who remained elected the "eminently apolitical" Ana Echegoyen Cañizares as president to lead the convention to its conclusion. Echegoyen's neutral political stance allowed women of varying perspectives, from Catholic conservatives to radical communists, to feel that their approaches to women's issues would be respected by the congress's leadership. Ideally, Echegoyen's presence helped ensure that no party shaped the direction of the congress. When controversies continued to disrupt the sessions, Echegoyen asserted, "Cuban women are building our future now, and that person who tries to take a line contrary to this thought is virtually obstructing it."[50] While successful in maintaining the support of the majority of delegates, she struggled to manage political divisions.

Black feminists continued to examine national politics and social equality from the perspectives of Black women during the congress. Included among them was the forty-three-year-old poet and teacher María Dámasa Jova. She helped outline an agenda for women's advancement and "national stability" for the congress in her speech entitled "La situación de la mujer negra en Cuba" (The situation of the Black woman in Cuba). Dámasa Jova argued, "The Black mother suffered most because she was the mother of the marginal Black child, the prostitute, the little newspaper vendor, the gang of robbers, the great number of unemployed and illiterate, and the ill-mannered Black child."[51] She went on to assert that discrimination in Cuba's schools undermined social equality, as they trained girls of African descent to become ironers rather than professionals. "When the Black woman is conceded her rights and when there is a [sizable] percentage of Black women in shops and offices, one can rest assured that women in Cuba are united in the struggle for the overall betterment and the interests of mothers and children," Dámasa Jova contended.[52] Thus, she asserted, any movement to bring about equality must include a commitment to securing the rights of Black women and children.

As a public figure committed to defending "school, primary education, veterans, and mothers," Dámasa Jova's speech highlights a rare instance in which a Black feminist critically examined the role of white women in Cuba's national development.[53] Dámasa Jova reiterated points made by African-descended feminists throughout the 1930s. She asserted that unity among Cuban women could occur only through the elimination of racial discrimination and that "the problem of racial discrimination called for the attention of white women to the situation of Black women."[54] She explained, "One must note that in this fight for the vindication of the white woman that she holds the greatest responsibility in being able to reject her unjust privileges. She must fight for a redistribution of resources by rejecting her privileges so that the Black woman might receive her rights."[55] Dámasa Jova thus implored white women to act on their stated commitment to racial solidarity. As Dámasa Jova called for cross-racial unity, she appealed to nationalist discourses and affirmed that racial unity was crucial to the realization of social equality.[56]

"La situación de la mujer negra en Cuba" by Dámasa Jova is the only available document in which a delegate specifically addressed the experiences of Black women at the 1939 Third National Women's Congress. The Santiago de Cuba educator Serafina Causse also presented a speech on racial discrimination, but I have been unable to locate this document.[57] Placing Dámasa Jova's address alongside synopses of other speakers' presentations suggests how leaders of the women's movement integrated matters affecting Black women into their agenda for legal reform. Aída Rodríguez Sarabia presided over a commission on women and racial prejudice that advocated against discrimination confronted by Black and Jewish women. The committee called for the agreements of the Lima Conference to be accepted "in the sense that Cuba respects racial problems." They demanded "that Article 4 of Act 1024, which determines the equitable proportion of Black women in the work in industry and commerce, be enforced, and sanctions against the offenders." They added, "And that in all political parties Black women have representation." They also called for equitable distribution of scholarships offered by the state, provinces, and municipalities between whites and Blacks; the creation of integrated athletic fields; and enforcement of racial equality for Black trained athletes. Finally, women of the commission called for the "Department of Education to print and disseminate in all the schools the story of the 'Muñeca Negra' by José Martí and 'Isaac el Mulato' by Gertrudis Gómez de Avellaneda, and . . . to publish the paper by Dr. Serafina Causse" addressing the problems confronting the Black woman.[58] Women of the congress called for social integration, which many linked to reforming the education system to validate the experiences of Black children.

During the final discussions of the congress, participants outlined a detailed proposal to submit to the 1940 Constitutional Assembly that reified their commitment to "women and children's improvement" and to "Cuban peace and progress."[59] A section entitled "La mujer y los prejuicios raciales" (Women and racial prejudice), presented fifteen points that they wanted the constitutional delegates to take into consideration. They explicitly based their suggestions for political reorganization on Article I of the Cuban Constitution, "All Cubans are equal before the law, and the law does not recognize exemptions or privileges."[60] The proposals included the creation of a "body of Congress capable of fighting against all forms of racial prejudice, to vigorously oppose acts of discriminatory injustice against the Black race in all activities of civic life, creating a bureau of statistics and research to that effect." Such a body would establish racial quotas for labor and education; it would enforce strict penalties for those professors and judges who discriminate against Blacks as well as for those who violated Blacks' rights in private schools and in public places such as parks, walkways, cabarets, and hotels. The women also called for the elimination of assigning racial descriptors when filing official documents "except in cases where required for personal identification." Finally, the women proposed an antiracism campaign to be carried out through the radio, the press, conferences, and "especially in primary schools."[61]

No doubt, attendees recognized the centrality of this doctrine to Cuba's legal order, as their desire for solidarity and absolute equality across racial, professional, and regional differences constituted a central tenet of the congress's discourse. The delegates to the National Women's Congress understood that racial discrimination had persisted because of the government's failure to implement and enforce legislation for those who violated the constitution. The majority of the points featured in the proposal put forth new policies such as maternity laws and public school curriculum reform that addressed discrimination within the legal system, employment, education, and public places. These policies were in line with reform issues identified by labor unions, the Communist Party, and the Federación of Sociedades Negras.[62]

It is difficult to fully comprehend elite white leaders' responses to Black women activists' calls for social reform beyond political rhetoric. Certainly, white women's incorporation of antidiscrimination policies into the final resolution demonstrates their willingness to endorse the demands of African-descended women in order to advance their own political goals. Yet the publication of an article in *El Pueblo* by the radical feminist Mariblanca Sabás Alomá reveals the tensions that continued to shape processes of cross-racial collaboration.[63] Weeks after the conclusion of the Third National Women's Congress, Sabás Alomá lauded the efforts of Black women to mobilize on behalf of all women's issues. The African-descended socialist Ángel César Pinto Albiol responded with indignation in a letter in *El Pueblo*.[64] Pinto Albiol questioned Sabás Alomá's right to speak on behalf of Black women. He accused her of racism, questioning her use of terms like "mestizo" and suggesting she harbored antimiscegenation attitudes. Sabás Alomá replied, again in *El Pueblo*, by expressing concerns with sexual relations between Black women and white men, particularly exploitive relationships outside of marriage in which white men fathered children they then left to live in poverty.[65] She determined that through such relations, white men weakened the "pure" Black race. Sabás Alomá's exchange with Pinto Albiol suggests how some elite white women maintained ideas of racial inferiority that contributed to Black women's marginalization.

The public exchange between two prominent activists, a white feminist and an elite man of African descent, shows how Black women continued to confront erasure in discussions regarding their experiences. I have found no record of Black women's responses to the social dynamics that unfolded during the Third National Women's Congress.

Women as a Voting Bloc

By the late 1930s, the diverse coalition of women activists that supported the Third National Women's Congress increasingly articulated itself as a unified voting bloc. The labor activist Inocencia Valdés presented a purposeful missive to the readers of *Noticias de Hoy* in which she championed the right of marginalized Cubans to pursue legal equality: "Every woman should fight. Women, Blacks, and workers need to set their sights on a constitution approved by a sovereign constituency. I, for my part, am creating an intense propaganda campaign among women tobacco workers."[66] Suggesting that women were entitled to pursue legal reform, Valdés underscored the need for a new constitution that would finally recognize the rights of all Cubans within a sovereign, democratic nation. She implored the newspaper's female readers to run for office and support political candidates who would break from the corruption of previous government administrations in order to build a more equitable society.

Communist activists advocated for women of different backgrounds to participate in the political arena in support of the popular classes. In *Noticias de Hoy*, the white journalist Emma Pérez described the "deep enthusiasm" that she believed animated Cuban workers, students, professionals, teachers, and peasants ready to support communist "Candidates of the People." [67] She cited the activists Edith García Buchaca and Consuelo Silveira of Havana as viable candidates. "And we have heard," she continued, "of a lot of women without a party who affirm that they will vote for 'those fighters who will defend me.'"[68] Among those who declared their intentions to vote were the twenty-year-old Black "servant worker" Amalia Rodríguez;

the public employee Rosa Martínez, who promised to vote as much for the rights of her daughter enrolled in the university as for her own; and the bus driver Josefa González, who viewed Garcia Buchaca and Silveira as "the great defenders of women." Most striking was the response of Adela Palacios, who announced, "I will vote for the Communist so that I will not die of misery."[69] Such women placed their hopes in the Unión Revolucionaria Comunista. Their commitment to its women leaders reflected a growing populist perspective that unified a diverse body of people across racial lines.

The cross-racial alliance of the Third National Women's Congress became critical for electing Esperanza Sánchez Mastrapa as a delegate to the Constitutional Assembly. Pérez used her *Noticias de Hoy* column to endorse Sánchez's candidacy.[70] Following her election, thousands of women gathered in Havana's Parque Central "to honor the women elected delegates to the Constitutional Assembly." María Josefa Bolaños, María Luisa Fafita, Catalina Pozo Gato, Delfina Chufal, Aida R. Saravia, Nila Ortega, Josefina Pedrosa, and Ana Echegoyen Cañizares proudly stood beside the delegates Esperanza Sánchez Mastrapa and Alicia Hernández Armentero.[71] The women, claiming public space, sought to mobilize other women in support of democracy and peace, a political issue of growing concern as World War II began. Women entered such discussions in defense of women and children. In this sense, women of all class backgrounds continued to forge alliances across political differences in support of a common agenda.

• • •

African-descended women activists stood at the intersection of national women's activism and elite Black men's club activism. At no time were all Black women of one mind about which political philosophy would best help them improve the social status of women. Some individuals pursued reform primarily through elite Black associations and women's groups, and others joined radical labor and communist organizations. Various groups of Black women forged strategic alliances with white women with the goal of achieving a wide range of reforms affecting African-descended women and their families. Building coalitions across racial and class differences created moments of tension. And following the conclusion of the 1939 congress, the vision of racial solidarity put forth by activists such as Dámasa Jova remained unresolved. Yet many women of African descent rose to national prominence as leaders of political movements by the close of the decade. The alliances they helped forge would be critical to securing the antidiscrimination clause of the 1940 Constitution.

Ultimately, the activism of elite and laboring poor women of African descent at the intersection of Black civic clubs and women's organizations reflects the overlapping nature of political activity among movements for legal reform. Race was not always central as a mobilizing factor for their activist strategies. Their strategic collaborations with white women in national political organizations, especially in the Communist Party, would continue to expand throughout the 1940s. The Communist Party became a major organization for supporting women's political activism. This dynamic would be framed in relation to the populist discourse that emerged during the late 1930s. Women of all races played pivotal roles in creating this brand. They continued to face marginalization in the communist movement, and most women held leadership roles only in auxiliary branches of the Unión Revolucionaria Comunista. Black women who embraced radical and moderate political approaches represented distinct political communities whose gendered approach to reform shaped their activist strategies.

6

The Limits of Democratic Citizenship in the New Constitutional Era

The ratification of the 1940 Constitution coincided with the beginnings of World War II, which reinvigorated democratic reform movements throughout the United States and Latin America.[1] Activists cautioned that weak political institutions would leave their nations vulnerable to fascism. African descendants, in particular, linked despotic regimes in Europe to anti-Black racism at home.[2] In Cuba, Black civic clubs of Las Villas announced the creation in 1943 of an alliance that would contribute to "national unity and the fight against Nazism" as well as "the defense of the civil rights of the Black population and the well-being of the Cuban people."[3] Civic activists of African descent thus considered the urgency of democratic citizenship from the standpoint of an Afro-diasporic community.

The 1940 Constitution, in many ways, realized the principles of democracy articulated by Black women activists who formed alliances with labor leaders, white feminists, and club men of African descent during the 1930s. It provided for free elections, universal suffrage, and the right to strike. Article 20 declared all Cubans to be "equal before the law" and deemed "illegal and punishable any discrimination on grounds of sex, race, color, or class and any other offense to human dignity."[4] The article helped establish an unprecedented legal foundation for addressing inequality: individuals could invoke their civil rights to pressure the government for labor and social welfare reform as well as protection from discrimination. Yet, ensuring equality would prove difficult, for declaring discrimination illegal would not eradicate the material disparities that existed between elites and the poor. Nor would it realize full political representation for women or provide Blacks with equal access to employment and social venues. Instead, many Cubans complained that the government lacked strong enforcement measures to successfully apply their new rights to daily life.[5]

The civic activist Ana Echegoyen de Cañizares navigated these political transformations as an advocate for all Cuban women and children. The University of Havana professor rose to national prominence during the 1930s through her leadership in elite Black associations and national women's groups. Her participation in sociopolitical movements preceded that of many elite Black women who pursued democratic reforms outside of the electoral sphere in the 1940s and 1950s. Elite women of African descent took a moderate approach to enacting citizenship in the new constitutional era. Echegoyen bridged her professional career with her membership in civic associations. Some civic associations provided access to state resources and opportunities for elite Blacks to socialize; others allowed a privileged multiracial membership to influence state reforms. By the late 1940s, sexism particularly within Black civic clubs led many African-descended women to establish independent groups that promoted national progress from their vantage point. Elite Black women employed the press to circulate their ideas about structural inequities, notably the failures of Cuba's education system. Schools became a critical site for pursuing social equality. Such strategies enabled elite Black women to seek reforms outside of political parties, as few women of any race held elected positions.

Elite Black women's moderate approach depended to some extent on the strategic alliances they had forged during the 1930s. Figures like Echegoyen joined organizations headed by privileged whites as advocates for racial equality. They addressed ongoing issues of labor discrimination alongside Black club men. Elite women of African descent sought to bolster their political influence through partnerships with Black club men and privileged white Cubans. Yet they refrained from directly confronting the racial and gender privileges held by their counterparts. Their moderate approach produced uneven results. While more women of African descent held positions in national civic clubs, their conversations regarding poor Black women's experiences that circulated during the 1930s became less frequent in public political discussions of the 1940s, and men led national campaigns for racial equality. Finally, the educators Adela García de Falcón, Consuelo Serra, and Serafina Causse joined Echegoyen in building ties with democratic reform activists across national boundaries. By the early 1950s, the inability of multiracial and, at times, transnational coalitions to achieve racial equality evidenced one of many limitations of elite Black women's moderate strategies.

Echegoyen and the Gendered Nature of Moderate Politics

Elite Black women's moderate political approach reflected the ambiguous position Cuban women held in society in the final decades of the republican era. The 1940 Constitution, besides affirming women's suffrage and prohibiting discrimination on the basis of sex, guaranteed women equal civil rights regardless of their marital status. Still, few women of any race ran for political office. Elite and middle-class women increasingly entered public affairs through civic associations and auxiliary branches of political parties.[6] Their lack of political representation supports the observation of the historian Johanna Moya Fábregas: "While organized female politicization often unsettled the dynamics of patriarchy by challenging the idea that women should refrain from political participation, they were not always concerned with breaking down traditional gender structures."[7] Indeed, most women continued to negotiate expectations of domesticity and modernizing gender norms in their pursuit of democratic reform.

This dynamic is exemplified by the civic activism of Ana Echegoyen de Cañizares. In January 1953 the Black magazine *Amanecer* profiled her attainments. Editors celebrated her involvement in organizations that addressed sociopolitical reform in Cuba and globally. The first set of organizations fostered intellectual discussions among elites regarding Cuban social dynamics. Notably, Echegoyen gave lectures on education and democracy before the Lyceum and Lawn Tennis Club, a cultural institution founded by privileged white women of Havana. She also lectured at a prominent intellectual society, the Institución Hispano Cubano de Cultura (Hispano Cuban Institution of Culture), founded by the anthropologist Fernando Ortiz to build relations between the island and Spain. During the 1940s, Ortiz devoted much of his work to investigating Cuba's race problem from a cultural standpoint. Ortiz selected Echegoyen to serve on the board of his organization, the Sociedad de Estudios Afrocubanos (Society of Afro-Cuban Studies). Ortiz used the organization to further the study of Cuban identity and culture, which he famously theorized as the product of "transculturation," the mix of African and Spanish traditions.[8] He brought Echegoyen into his institutions to promote racial equality through the gradual erasure of racial distinctions.

Echegoyen also engaged racial politics through her involvement with activist organizations that promoted democratic reform during the 1950s.

Among them, the Frente Cívico Cubano contra la Discriminación Racial (Cuban Civic Front against Racial Discrimination), established 1951, and the Instituto Interamericano de Lucha contra la Discriminación Racial (Inter-American Institute for the Struggle against Racial Discrimination) unified Black civic leaders, student activists, and Confederación de Trabajadores Cubanos (Confederation of Cuban Workers) members in support of racial reforms. The Instituto Interamericano addressed racial equality as a democratic issue that drew inspiration from the US civil rights movement. Echegoyen also joined the global movement for equality as a member of Josephine Baker's World Cultural Association against Racial and Religious Discrimination.[9]

At yet another level, Echegoyen participated in international organizations for education reform. She served as an education faculty delegate for UNESCO, and she was appointed the director of the School Forum for the United Nations and its specialized agencies.[10] Her work in international educational organizations brought her into contact with teachers from other nations. They affirmed her belief that strengthening Cuba's school system was crucial for building a strong democracy. Educators who joined international organizations for education reform asserted that obtaining an education remained an important path for pulling oneself out of poverty and entering the middle class; they sought strategies for expanding access to schools within their respective nations. Echegoyen worked with three Cuban government agencies that enabled her to shape national policies on education: the Office of Social Affairs of the Ministry of Information, Review Commission of Cuban Study Courses, and Culture Section of the Havana Pedagogues College, as its president.

Published photographs of Echegoyen complemented the written profiles that praised her organizational activities. Black press editors and female subjects continued to deploy visual images as a political strategy. Similar to the magazines and newspapers that featured studio portraits during the early years of the republic, those that circulated in the 1940s and early 1950s incorporated contemporary stylistic trends. *Amanecer* editors used photojournalism to evidence Echegoyen's professional activities. A two-page spread featured a photograph of Echegoyen descending the main staircase at the University of Havana (figure 6.1). Other photographs included in the spread portrayed Echegoyen in the act of working, seated at a desk reading papers in what appeared to be an office and standing before a classroom

Figure 6.1. The educator and civic activist Ana Echegoyen de Cañizares at the University of Havana. From "Ojos y olbos," *Amanecer*, January 1953.

chalkboard as she engaged a room full of students. Collectively, the three images affirmed her intellectual authority as a prominent educator.

The *Amanecer* editor, by placing photographs alongside text, gendered Echegoyen's civic engagement beyond the classroom. Her modest attire helped convey an image of modern femininity. Readers would have observed and perhaps admired her two-tone shirtdress, her watch, and her wedding band. The caption to the classroom photograph describes her work ethic: "In Doctor Echegoyen, as a professor, exists tenacious dedication and enthusiasm that never wavers. The students become disciples, the disciples become friends, the friends become children. *A deep maternal feeling governs her.*[11] The editor and article author stressed the emotional labor that she took on as a teacher. Rather than simply provide her students with career skills, Echegoyen built motherly relations with the students who fell under her guardianship. The caption reflects how Cubans continued to view teaching as an extension of women's domestic role as caretakers.

Characterizing Echegoyen's professional labor as a form of mothering helped feminize her organizational activities. The published profile also included two photographs that depict Echegoyen wearing formal attire as she advocated for educational reform at the United Nations in Geneva. One image shows her receiving an award, and the other captures her working alongside fellow delegates. The *Amanecer* profile positioned her as an accomplished advocate for democratic reform through education. Framing her organizational activities and international travels as an extension of her caretaker responsibilities in the classroom validated her public engagement.

Published photographs of figures like Echegoyen centered professional Black women as modern feminine subjects. Editors employed such images to promote a particular class-based vision in which women of African descent navigated the public sphere as refined workers. They countered the stereotypical images of Black women that continued to depict poverty, Afro-Cuban cultural practices, and hypersexuality. Other Black press editions from the period featured the internationally renowned soprano Zoila Gálvez, the pianist and educator Zenaida Manfugas, and the journalist Calixta María Hernández de Cervantes as accomplished leaders in their fields to be admired and celebrated. Such profiles called attention to practices of racial discrimination in the labor force. They used clothing, gestures, setting, and text to demonstrate elite Black women's adherence to dominant standards of femininity.

The *Amanecer* profile of Echegoyen conveys a sense of her sociopolitical concerns as a prominent professional who negotiated gender expectations through her professional and association activities. But how did she enter such groups? What did she accomplish through these affiliations? How did her participation in each organization allow her to navigate the political realm? It is possible to piece the limited records on Black civic associations together to better understand how she carried out her political mission.

More than "Club Ornaments" and "Instruments of Propaganda"

By the early 1940s, women experienced greater opportunities in traditionally male-headed Black civic clubs, and several associations elected women to their executive boards. At the 1946 Convention of Black Societies in Camagüey, delegates advocated for women to be fully incorporated into social organizations as participants "and not regarded only as club ornaments or as instruments of propaganda."[12] Several organizations responded. Felicita Ortiz, a prominent communist leader in the region, became vice president of the Black Camagüeyan club La Victoria. Esperanza Sánchez Mastrapa was an active member of the Federation of Societies of Color of Oriente Province at the same time that she served in the national Communist Party. The election of both women to leadership positions in the federation affirms that the Communist Party elevated women within its ranks as it solidified ties to Black civic clubs.

Most Black civic associations reinforced a masculinist approach to political activism, however. Black civic club and Communist Party leaders who sought to shape government policy included prominent men like Lazaro Peña, Salvador García Agüero, Blas Roca, and Jesús Menéndez Larrondo. The intellectuals Gustavo Urrutia, Ramón Vasconcelos, and Pedro Portuondo Calá protested anti-Black racism and government corruption through the press. Men of African descent appeared as the most vocal critics who leveraged their electoral influence on behalf of racial reform. Such figures acknowledged how women of African descent confronted labor discrimination, but few women radically challenged patriarchal dynamics within Cuban society.

Black women's lack of power within the civic club movement paralleled their lack of power in the national political sphere. Women won suffrage rights in 1934, yet few women of any race held elected positions in the major political parties more than a decade later. The African-descended journalist Juana Oliva Bulnes complained that only one woman, Adelaida Oliva Robaina, had been elected in 1944 to the House of Representatives from Havana Province.[13] Twenty-six women served in Congress between 1934 and 1958, and they sought to legislate the social welfare initiatives of the national feminist movement. Most hailed from elite white families with established government ties. The Communist Party was an important exception, but it likewise sent few women to Congress relative to its male representatives.

The leadership of Ana Echegoyen de Cañizares exemplifies the approach of elite Black women who established autonomous civic clubs. During the 1940s the Asociación Cultural Femenina (ACF) continued its mission of uplifting the Black population by hosting events such as a conference on social work and offering night classes for poor women.[14] In 1948 the association established a prize in Echegoyen's name for night school students. Members organized a Women's Cultural Festival as a fundraiser to cover educational expenses for illiterate women. The event featured well-known artists from Havana.[15] Elite Black women therefore continued their work of providing poor families with formal training while hosting exclusive cultural events.

By the late 1940s, the ACF was one of several civic associations for elite Black women of Havana. A younger cohort of women of African descent founded the Thesalia Club; the selective group identified Ana Echegoyen de Cañizares as one of its mentors.[16] Havana women also established the Catalina Pozo Gato organization in honor of the prominent feminist activist. Both groups followed the model of the ACF by combining social events with educational programs and celebrations of Black heroines.

Yet times had changed. Unlike the elite women who organized during the previous decade, those who established associations in the mid-1940s formed clubs that affirmed the leadership of Black women. At least six clubs appeared in Santiago de Cuba that were named after Mariana Grajales and María Cabrales, respectively the mother and wife of the Liberation Army General Antonio Maceo. The two women went to the battlefront during the Ten Years' War as nurses. Their familial descendants Felicita Maceo and Emilia Cabrales founded the Daughters of Mariana Grajales Veterans Association (1955–1959) "for the purpose of raising patriotic sentiments, maintaining respect for the heroes who led us to freedom, and giving attention to all Cuban mothers."[17] The founders emphasized how the heroines represented mothers across racial groups. They celebrated the work of Mariana Grajales in particular as an exemplar of motherhood. A separate group of Santiago women founded the National Association of Descendants and Admirers of Mariana Grajales in 1956 to "cooperate in the defense of the nation and to work toward maintaining pure social status, based on the development of the Cuban people and the love of country, with its free institutions."[18] The Centro Cultural Artístico Popular Mariana Grajales of Guantánamo was founded in 1947 with Isabel Luisa García Polanco as its president. Its purpose was to unite political and civic organizations on behalf of "the creation and sustainment of the education campus . . . as a tribute to the exalted patriot, to study music, modeling, drawing, and painting."[19]

Women of African descent established civic clubs as they envisioned the nation from a Black female standpoint. In the process, they venerated each other as national heroes. These groups affirmed the refinement of Black women like Ana Echegoyen and Catalina Pozo Gato as models to emulate. The formation of such groups suggests ongoing experiences of marginalization within multiracial groups and male-headed mixed-gender civic groups even as the 1940 Constitution granted women full legal equality.

"The Cuban Negro Woman in Her Battle for Liberty"

The civic clubs established by women of African descent in the late 1940s and the 1950s reflect how their leaders recast national narratives to center the contributions of Black women. While few archival resources exist that would provide detailed insight into their organizational activities, collaborations between Black Cuban and African American women illustrate how they theorized the nation's formation.

In late August 1940, women of the ACF welcomed a delegation from the National Council of Negro Women (NCNW), based in Washington, DC.[20] The exchange reflected the nature of African American–Cuban sociopolitical connections that evolved during the 1930s, a decade in which elites of both communities increasingly compared their achievements and struggles in the press and in public events in both countries.[21] NCNW members received an enthusiastic welcome from "official representatives from each of Cuba's unique and interesting Negro organizations" and Eusebio L. Dardet, commissioner of the Cuban government's National Tourist Division. In attendance was the NCNW member Sue Bailey Thurman, a former president of the YWCA and the wife of the scholar Howard Thurman. The organization "chose Cuba for the Latin American country in which to initiate the Summer Seminars or missions of contact and study" as part of a "significant tour of friendship to the Latin American Republic."[22] The tour extended to Haiti the following year. NCNW President Mary McLeod Bethune organized the event with the help of the Black Cuban Americans Henry Grillo, his sister Sylvia Grillo, and Sylvia's husband, José Griñán, as well as Ana Echegoyen de Cañizares. Echegoyen served as the intermediary between the two organizations.

Though the women of both groups confronted racial and gender discrimination as community leaders, the functions of their organizations reflected the distinct strategies that national political circumstances required for pursuing rights and social advancement in each country. Bethune and the NCNW maintained a commitment to sociopolitical affairs at home and abroad during the 1930s and 1940s. The NCNW, while supporting US foreign policy, drew attention to the government's hypocrisy in fighting for democracy abroad while failing to ensure rights of African Americans.[23] The ACF, on the other hand, distanced itself from politics to avoid conflict among its members.

NCNW and ACF members interacted as ambassadors of their respective nations. Adela García de Falcón, an educator and recipient of Cuba's Gold Medal of Merit for distinguished service, presented on "The Cuban Negro Woman in Her Battle for Liberty." Her presentation placed "the Cuban woman in the role of heroic fighters for liberty in the War of Independence, equal to men."[24] She emphasized that Cuban men and women, Black and white, contributed equally to the anticolonial movement. García likely referenced this point to underscore the distinct national narratives of Cuba and the United States: Cuban nationalist discourses emphasized the crossracial brotherhood that emerged during the nation's fight for independence, while US narratives of the revolutionary movement centered primarily on the contributions of elite white men. Carmen Panivino, a cofounder of the ACF who taught in Havana and vice president of the District Session of the Educational Association of Cuba, discussed "History of Education and Culture of the Negro Woman in Cuba."[25] ACF representatives discussed in great detail the experiences of women of African descent during Cuba's struggle for independence and within republican society.

Echegoyen gave the only speech that appeared in its entirety in the NCNW publication, *The Aframerican Woman's Journal*. Titled "Cuban Social Life and the Negro Woman," her speech highlighted the gendered integration of the races within national life. Echegoyen emphasized the role of the family in the historical formation of Cuba's racial structure:

> The institution of the family, which is losing its strength and importance in not a few countries of the world, maintains, among us, its

unity and even a certain hegemony. It constitutes, thereby, a certain point of departure, a firm basis, for interaction among the largest social communities. Our country lacks those deep and firm roots—roots anchored securely in a spirited unified past—, which give precise, definite outlines to other human groups. Therefore, the soul of the nation depends to a great extent upon a coincidence of location, rather than upon the spiritual bonds of a common tradition, a unique pattern of life, or a vigorous and enthusiastic love for that which is genuinely indigenous and national. This has been referred to as "*Cuba's Negro Problem.*"[26]

Echegoyen located persons of African descent in the national process of *mestizaje*, racial intermixing. This process began with the initial stages of the Spanish conquest, during which the native populations were drastically depleted and Africans were imported as an alternative labor force. Echegoyen noted that each racial group held distinct affiliations; colonialism rendered indigenous communities powerless, maintained Spaniards' emotional attachments to their homeland, and constructed Blacks as "a negative element" in society. This, she determined, undermined national unity, producing conditions that she observed "may seem a trifle obscure to many."[27]

Echegoyen prudently outlined how continuities between gendered racial ideals of the colonial era and the contemporary period shaped domestic relations.[28] She pointed to the desire of some Black women to partner with white men in the hopes that their children would have social advantages because of their lighter skin color in addition to the economic opportunities afforded to white men that would benefit their families. Yet she maintained a critical perspective regarding the ways many Black women were mistreated in such relationships.[29]

Even as she suggested that racial intermixing contributed to inequitable gender dynamics in Cuba, Echegoyen determined that "race prejudice cannot actuate with the same vigor in our country as in the United States."[30] Despite the history of racism within the colonial system and its remnants in contemporary society, the 1940 Constitution made discrimination illegal. Echegoyen was likely conscious of the Jim Crow system that undermined African Americans' civil rights. She thus highlighted the differences in legal equality for African Americans and Black Cubans, noting that well-established Cuban Blacks had more opportunities to interact with whites without conflict. She remarked that racial discrimination in Cuba occurred largely in social settings, especially in racially segregated clubs. Echegoyen concluded that racial prejudice had been intensified due to its proximity to the US southern states. At the same time, she provided an interesting perspective: rather than criticize the United States, she hoped that it might learn from Cuba.[31]

As Black Cubans drew inspiration from African Americans, the work of the NCNW figured prominently in the minds of many women, informing their strategies for building institutions to address racial inequities from a Black female perspective. In 1950, the Santiago de Cuba resident Celia Planos wrote a letter to Bethune regarding the NCNW. Bethune received two versions of the letter, a hand-written original by Planos in Spanish and an English translation typed by Evelio Grillo. Planos began the letter by affirming her familiarity with and admiration of Bethune's work toward uplifting Black women: "Distinguished Mrs. Bethune, inspired by your noble mission as a mandate of all women of culture, I appreciate your generosity and kindness and that out of this generosity and kindness that you will include me in your noble and just mission of all women of color."[32] Planos visited the council house in Washington, DC, the previous year and since "remained united" to Bethune's purpose. She sought to formally commit herself to Bethune's sociopolitical work by joining the NCNW. "I would like to enroll in this institution as one more soldier on the battle front," she wrote. Planos compared the work of the council to physical conflict, but she was careful to distinguish these efforts from the "bloody battle that ruin[s] so many cities" during times of war. She declared her devotion as "a soldier who fights and will fight for the peace, for the culture and for the solidarity and well-being of the human community."[33]

Planos maintained a patriotic perspective even as she affirmed the mission of the NCNW. She wrote that the council was a vital organization for "carrying out one of the most beautiful works that the world needs for peace, for international unity and culture, and for general progress."[34] She carefully arranged her letter in a manner that linked international goals for political stability and development with Cuba's national mission. Planos requested that Bethune confirm her membership to the organization "in memory of the two great men of Cuba, Maceo and Martí and the many others who died for the well-being of the progress of my nation." Clearly, she saw the NCNW as an institution through which to advance nationalist goals identified by Cuban independence heroes. She promised, "From the moment of my enrollment in your noble institution, the National Council of Negro Women will radiate in Cuban soil as a brilliant ray of the sun in all directions."[35] Planos's letter suggests the transformative power of connecting to this transnational vision of Black womanhood for political empowerment as Cuban citizens. "I want it to be my testimony," she declared, "that my visit to the NCNW has been a new triumph in my life and has been the beginning of a new chapter of my existence." She concluded, "All the women of progressive communities in the world should follow this flag that so well protects the world and the women."[36]

It is likely that Planos's letter reflected the perspectives of numerous Cuban women of African descent who valued the mission of the NCNW. In a note that Grillo included with his translation of Planos's letter, he wrote, "I am of the opinion that there are many women in Cuba like Miss Planos who would be greatly interested in [the NCNW]."[37] Grillo expressed his hope that during an upcoming trip to the island he might be able to help set up a branch of the council in Cuba. Future research may reveal Planos's subsequent involvement in the NCNW. However, no document that I consulted provided Bethune's response or the establishment of the council in Cuba.

Planos's 1950 letter to Bethune indicates the likelihood that many Black Cuban women adopted African American women's activist strategies to pursue their specific goals. The belief that Black women living in the United States confronted similar issues of racial and gender discrimination facilitated this understanding as well as their commitment to international democratic discourses that circulated during the period. As such, Planos articulated an understanding of racial womanhood that simultaneously reinforced and transcended national affiliations. By communicating with Bethune through a private letter rather than a public conference presentation, Planos sought to establish a personal connection in which she highlighted their ideological commonalities. This would have created an intimate dynamic that differed from ACF members' leaders' role as ambassadors who felt the need to interpret their national differences.

To "Educate for Democracy"

As elite Black women moved between civic clubs and educational organizations, many emphasized the classroom as a critical site for achieving
democratic reform. Cuba's education system remained in crisis throughout
the republican era. The number of children enrolled in schools increased
throughout the 1940s and 1950s. Literacy rates of Cubans also rose, from
71.3 percent in 1943 to 76.3 percent a decade later. Yet improvements in literacy and educational access remained uneven. In 1953, slightly more than
half of all children attended school.[38] Most students did not complete secondary school. Less than 2 percent of students obtained university degrees.
Educational disparities were particularly apparent in rural communities,
where illiteracy rates averaged 42 percent.[39] Improving Cuba's school system thus would benefit the majority of its citizens.

Consuelo Serra called attention to racial inequities in Cuba's education
system during a 1941 interview for the African American newspaper the
Atlanta Daily World. Serra discussed the discriminatory practices in private
schools that excluded Black students "of the same color as [patriots Rafael]
Serra, [Antonio] Maceo, and Guillermon [Moncada]." She established her
own school to deal with this issue. Serra noted that most private Catholic
schools only admitted students "light enough to pass for white." She complained that admitting fairer-skinned Blacks did not address issues of racial
inequality but instead "aggravated the problem."[40] As she observed, such
practices alienated Black Catholics. Further, separating lighter-skinned African descendants from other Blacks would "mean creating a race of inferior men who will have learned to do what one should never do: deny one's
ancestors." She went so far as to call for the nationalization of all private
schools to "educate for democracy" by teaching Black and white students
together.[41]

Serra's critique of discriminatory practices in Catholic schools point to
the growing reliance of middle-class Cubans on private schooling. Public schools experienced budgetary cuts during periods of economic crisis, while the number of private schools increased. Many of the private
institutions relied on US teachers and curricula. In comparison to public institutions, private schools better prepared students for professional
employment, with many serving as pipelines to universities in the United
States. Practices of racial discrimination thus aggravated inequities in em-

ployment.[42] Communist Party and Black civic activists partnered during the 1940s to propose legal restrictions on private institutions. However, the largely elite-class Congress rejected such measures. The number of private schools, as a result, continued to increase throughout the decade.[43]

The work of Black women like Consuelo Serra in the classroom challenged discriminatory practices that occurred frequently throughout the republican era. Elite whites considered access to private education the right of whites only; they used private schools to buttress their sense of racial superiority. Many affluent white families justified practices of racial exclusion by suggesting that Blacks remained incapable of fulfilling the dominant standards of moral respectability. They mocked Blacks' aspirations for socioeconomic mobility while insisting that African descendants were better suited for low-skilled, low-paying employment. Catholic schools enforced this idea of Black racial inferiority through practices of racial segregation. Yet, as Blacks' challenges to racism in the education system illustrate, most elite whites excluded persons of African descent, regardless of their economic backgrounds, from all spaces they deemed refined.[44]

By the early 1940s, a small number of Black women educators attained national prominence as pedagogues. In Santiago de Cuba, Serafina Causse became the school superintendent. Haydee Arteaga Rojas of Havana founded the children's educational program Charlas Culturales (Cultural Talks) in 1935; she directed the Estímulo Cultural entre Selectos Amigos (Cultural Stimulation among Select Friends) in the 1950s.[45] Ana Echegoyen held positions as a professor of methodology and special methodologies in the Department of Education at the University of Havana. She joined Arteaga in shaping pedagogy between the 1930s and 1950s.[46] Echegoyen began this work alongside Consuelo Serra when they published articles on parenting and juvenile education in the *Adelante* column "Pedagogías." Echegoyen later wrote pedagogy books that included *Mi libro: Libro pre-primario* (1946) and *El continente de la esperanza: Unidad de trabajo* (1947), the latter with Calixto Suárez Gómez. Echegoyen coedited the *Enciclopedia de educación científica*.[47] Women of African descent enhanced their professional profile as they bridged theory, performance, and classroom instruction.

Despite successes, Black women remained underrepresented as teachers. In 1948, the African American journalist George Schuyler estimated that 35 percent of the 10,000 students enrolled in the University of Havana were persons of color.[48] He lamented that Echegoyen was the only Black instructor. Schuyler's critique called attention to Cuban Black women's ongoing marginalization in the profession. African descendants, though 24.9 percent of the public school student population from 1925 to 1929, made up 16.3 percent of teachers. The number was even lower at private schools for the same period; Blacks comprised 7.9 percent of the student population, which fell to 6.9 percent in 1929, but 3.4 percent of teachers.[49] By 1943, the number of primary school teachers of color remained relatively unchanged at 17.6 percent, compared with 15.4 percent of professors. Only in the field of music did persons of color comprise 45.8 percent of all professors, though women of African descent remained severely underrepresented, as 188 of the 3,296 music professors employed in 1943.[50]

Teachers of African descent contributed to reforming Cuba's democracy through their work in the classroom. They provided opportunities for poor children, especially poor Black children, who experienced exclusion from elite private institutions. Their work as educators presents new temporal frameworks for understanding Black activism, as African-descended women entered the classroom to teach by the late eighteenth century. Black female teachers asserted their feminine respectability in accordance with dominant gender norms; they brought women and children of all races into educational institutions to address material inequalities.[51] This trajectory placed Echegoyen on the same continuum as turn-of-the-century Black educators such as Cristina Ayala and Úrsula Coimbra de Valverde. Finally, the commitment of Black women teachers to reforming the education system responded to discriminatory labor practices that continued into the new constitutional era.

Enacting the Constitution

In theory, the 1940 Constitution provided a legal foundation for addressing social discrimination. Architects of the new constitution established rights particular to women of all races. The constitution established equal pay for equal work among men and women as well as for married and single women. Article 68 outlined protections for working mothers. Pregnant women received guaranteed employment leave. The article stipulated that employers could no longer terminate the employment of an expectant mother within three months of her giving birth or require her to "do work that may require considerable physical effort."[52] It guaranteed twelve weeks of leave with pay and required that employers hold women's positions for them during their maternity leave. Employers were also required to provide two daily breaks for new mothers to nurse their infants. Legal reforms initiated by the 1940 Constitution, in these ways, supported women's labor in a modernizing society.

In reality, the 1940 Constitution did little to transform gender hierarchies. The scholar Graciella Cruz-Taura has demonstrated that many of the rights granted to women "needed complementary laws, or amendments to existing legislation, to be passed in order to enter into force and take effect."[53] While some laws went into effect immediately, more than 280 existing laws, codes, and decrees contradicted the new articles and undermined others. The government thus needed to pass new legislation to address these discrepancies and provide mechanisms for the state to enforce social equality. Cruz-Taura observes, "This later process, however, was destined to drag on for years. . . . Consequently, it was not until 1950 that the Cuban Congress finally passed the enabling legislation (20 December 1950) which made Cuban equal rights law a reality."[54]

Discrepancies between the constitution and existing legislation prompted a series of reform efforts among Cubans of different political factions. Campaigns led by teachers such as Consuelo Serra to improve Cuba's public education system represented one such faction. Black women who worked as domestics represented another. In 1946 Elvira Rodríguez, the African-descended leader of the Sindicato del Servicio Doméstico (Domestic Service Union), approached the Ministry of Labor to advocate for mandatory benefits for the members of her organization.[55] Throughout the 1930s and 1940s Rodríguez advocated for legal reforms to protect domestic workers.[56] The two groups reflected cross-racial collaborations among political activists in different sectors that achieved legislative victories.

Black civic club members of Camagüey devoted some of their 1947 regional convention to the matter of African-descended women's labor. Concerned by discriminatory acts against Black women "and all women in general," the delegates outlined a list of grievances of how women of African descent were marginalized in their "social life" and "work opportunities."[57] They noted Black women's lack of access to the trade and production industries, exacerbating their need to rely "solely on domestic service."[58] While the convention attendees did outline issues pertaining to working Black women, they neglected to directly address the economic consequences of racial discrimination. They discussed African-descended women's access to labor and professional training as a right they merited as citizens. Discussing labor discrimination in particular, they resolved to "fight with all our might for the approval and enactment of laws supplemented by the articles 20 and 74 of the Constitution of the Republic." The delegates underscored that, "only with the equitable distribution of work would discrimination cease to exist."[59]

Participants outlined a series of workers' rights, with the goal of protecting women of African descent from various sectors of labor. They determined that Black women should be considered in legislation that established a "maximum hours of work, rest, and retribution."[60] All women, from peasants to intellectuals, merited protection under workers' laws and were entitled to equal pay and maternity rights "to improve the conditions of her children." They thus defined women's rights primarily within the framework of motherhood. Convention delegates further demanded increased wages for women in "female preferred sectors." Finally, they proposed ways to bring about reform by uplifting sex workers through educational opportunities. The convention attendees advocated for the establishment of social institutions to "save [poor Black women] from vice and corruption" and to "make them useful to society."[61] Such institutions, they suggested, might provide classes in cutting and sewing similar to the work of organizations that focused on occupational training and protecting the legal rights of women, like the Commission of Women's Affairs.

Black activists, beyond outlining their concerns during civic club conventions, sought clear legal definitions of terms such as "discrimination" to enhance enforcement of the articles prohibiting anti-Black racism. They worked with communists to campaign for the passage of an antidiscrimination law. Many club members were also prominent communist leaders, among them the House Representatives Lazaro Peña (also an executive leader of the Confederación de Trabajadores Cubanos), Salvador García Agüero, Blas Roca, and Jesús Menéndez Larrondo. As early as 1941, Roca introduced the Education and Sanctions against Racial Discrimination bill that would regulate the constitutional provision that outlawed racial discrimination. The bill did not pass. In 1944, Salvador García Agüero again introduced the bill, this time in the Senate. Despite numerous attempts to hold businesses responsible for not hiring African descendants and to create government-sponsored antiracism campaigns, activists struggled to get a bill passed. As communist leaders sought to create a Democratic National Front to regain their political grounding during the early 1950s, they proposed an antidiscrimination bill before Congress.[62] In November 1951 the bill finally passed. President Carlos Prío Socarrás (1948–1952) issued a decree that helped enforce Article 74 of the Constitution on equal access to work.

The decree had limitations. For one, it did not ensure opportunities for Blacks to be promoted or hired in particular but instead called for color-blind hiring processes. The article stated, "Violators of this decree will be considered responsible for encouraging hatred between races and social classes, a warning that will be issued, officially, to the industry or business that breaches or circumvents the cited constitutional principal."[63] Editors of *Prensa Libre* reminded readers that those found guilty of racial discrimination had violated more than legal codes; they also violated the very text that served as a foundation for Cuban citizenship.

Despite such reforms, discriminatory practices continued to limit Black women's mobility in the workforce. During the winter of 1951, thirteen Black and mulatto women were hired to work at El Encanto, Fin de Siglo, and La Filosofía, upscale department stores in Havana's prominent shopping district. This marked a significant change in the stores' hiring practices as the first time that women of color had been hired to work as sales clerks. The women were fired shortly after the end of the holiday season. As explained in *La Prensa*, "The young Black women who began to work during the past month of December in the great commercial stores of the capital were thrown into the streets!"[64] The writer reported that each woman hired had been dismissed without reason and implored President Prío to take action. From the writer's perspective, the government's response to the sudden firing of the thirteen sales clerks was an opportunity to test the efficiency of Cuba's antidiscrimination policies. More specifically, Prío's treatment of the situation would demonstrate his commitment or lack of commitment to the cause of racial equality. Possibly wary that Prío had made bold statements without following through on his promises, the writer challenged the president to "make his demagogic propaganda" useful by enforcing the antidiscrimination decree.[65]

Black civic club activists also entered the discussion in support of the young women who had lost their positions. Executive board members of the Federación Nacional de Sociedades Cubanas protested the dismissal of the sales clerks. They contended that the workers' civil rights had been violated, and they argued that the antidiscrimination decree was "an ineffective measure that does not resolve the discrimination problem."[66] This provocative allegation implied that the government had not adequately addressed racial discrimination in the workplace. The board members stressed the emotional impact that the firing might have had on other young women of color: "Hundreds of other girls, inspired by that group [of women hired], have watched the illusion of finding employment as they were promised collapse."[67] Appalled, the board asserted, "Everything has been a political move, demagogic."[68] The board thus accused the government of having little interest in protecting the rights of Cubans of African descent. They continued, writing:

> We have also tirelessly defended Cuba's Black population, fighting discrimination in all spheres of national life. We advocate against it as a valid compliance with the Constitution and support the approval of the Education Act and Anti-Racial Discrimination bill recently passed by the House and Senate. We denounce before the people of Cuba this mockery and demand the right for these girls to work. The ranks of exclusionary unions have to be open for Black men and women, as a guarantee of the fulfillment of equality in the workplace.[69]

They used the experiences of the young women to speak to the larger issues affecting all African descendants of discrimination within the workplace. The board members noted that the struggle to protect Black worker's rights constituted part of an ongoing movement tied to unions and educational institutions. Moreover, they called for more effective measures to make labor and labor unions more inclusive spaces. By demanding that the government take action on behalf of men and women of African descent, the board brought race to the forefront of democratic reform discourses.

Three years later, *Orientación Social*, a monthly magazine published by Santiago de Cuba's Black club members, reported another prejudicial incident. Two "dark-skinned" young women approached the Ten Cent store in Havana seeking employment as clerks. According to the article, they "tested very well" and demonstrated their aptitude for the positions. When they were refused employment, representatives of two Havana societies approached the Labor Ministry to request assistance. The labor minister promised to contact the director of the establishment, and he later reported that he had no reason to suspect that an act of discrimination had taken place. In response, *Orientación Social* editors posed the following questions: "What happened afterward? Did they contact the young women? Has anyone been hired?"[70] While they applauded the labor minister for attempting to investigate the store's hiring practice, they questioned his methods of inquiry. It was not enough for officials to merely accept the explanation that the women had failed the store's "capability tests." They wanted a reformed system through which more women of color could qualify for employment. They asserted, "These ladies, like the others, have the right to work. Segregation and discrimination are incompatible with democracy. Words are not enough. We need facts."[71] Because laws were rendered meaningless if those who suffered from prejudice were unable to provide proof of discrimination, the club members' actions underscored the importance of implementing effective laws that could be enforced to maintain the integrity of Cuba's political system.

One month after the Havana civic club leaders approached the Labor Ministry, *Orientación Social* reported that no progress had been made. They perhaps desperately appealed to nationalist narratives to articulate their concerns. Editors protested, "This is not just! We want public places for all, workplaces without exclusions, and equal education for all. This is what Martí, Maceo, [Máximo] Gómez and his followers wanted, noted in Articles 20, 73 and 74 of the 1940 Constitution."[72] Editors also referenced the UN Declaration of Human Rights as they invoked the rhetoric of equality.[73] The writers moved beyond addressing Black women's employment through the rhetoric of citizenship by articulating labor discrimination as a global human rights issue.

The nuanced approach of *Orientación Social* editors reflected a key trend of the early 1950s. While persons of African descent viewed access to the workplace as a legal right for all citizens, other individuals and even some institutions attempted to approach the matter through the global discourse of human rights as recently promoted by the United Nations. Ana Echegoyen Cañizares, following her tenure as a director of the UN School Forum, gave a talk on the United Nations and human rights for the club Jóvenes del Vals, facilitating such conversations.[74] The inability of Black women to achieve social equality took on global significance as Cuba's political system remained in crisis.

Most elite Black women employed moderate political approaches to achieving reform after the ratification of the 1940 Constitution. Refashioning racial regeneration philosophies to fit modern expectations of Cuban women's public engagement, they established organizations to provide Black women and children with opportunities for socioeconomic mobility. African-descended women's entrance into organizations beyond the Black public sphere corresponded with the democratization of the national political sphere that began during the 1920s. Two decades later, women such as Ana Echegoyen de Cañizares expanded their sociopolitical networks as they embraced global discourses of democracy. As democratic discussions centered on racism, white and African-descended men led the fight for racial reforms. Men's leadership as political officials, press editors, and civic club members sustained Black women's marginalization even as women gained full citizenship rights. Gender dynamics reflected struggles for all Cuban women to build political power in the electoral system.

The moderate approach employed by elite Black women enabled them access to a broader range of civic institutions as they sought democratic reforms. Figures like Echegoyen joined established organizations as a strategy to address the distinct issues confronted by women, African descendants, and teachers. Echegoyen recognized the inadequacy of focusing on a single social group, especially as a Black woman educator, and thus opted to confront the multiple, overlapping forms of discrimination experienced by women of African descent and Cubans in general. Her approach allowed her to collaborate with elite male leaders who held power in shaping national and international policy. In doing so, she circumvented a lack of formal political power by bringing issues affecting women and children within her social networks to the forefront of public discussion.

Ultimately, the difficulty men encountered as they pursued an antidiscrimination clause to supplement Article 20 of the 1940 Constitution demonstrates the limitations of cross-racial alliances of Black civic leaders and political parties. Black civic activists' campaign to have an antidiscrimination clause added to the constitution intersected with the work of the Communist Party. Both political communities rarely elected women to high-ranking positions, although communist women actively participated in electoral politics. Elite Black women responded to their marginalization in formal politics by engaging in their professional careers and public affairs, while Black women of the Communist Party organized across class backgrounds as they targeted economic inequities. African-descended women who entered into the communist movement hailed from a range of socioeconomic backgrounds; their activism helped propel the Communist Party to national political power by the 1940s.

7

"A Heroic and Revolutionary Undertaking"

African-Descended Women of the Communist Movement

In 1939, the year the Third National Women's Congress brought together more than two thousand women in support of democratic reform, the Unión Revolucionaria Comunista (URC), elected Esperanza Sánchez Mastrapa as a delegate to the Constitutional Assembly. Later, she became the first Black woman elected to Congress. Her ascendance to the national political stage paralleled the peak of communist influence in the labor movement and broader electoral system. The Communist Party was established in 1925 and reorganized in 1937 as the URC. The URC gained recognition as the party that ardently defended the interests of women, workers, and persons of African descent. The party's success stemmed from its reciprocal relationship with President Fulgencio Batista. Party leaders mobilized citizens across the island in support of the president's administration. In exchange, Batista supported labor strikes for higher wages.[1] The URC, as a result, empowered African-descended women like Sánchez as political activists who further transformed the nature of the government on behalf of the working classes.

Radical Black women like Sánchez employed communism as a strategy for democratic reform between 1940 and the 1959 Revolution. Scholars have examined how communists and Black civic activists formed alliances to demand labor rights and antiracist legislation.[2] Historians have analyzed how the Cuban Communist Party mobilized working-class women on behalf of a progressive platform for labor rights.[3] Here I emphasize how Black women communists broadened their intersectional analysis of racial, gender, and class oppression, articulated during the 1930s, to unify a broad contingent of laboring women. Communist activists of all races critiqued capitalist exploitation on the island and globally; men and women promoted workers' rights including the right to strike as well as equality for women and Blacks, government regulation of major industries (sugar, tobacco, railroads), and the creation of social welfare programs. Black women communists, as they embraced these perspectives, aligned themselves politically with the laboring classes—whether they were professionals, agrarian or factory workers, or domestic workers—and called for state intervention on their behalf. Many took on elected positions within the Communist Party during the early 1940s, and they elevated campaigns for antidiscrimination legislation while achieving improved working conditions. With the rise of anticommunism by the late 1940s, African-descended women communists helped refashion the party's image to present its women supporters as guardians of democracy, at home and globally. As such, they maintained a political bloc that actively organized women through the 1950s.

Sánchez's political career elucidates the evolving political strategies of elite Black women since abolition in 1886. In the late nineteenth century, most elite women of African descent challenged racial and gender discrimination through the Black public sphere. They penned articles, submitted letters, and supported civic clubs as part of a collective effort to "regenerate" the race. This approach continued into the 1920s, when a younger generation of elite Black women activists began to collaborate with white feminists and working-class activists on behalf of legal reform. Sánchez also tapped into a long-standing tradition of labor activism forged by poor women of African descent, especially those working in the tobacco industry. The historian Joan Casanovas notes that Black women tobacco stemmers protested low wages and sexual abuses in the workplace in the late colonial period.[4] The scholars Pedro Padrón and Jean Stubbs in their respective studies demonstrate that tobacco stemmers continued to lead strikes and boycotts throughout the republican era, shaping the business strategies of US corporations as well as Cuban labor policies in the 1910s and 1920s.[5]

Inocencia Váldes used her elected positions in tobacco guilds to mobilize women across racial lines. Black women's activism in the tobacco sector contributed to arguments made in 1915 by the Santiago resident Maria P. Garbey, who asserted that globally, women played an integral role in the industrialization of the modern workforce.[6] By the 1920s, this mobilized constituency helped shift political power away from that of the oligarchic classes to the concerns of the popular classes.[7] Few radical Black women activists publicly addressed how race shaped laboring women's experiences prior to the 1930s. African-descended women's participation in popular movements during the Revolution of 1933 and the evolving feminist movement helped create a cross-racial alliance that elevated Sánchez and others to national prominence.

Black women of the Communist Party continued the collaborative strategies of the late 1930s following the ratification of the 1940 Constitution. Women of African descent shaped the Communist Party agenda and helped ensure its most noteworthy successes. They served as writers, union members, newspaper vendors, and elected officials. Individuals including Consuelo Silveira and Teresa García joined Sánchez in criticizing US imperial control of the nation's economy. They called for government transparency and the establishment of programs that benefited poor mothers and their children. Those who worked in the tobacco industry led successful strikes for higher wages. As elected leaders, communist women of African descent helped incorporate other women into the political realm as members of the popular classes.

African-descended women's involvement in the communist movement reflects patriarchal norms that continued to limit women's political activism in Cuban politics more broadly. By speaking to the concerns of women in general, women of all races enacted a model of activism that paralleled that of men. Those who supported the URC did so largely through women's newspaper columns and organizations. Despite Sánchez's visibility as a party official and member of Congress, most leaders who emerged at the forefront of the URC and major labor unions were men. Black women who supported the communist movement exercised greater influence in formal politics than those who employed moderate strategies. Yet women from the various factions remained marginalized in the political system due to their gender.

The Revolutionary Struggles of Esperanza Sánchez Mastrapa

Born in the town of Gíbara in eastern Cuba, Sánchez Mastrapa completed high school in Santiago de Cuba and moved to Havana to study pharmacy. It was during her tenure at the University of Havana that she established what she called her "firm Marxist convictions." Sánchez said she met the communist leader Julio Antonio Mella and witnessed his work on behalf of "the rights of the people and for national independence."[8] Perhaps she connected his critiques of capitalism to the concerns of poor women from her family or hometown. Her observation of working-class populations in Havana and their activism during the 1933 Revolution may have led her to sympathize with labor activists. She eventually returned to Gíbara to pursue her profession and continue her revolutionary struggles throughout Oriente Province.

Like moderate Black women activists such as Ana Echegoyen de Cañizares, Sánchez traversed political boundaries in her organizational activities. Both women participated in the Third National Women's Congress, and Sánchez was a voting member of its executive committee. Yet unlike Echegoyen, Sánchez bridged radical perspectives on women's labor and legal reform with the sociopolitical agenda of Black civic organizations. She joined the URC, the communist-organized Unión Radical de Mujeres (Radical Women's Union), and the Federación Provincial de Sociedades Negras de Oriente. The Unión Radical de Mujeres, later renamed the Unión de Mujeres Laboristas, promoted gender equality and worker's rights in addition to challenging US imperialism.[9] Moving between the communist, women's, and Black civic activist movements brought her into contact with diverse social constituencies; her strategic movement resembled the political activities of Black communist women like the Camagüeyan educator Felicita Ortiz. Both women's work in the URC facilitated their engagement with the antiracist movement for economic reform.

Sánchez's rise to prominence came at a moment when the Communist Party reached its peak as an influential political force. Communist leaders reluctantly collaborated with then military general Fulgencio Batista, who was running for president, to advocate for labor reform. They began publishing the daily newspaper *Noticias de Hoy*, and as it circulated it expanded the URC membership and advertised Batista's proposed populist reforms such as health programs and new tax structures. URC leaders, recognizing that they represented only 8 percent of the voting power, fostered alliances with other political groups during the 1940 Constitutional Assembly to enhance their influence. They joined the government bloc of delegates who also supported the populist vision of Batista as a presidential candidate; the coalition included representatives of the Partido Liberal, Unión Nacionalista, Conjunto Nacional Democrático, and Partido Revolucionario. After Batista's presidential election in 1940, he allowed the URC to reorganize the Central de Trabajadores de Cuba (CTC, Federation of Cuban Workers), the umbrella organization for most labor unions. This established a reciprocal relationship between Batista and the communists; in exchange for mobilizing workers in support of his presidency, communists could ensure that "most of the strikes that developed in early 1940s were settled in favor of workers."[10] Labor unions quickly realized that their affiliation with the CTC granted them access to government power. By 1940, the organization included an estimated 1,500 delegates who represented 576 unions throughout the island and boasted a membership of 350,000 individuals.[11]

That the URC addressed both racial discrimination and poverty made the party especially appealing to persons of African descent. US government officials observed large numbers of Black supporters at communist rallies throughout the island. The *mulato* CTC leader and secretary general Lázaro Peña issued a message of racial unity that at the same time called attention to the exclusion of African-descended workers from opportunities for advancement.[12] The Black labor activist Jesús Menéndez argued for merging the unions of cane cutters and technicians to bridge the predominantly segregated organizations of the sugar industry. Such ideological stances, coupled with successes in obtaining higher wages, brought Black women into the fold.[13]

That the leadership of the URC reflected its multiracial membership set the organization apart from other political parties. African descendants represented nearly a third of delegates sent to the URC's national assemblies.[14] The proportion of Black URC members elected to the House of Representatives was even higher. In 1944, persons of African descent comprised 33 percent of Cuba's senators and 50 percent of House representatives. The high representation of Blacks as party candidates could be found at all levels of the organization. *Noticias de Hoy* featured photographs of African-descended men and women who ran for national, municipal, and neighborhood positions. Men made up the majority of Black leaders at the national level; women successfully ran for positions at the municipal and neighborhood levels. The number of women elected to formal positions may have been lower due to opportunities to support the organization through women's branches of the party. In this sense, the URC lagged in obtaining political equality for women but succeeded in its commitment to racial equality in the electoral arena.

The historian Alejandro de la Fuente explains that the URC "was the only party that had taken the recommendations of the National Federation of Societies of the Colored Race into the [constitutional] convention." This reinforced the image of the Communists as the most unwavering advocates for Black Cubans' rights.[15] As the URC's delegate to the upcoming Constitutional Assembly, Sánchez mobilized the popular classes on behalf of legal reform, notably as a speaker at the Provincial Assembly of Oriente Women in March 1940. The assembly brought together individuals from the region to demonstrate that "women play a vital part in successfully carrying out the nation's objectives through progressive and democratic means."[16] She declared in her published summary of the event that "revolutionary women, linked to the heroic working class" stood with the URC "at the forefront" of the movement for national reform. Sánchez contended that "huge, mass mobilizations" would illustrate the party's commitment to progressive men and women. The Provincial Assembly rallied a large, visible electorate of women who demanded "clear and comprehensive constitutional requirements" that recognized the "legitimate human rights of all those exploited and discriminated against." Sánchez determined that, to ensure this development, the women of the Provincial Assembly should affirm the "core liberal platform" of the URC, hoping for "a triumph" in the upcoming presidential election of Fulgencio Batista.[17]

The Provincial Assembly of Oriente Women used the framework of working-class issues to unify women across racial, class, professional, and geographic differences. Sánchez strategically drew from these subjective positions to articulate a cohesive constituency. She issued the following statement regarding the women of eastern Cuba:

> White and Black *compañeras*, factory workers, and those from shops and domestic service; peasants from distant corners, tobacco fields, and sugar plantations; teachers and professionals aware of their high responsibility to their homeland have definitively united to achieve true liberation and our emancipation. They created such a unique Assembly, a heroic and revolutionary undertaking.[18]

Though women of the assembly came from varying social backgrounds, the participants shared a patriotic duty to emancipate the nation from political corruption and foreign control. Sánchez noted that as the assembly delegates came together, they called for equal employment opportunities for both men and women, articulating their agenda to "make reality the [URC] slogan of Democracy, Social Justice, Defense of the National Economy" and "to keep Cuba out of the Imperialist War."[19] Cuba entered World War II on the side of the Allies in December 1941. Sánchez emphasized that the war, which communist leaders characterized as imperialist, presented a serious threat to national progress. Her assertion that the war grew out of "the markets and spheres of capitalist influence" mirrored views of anti-war activists in the early 1940s. Rather than support a particular side, she charged the national leaders of both Ally and Axis nations with pursuing selfish aims that "strangle the people," and she emphasized that the women of the Provincial Assembly desired to prevent "our fathers and brothers from marching on European ground for the greater enrichment of Wall Street and the international financial capital."[20]

Sánchez's summary reflects the shift in nationalist political discourses that responded to growing concerns over fascism, with many activists drawing parallels between fascism and racism on the island. She formulated an anti-imperialist critique that called attention to how Cuba's support of Ally nations undermined its domestic economy. In doing so, she implied that the war benefited powerful nations that exploited Cuban workers, not everyday citizens. She did not simply emphasize the role of Cuban women, but interpolated women as members of a politicized constituency obligated to fight for reform as members of the working classes. Thus she incorporated the language of revolutionary womanhood that entitled women to political participation as *workers*. Such discourses broke with the language of women as caretakers with moral superiority, and they reflected broader trends throughout the international communist women's movement.

Sánchez devoted substantial energy to the growth of the URC, which was again reorganized in 1944 as the Partido Socialista Popular (PSP, Popular Socialist Party). While she rarely discussed issues of racial inequality as a public figure, a *Noticias de Hoy* interview shows that Sánchez valued the PSP as a group that enacted social equality.[21] She proudly stated that no racial or sexual discrimination existed within the organization. Noting that women historically lacked representation at all levels of government, she declared that the PSP fought for the "absolute equality of women and men, the constant battle to achieve, in practice, the realization of this right and equality." Sánchez affirmed the PSP as an organization that fought for the "abolition of racial discrimination." Further, she critiqued political factions that supported the exploitation of the popular classes, asserting that the

PSP was "the only party that loyally defends [popular class] economic and social interests."[22] Sánchez contrasted the socially egalitarian PSP with the discriminatory practices embedded in Cuba's broader political system.

During Sánchez's term in the House of Representatives (1944–1950), her stated goal was to change the political culture; she pursued it by advocating for complementary laws to enforce civil rights and antidiscrimination guarantees, economic justice through new "lease and partnership contracts," and social security programs.[23] She proposed bills to establish schools as well as arts and domestic science programs in municipalities across the island. She recommended the creation of rural, technical, and vocational schools "to elevate the education of women and to achieve the improvement of the educational system in the country."[24] Sánchez also called for special protections for mothers that included maternity and health care benefits, and she asserted that breaks for breastfeeding mothers be considered work during their eight-hour shifts. She consistently advocated to have the civil code edited to protect married women. Including rural women in her work, Sánchez proposed medical assistance for workers in the countryside and a permanent organization to serve their interests.[25] Her proposed reforms aimed to protect women across labor and geographic backgrounds.

Sánchez pushed for government reforms that benefited women who worked in various sectors of the economy. Her attention to educational opportunities echoed the reformist calls put forth by tobacco stemmer Inocencia Valdés at the 1925 Second National Women's Congress. Sánchez's calls for social welfare programs helped institutionalize the democratic visions outlined during the 1939 Third National Women's Congress. She held the state accountable for protecting laboring women in the workplace and at home. Whether people found Sánchez's characterizations inspiring or mere political rhetoric, her populist views were certainly timely; the PSP's broad commitment to workers' issues drew thousands of women into the party in support of economic and political reforms.

"Our *Compañeras* of the Party"

Not all women of African descent who supported the URC embraced communist doctrine. Their interviews in *Noticias de Hoy* emphasized their personal struggles to improve their living conditions. Black women's affiliation with the party, mainly through reading its publications and voting for its candidates, demonstrates their willingness to align themselves with the party in order to overcome racial, gender, and class discrimination in the labor force. In the 1940s, women of African descent were employed in the largest sectors of the Cuban economy that paid some of the lowest wages: agriculture and manufacturing. In fact, 65 percent of all Cubans in the labor force were employed in these industries and thus formed a large working class. The income differentials by race were lower among this group, suggesting that class played a significantly greater role than race in determining Black women's circumstances.[26]

Individuals of African descent in general and Black women in particular remained underrepresented in the professions. According to the 1943 census, 68 of 5,427 lawyers in Cuba were women of color. Women of African descent comprised 39 of 1,322 dentists; 69 of 1,848 nurses were Black women, compared to 1,178 white women nurses. In commerce, they held 817 of the 146,572 positions available; white women accounted for 7,211 of commerce workers. Only in domestic and personal service were Black women overrepresented. There were more Black women domestics (19,246 of 73,963) than white men, Black men, or white women as groups in the same labor category.[27]

Economic grievances led Black women into the communist movement, and many ran for elected offices at municipal and neighborhood levels as PSP candidates. They aimed to sway campaign outcomes as they declared their support for other candidates. They raised funds to support the development of unions. They varied from individuals like Concepción Núñez, who sold copies of the socialist magazine *Mella* in her neighborhood of San Antonio de los Baños, and Aurora Santiago, who sold two hundred copies a day of *Noticias de Hoy* in Placetas to bring money into the home, to elected officials like Francisca Romay, who ran for a position as councilwoman (*consejal*) on the PSP ticket in Havana.[28] In all, Black women's efforts demonstrate a grassroots movement to shape the philosophies and outcomes that sustained the PSP's influence.

Their routes into the movement varied. Consuelo Silveira entered formal politics through the Communist Party of Havana. Born into a poor family, she overcame financial constraints to become a schoolteacher and then earn a doctorate in pedagogy. Silveira joined the student movement led by Julio Antonio Mella in the Sindicato de Trabajadores de la Enseñanza (Union of Educational Workers) to improve conditions in Cuban schools.

The union's leaders were radical activists such as the Black educator Rosa Pastora Leclerc; they promoted an anticlassist movement to unionize all employees at schools for teachers. Union members launched strikes to demand that the government expand education spending to 25 percent of the national budget. Silveira emerged alongside Pastora Leclerc and others as part of a URC-sponsored contingent within the union.[29] Silveira's activism eventually expanded from a focus on children and class equality to "the emancipation of women." Silveira participated in the 1939 Third National Women's Congress as an organizing member and joined the General Committee of the Communist Party.[30]

Silveira advocated for the existence of a politically influential URC that served "all people in the struggle" under a "constitution that meets the popular desires."[31] For her, addressing the needs of the popular classes required that the party incorporate all laboring women into its movement for democratic reform. She proclaimed,

> Our *compañeras* of the party must be the most effective builders of this work front. They *must* go to the countryside and the city, reaching the factories and workshops, invade the streets and markets; but above all things, they *must* enter homes and talk with the mass of women who know the intricacies of low wages and unemployment, the rising cost of bread, meat, and medicines; because they have suffered in their own flesh from barbarous evictions, endured abandonment, sickness, and malnourishment; in a word, pain and misery in all its nakedness.[32]

Silveira bridged the public and domestic spheres as sites of political mobilization. She characterized women of all backgrounds, qualified by their experiences with economic exploitation, as figures of authority.

Silveira's attention to the struggles of working families responded to shifting economic dynamics of the period. Cuba's economy experienced a brief boom as sugar prices rose during World War II. President Fulgencio Batista took advantage of this moment of prosperity to expand public works programs and government bureaucracy. However, not all sectors of the economy benefited; some suffered greatly. Because of wartime restrictions in overseas trade and shipping, Cuban exports to Europe declined and shortages frequently took place. Agricultural producers and cigar factory owners lost their European markets. Many owners closed their factories' doors. As economic segments waned, the costs of products from food to household goods skyrocketed. Some taxes were raised and new ones were implemented. In light of these events, householders, particularly those of the laboring poor, struggled to find employment and feed their families.[33]

The employment crisis of the early 1940s led communist activists like Silveira to call for national economic development on behalf of working women and their families. In December 1942 she and other prominent activists from across the island gathered at the Amas de Casa Conference (Housewives Conference) to address how speculation and profiteering had affected the lives of the laboring classes since the war began. The Asociación Pro-Enseñanza Popular de la Mujer (Association for Women's Popular Education) sponsored the event as part of its mission to defend the "genuine interests of the popular classes, particularly those concerning women."[34] The conference began at nine o'clock on a Sunday morning at the prominent Campoamor Theater in Havana. Eight hundred delegates, among them the Havana tobacco worker Teresa García and the Santa Clara lawyer Ofelia Domínguez Navarro, began the event by singing the national anthem. The conference was aired over the national radio stations Radioemisoras Coco and CMX Casa Lavía.

In her keynote address Silveira appealed to working women.[35] She said when the national economy shifted after Cuba entered World War II in December 1941, "speculators and jobbers, who accumulate their plunder by inflating prices, throw their load on the backs of the people, place the blame [for high prices] on the war, and assert that Cuban product costs have been raised in the same way as foreigner products."[36] Silveira determined that citizens could not continue to live "without taking measures to ensure a better life" and needed to fight to protect the masses from capitalist exploitation. She contended that the government should work to ensure the domestic supply of food and other consumer goods and replace imported products through "an industrial plan that meets the needs of the country." The government, she declared, should diversify agriculture by cultivating "root vegetables, beans, and other essential items of consumption." The state should defend "to the maximum" workers' wages and prevent employers from slashing or freezing wages. Doing such, the government would "ensure the standard of living in accordance with the obligations and sacrifices that war imposes."[37] Silveira asserted that a basic quality of life, including the availability of food and the protection of wages, was a fundamental right that the government had to ensure.

Silveira incorporated an antiwar critique similar to that of Sánchez two years earlier, that political corruption threatened Cuba's economy. She declared to her fellow assembly participants,

> We work, therefore, relentlessly to ensure our national defense, going to the richness of our own soil to find the elements that allow us to ensure domestic supplies from its own resources, we work tirelessly for the diversification of agricultural products; [we] fight so that capital accumulation may be put at the service of the nation and the big capitalists contribute not just with a little effort while working people are giving everything in the effort to win the war.[38]

Silveira proposed that the government create facilities for developing the domestic economy through social programs. Her speech was part of an ongoing campaign to protest Cuba's participation in World War II; she had given a similar address in October 1942 at the Asociación Pro-Enseñanza Popular de la Mujer event held in honor of Inocencia Valdés.[39] The following year, the Amas de Casa organization announced an official campaign against "profiteering and speculation."[40] Silveira's speeches and activism helped fuel a larger antiwar campaign among women activists that reinforced communist discourses.

As specific concerns and local exigencies compelled marginalized Cubans to pursue economic reform through state institutions, Black women challenged political corruption at varying levels of government. Havana's tobacco stemmers union leader Teresa García rose to national prominence as propaganda secretary of the CTC's executive committee. In fall 1941, García challenged corruption in the government's Central Board of Health that, following accusations of embezzlement, sparked a national scandal and motivated many workers of Havana Province to question the state's commitment to working people. García told *Noticias de Hoy* reporters that the Central Board of Health had arbitrarily been withholding workers' maternity insurance checks; the checks were to come from an insurance fund created to cover health care expenses of working mothers and male workers' wives.[41] She said that the Central Board withheld the checks to cover the large expenses incurred in the construction of a provincial maternity clinic. García explained she initially lauded the government's decision to construct a clinic that would make medical care more accessible to expecting mothers throughout the region. However, she soon became concerned with the process of its construction. She approached the organization's office to protest some practices. García asserted that the Central Board of Health had adopted an aggressive attitude "against the interests of the workers."[42]

García underscored how the Central Board of Health had ignored the rights of laborers. She stressed that if the agency had the intention of building a facility for workers and their families, it should have taken into account the needs of the popular classes in developing a spending budget. Instead, the Central Board of Health had created a "useless bureaucracy," including a director, assistant director, and clinic administrator who drained workers' funds to cover their salaries. García complained, "It is a shame that workers' money be wasted so outrageously." She pronounced that the "national proletariat" energetically and strongly opposed the "immorality" and "pretension" of removing the funds set aside for workers.[43]

At the heart of her complaint was the lack of transparency and popular representation within state institutions. For García, working women and their families, who would eventually patronize the maternity clinic, should have had a voice in the construction of the health care system. Workers' input was especially important to García since labor organizations initially identified the need for such a facility. Therefore, she requested that the budget of the provincial maternity clinic be made public.[44] While it is unclear if her campaign against the Central Board of Health succeeded, the protest furthered García's activism on behalf of the laboring class.

Two years later, she organized a regionwide campaign to increase pay for tobacco workers. García, then general secretary of the tobacco workers union executive committee, spoke before a special assembly held by the union. One attendee later compared her address to those given by such famous fighters as the prominent labor leaders Julia Rodríguez, Ramona Vargas, Inocencia Valdés, and Evelia Somonte.[45] In her address García criticized recent pay reductions that affected more than fifteen thousand tobacco workers throughout the country. The pay cuts and increased living expenses coincided with higher demand for tobacco, which led to higher tobacco prices; the convergence of conditions made an organized protest for higher wages a logical decision. Following her speech, the seven hundred union members in attendance deliberated and agreed to fight for a 50 percent raise. At the conclusion of the special assembly, the union delegates approved to create a "resistance fund" to ensure the "proper oversight of laws" affecting working conditions and workers' wages.[46] The women's campaign for wage increases proved relatively successful. Shortly after the assembly, García and CTC head Lázaro Peña met with Labor Minister Suárez Rivas and negotiated a 25 percent increase for all tobacco stemmers.[47]

While challenging government corruption was not always effective, campaigns organized by women like García gained a measure of popularity among communist supporters, many of them laboring Black women. This can be explained in part by changing political and economic factors. Cuba recovered from the economic stagnation of the 1930s and then experienced an economic boom toward the end of World War II. Yet poor government management meant that funds were not invested into building solid infrastructure to support future growth. In addition, as labor union leaders leveraged their affiliation with the PSP, they garnered national attention for local issues affecting workers across the island. In this sense, women of African descent helped achieve major party victories of the 1940s that reinforced its position as the authentic representative of the popular classes.[48]

Demands for Cuban sugar boomed when cane and beet production dropped in Asia and Europe. The recovery of this sector was offset by declining demand for cigars and produce as well as disrupted access to raw materials, merchandise, steel, and iron.[49] Disruptions in ship transportation shifted control of moving products from the docks to the railroads. Tourism faltered. Economic concerns exacerbated the racialized critiques of many middle- and upper-class whites, a demographic that resented the Communist Party's political dominance and Batista's position as an official with African ancestry.[50]

"The Hopes of the Great Masses of Women"

The end of Batista's presidency in 1944 and World War II marked a shift in Cuba's political culture. The ascendance of the Partido Auténtico to power, led by President Ramón Grau San Martín, and the rise of the Cold War diminished the influence that communists held in national politics. Batista's Prime Minister Carlos Saladrigas lost to Grau in the 1944 elections, with Grau nostalgically reflecting on his hundred-day presidency during the provisional government period (1933–1934) to assert that he was the most qualified candidate. Grau's previous political successes included ending the Platt Amendment and granting women suffrage. He also empowered Cubans in the labor force through legislation to remove foreign workers. Cubans hoped that with the reinstatement of Grau the nation would enter another age of prosperity. However, Grau would fail to meet Cubans' expectations. Government corruption came to characterize the administrations of Grau as well as Batista. Citizens became cynical toward the government as gangsterism took over political operations, creating an era defined by violence and government embezzlement.[51]

The 1944 elections threw the PSP into a state of crisis. Partido Auténtico leaders stripped the PSP of its control over the CTC. Communist leaders found themselves alienated from the other major parties and unable to build coalitions that had been central to achieving reform on behalf of their supporters. The Grau administration violently targeted radical activists, and the labor leaders Jesús Menéndez and Aracelio Iglesias Díaz of the Maritime Workers Union were assassinated. Auténtico leaders ordered the closing of the PSP radio station and targeted the party newspaper for harassment.

On the eve of the 1948 elections, the Black PSP activist María Argüelles issued a plea in the newspaper *Noticias de Hoy* to "the great feminine masses" to reclaim control of the island's political system.[52] Argüelles published her plea as part of her candidate's statement to represent the PSP of Havana. She called on all women: "You, housewife, worker, *campesina*, employee, professional, student, white or Black, young or old, you have the sacred duty of selecting the best. In 1944, you wasted your vote by selecting the worst deception committed [by a candidate] through demagogic promises." Argüelles implored them to vote for a different outcome. She asserted, "If you vote for the puppet candidate from the third floor [of the presidential palace], you will vote for the *bolsa negra* [black market], the alienage of the foreigner, the divisiveness of the gunmen, and assassinations of workers as worthy as Montoro, Fernández Roic, Lezcano, Cabrera, and the great Jesús Menéndez, and other men of the people and students who have fallen in the last three years." Voting for the "conventional opposition" also meant Cubans would subject the country to the "North American chancellery, to Yankee imperialism and the resurgence of an opprobrious past." Argüelles encouraged them to vindicate the PSP by voting for the presidential and vice-presidential candidates, Juan Marinello and Lazaro Peña, as well as the congressional candidates Salvador Agüero, Blas Roca, and Carlos Rafael Rodríguez.[53]

Noticias de Hoy echoed Argüelles's call for women to vote for PSP candidates in order to end government corruption. A June 1948 article described that discontentment among Cuban women spread throughout everyday places. The article's author stated, "Popular disenchantment is apparent wherever the public convenes."[54] The writer identified rumblings against the "traitorous government" throughout the public sphere, in popular cinemas, buses, and trams. They explained that, through such acts, women collectivized their complaints about government failures. The author surmised, "The commentaries clearly speak of how the result of these elections have been adverse to the hopes of the great masses of women."[55] Women were disappointed with the 1944 election of the "myth," Grau, whom they hoped would "end the scandal of the *bolsa negra*."[56] Instead, Grau exacerbated women's concerns as the government fell into a series of scandals. The author asserted that the great majority of women voted against the Partido Auténtico candidate Carlos Prío Socarrás, and they accused his party of fraud not only in the electoral area but also the public treasury and public posts handed out to ensure the "amount of votes necessary to circumvent the will of the people."[57]

Despite PSP efforts to elect Juan Marinello as Cuba's president, Prío was elected president in 1948. Subsequently, leaders of the PSP women's committee issued a collective critique of government corruption and linked it to the economic concerns of all women. "Is it not time," they asked, "to protest against abusive rents, against the increase of meat to 50 cents, of bread to 20, of condensed milk to 20 and 25, of beans to 38, butter to 60, and so many articles that have prohibitive prices?"[58] The women protested rising food costs that maintained the impoverishment of Cuban families. The PSP women reminded voting women that beyond confronting economic precarity, mothers faced the terror of anticipating news that their children, whether headed to the factory or the university, would be attacked and murdered, while gangsters received protection from politicians. They called for all women to condemn the "politics of divisionism, of attacks and assassinations."[59]

Ultimately, Carlos Prío Socarrás became president (1948–1952). The PSP maintained a visible presence in electoral politics. The party held nine seats in the House of Representatives until Batista led a coup against the government in 1952. While PSP women activists never achieved the level of political influence that communists held during the early 1940s, they maintained their base through grassroots organizing.

Full Equality "Has Not Yet Been Achieved"

As the communist movement lost its hold on national politics and communist supporters confronted government suppression, women of the PSP shifted their attention to global discussions of democracy. At the 1945 International Women's Congress in Paris, a multinational group of women established the Women's International Democratic Federation. Its founders aimed to prevent future wars or the resurgence of fascism, and they critiqued how war threatened the security of women and children. Women established national branches of the federation in various countries in the next few years. In 1948, the PSP activists Edith García Buchaca, who was white, Sánchez Mastrapa, and Argüelles established the Federación Democrática de Mujeres Cubanas (FDMC, Democratic Cuban Women's Federation) as a branch of the international federation. They linked local issues affecting Cuban women to global struggles for democratic reform.

García and her peers utilized the FDMC to help bridge Cuban women's political interests with those of activists from other nations. They called for a "popular and democratic movement" committed to equality and the "defense of our democracy and independence."[60] They appealed to communities of women who had been mobilized by the Communist Party in the late 1930s and early 1940s. Their efforts proved fruitful, as women established FDMC branches throughout the island. Leaders of the FDMC asserted that the organization would address issues that had not yet been resolved since the ratification of the 1940 Constitution:

> After long and difficult struggles in close liaison with the progressive forces of the country, Cuban women have conquered many of the rights for which women of other nations are still fighting: the electoral vote, the constitutional right to receive equal pay for equal work, working mothers' rights, etc. . . . Yet the full equality to which the Cuban woman had always aspired has not yet been achieved.[61]

FDMC leaders called on Cuban women to "coordinate our activities with women from around the world, British or Soviet, American or Chinese, Yugoslav, Greek, Italian, French, Spanish, Latin American." By uniting with women across the world, they sought to prevent the political corruption "that brought our sons and brothers into an unnecessary war, only to meet the economic appetites of financial tycoons."[62]

The FDMC became an important force for organizing radical women in the postwar years of the late 1940s and early 1950s. FDMC delegations held national forums in defense of children, at which they emphasized youth education, health, and living conditions. They published a monthly magazine, *Mujeres Cubanas*, to disseminate information about the global women's movement. The magazine demonstrates the wide reach of the organization across the island. In some rural towns, the FDMC was the only political group solely devoted to women's issues.[63] The Black activist and *Mujeres Cubanas* reporter Zoila Castellanos Ferrer, married to Lázaro Peña, profiled the living conditions of poor women from rural and urban communities.[64] Castellanos continued communist women's approach by addressing a broad base of citizens unified in the struggle for legal reforms on behalf of the popular classes.

Part of the FDMC's appeal to Cuban women lay in its commitment to addressing discrepancies between the constitution and civil codes that affected women. The 1940 Constitution conflicted with many laws from the colonial era that had legalized women's subordination. This discrepancy became one of the key issues addressed by the FDMC. During the late 1940s, FDMC members worked to obtain a Woman's Equalization Law to establish enforcement provisions for cases of discrimination against women. President Prío signed the law into existence in December 1950.

Legislative efforts to enforce the antidiscrimination tenets of the constitution left much to be desired. In January 1951, leaders declared the following in a *Mujeres Cubanas* article:

> Our organization, which fights for the advancement of women, supports all initiatives through which they might claim their equal rights granted by the Constitution of the Republic. That is why, although we believe that this project is not yet comprehensive and complete enough to pull down all the absurd prescriptions of the Civil Code as it stands, it represents, without a doubt, an appreciable step toward advancement, which is why it has our full support and sympathy.[65]

FDMC members contended that the government had not gone far enough in its efforts. Further, that the issue remained unresolved highlighted ongoing issues of sexism in Cuban society. The article's authors stated, "We Cuban women are closely following the discussions that are taking place in this legislative session regarding this matter, and naturally feel profound repulsion by those who oppose that which we have already been granted in the established [1940] Constitution." FDMC leaders advocated for social reforms that would lead to the recognition of women's full legal rights. They issued a hopeful message to Congress: "We are certain, however, that the spirit of democracy that brought the representatives to their positions, in which many supported women's suffrage, ultimately prevails in that women's proposed equal rights shall be approved."[66] Their call for legal equality continued the movement for women's political empowerment put forth during the 1920s and 1930s; it connected women's ongoing political marginalization to the colonial era to call attention to the absurdity of such contradictions in a modern, independent nation. Notably, the women did not acknowledge the parallel movement enacted by men to achieve a racial antidiscrimination clause. Perhaps in this sense they supported patriarchal perspectives that characterized women's political efforts as complementary to those of men.

Certainly, women of the FDMC recognized how women of African descent stood to benefit from an antidiscrimination clause that would protect both Blacks and women. In 1948, Esperanza Sánchez Mastrapa spoke on behalf of Cuban women at the Second International Women's Congress in Budapest. She issued a critical message for those who viewed Cuba as a progressive, democratic state. Although the Cuban Constitution contained "multiple provisions and undeniable progress and justice" for women to "exercise political and civil rights," she asserted that the colonial-era civil codes, which placed women under the guardianship of a male patriarch and denied them legal rights, contradicted the more recent text and thus undermined women's equality.[67] She explained, "All our civil law is the hallmark of monarchical conservatism that implanted it on the island, and for the purpose of this legislation—a clear reflection of the times—the woman is a man's property and must act as such."[68] She argued that to address this discrepancy, women must challenge the colonial legal codes that undermined their constitutional rights. Sánchez was on a mission at least partly motivated by anxiety over citizenship rights. She declared, "As is characteristic of a capitalist democracy, equality in practice is limited by the prejudices and inferiority maintained and cultivated by the dominant social political regime in our countries."[69] She contended that marriage, labor exploitation, and racism maintained women's social marginalization.

Sánchez issued a critique of social discrimination that departed from the race-neutral rhetoric articulated by most women of the FDMC.[70] She made clear that racial prejudices "extended and sustained by the dominant classes" maintained "the opprobrious conditions for thousands of Black and mulatto women." She poignantly noted, "Dark-skinned women, identified as Black or *mulata*, also suffer from disadvantages because they are women. Yet complete parity [between Black and white women] does not exist in our country due to their skin color. If [Black women] are also workers, they suffer a *triple discrimination*."[71] Women of African descent, like Black men, continued to struggle with access to employment in stores, offices, nursing, and the public sector. Though Cuban law prohibited racial discrimination, Sánchez claimed that employers continued to evade hiring those "struck by the color of their skin." She lamented that even as the constitution established equality among all Cubans, "many possibilities for progress" were closed for Black and *mulata* women.[72]

Sánchez's presentation marked a rare moment in which she publicly centered the experiences of African-descended women. She noted that the 1940 Constitution, though progressive when compared to other nations' charters, still failed to bring about gender equality. Yet she stressed the intersection of race, gender, and class in defining the experiences of women, factors that the 1951 *Mujeres Cubanas* article on the Women's Equalization Law overlooked. Her speech resonated with a 1949 essay by the Trinidadian communist activist Claudia Jones. In the essay, "An End to the Neglect of the Problems of the Negro Woman," Jones also theorized Black women's struggles at the intersection of racism, sexism, and classism, especially those living in the United States.[73] While Jones is remembered as one of the first women to theorize intersectionality, Sánchez should also be recognized for her contributions to framing African-descended women's experiences before global communist circles. Her attention to the plight of Black and *mulata* women within a nationalist framework fits a tradition of Black feminist theorizing put forth by María Dámasa Jova, Catalina Pozo Gato, and others in the 1930s.

Blacks as "Soldiers of Freedom"

After more than a decade-long career in the Communist Party, Sánchez abruptly left the movement she helped build. I have found no document in which she explains her departure. In 1951, the executive committee of the FDMC announced its decision to strip her of her positions in both the FDMC and the global women's organization, the Federación Democrática Internacional de Mujeres (Women's International Democratic Federation) "after repeated efforts" to solicit Sánchez's attendance at meetings and "to discuss her attitude and behavior toward said organization."[74] The FDMC portrayed Sánchez as a traitor to its movement for democratic reform. Committee members asserted that her actions stood in "direct contradiction to the principles that sustain the FDMC, which defends peace, democratic rights, and public liberties, [principles] attacked and ignored by the government."[75] The organization's announcement reinforced the November 1950 accusations by PSP leader Blas Roca that Sánchez abandoned her allegiance to the party in order to form a political alliance with Fulgencio Batista.[76]

The FDMC announcement, which the executive committee reprinted in multiple PSP publications, prompts more questions than answers. *Oriente* countered that Sánchez renounced "her political militancy" and settled "comfortably" into her newfound independence from the PSP, including the expectation that she would return her monthly check of 2,000 pesos from the FDMC in exchange for a monthly salary of 250 pesos from the party.[77] Sánchez appeared as an elected official of a lesser-known political party a year later. That she remained active in national politics suggests that she chose to abandon the communist cause. Anticommunist backlash may have affected Sánchez personally and led her to break her affiliation. She may have had a disagreement with FDMC or PSP leaders about the direction of the party. It is also possible that Sánchez formulated a political perspective incompatible with the approach of the FDMC.

Sánchez's 1948 analysis of the "triple discrimination" confronted by women of African descent, coupled with her subsequent departure, also prompt questions about the role of Black women in the communist movement in the 1950s and beyond. Unlike Sánchez, María Argüelles remained active in the PSP through the *comités de amas de casas* (housewives committees), which she organized alongside Candelaria Rodríguez.[78] The government outlawed the PSP and its newspaper in 1953, and Argüelles and others moved their activities underground. US State Department officials speculated that the *comités de amas de casas* served as one of the PSP's "various front or collateral groups to determine which ones can continue to operate and infiltrate official organizations of a similar nature." Officials indicated that through such efforts, "many have joined the movement without being aware that it is Communist-inspired and controlled."[79] The establishment of the committees suggests how Argüelles and other activists remained active in mobilizing women on behalf of the communist movement. Scholars cite few women of African descent who participated, and this topic merits further study. Men of the PSP led the antidiscrimination campaign throughout the decade. Future research may reveal the range of activities led by women who joined the committees and of women of African descent who supported the insurrectionary activities of the 1950s.

In January 1959, shortly after the triumph of the Revolution, race momentarily reemerged as a subject of public discussion among women of the PSP. That August, in its weekly women's column, *Noticias de Hoy* featured an article by María Argüelles on "the progress of the revolution and the fight against racial discrimination."[80] Argüelles identified the stakes that Blacks had in supporting the new government. Her statement likely stemmed from hearing the army leader Fidel Castro deliver a speech at the Presidential Palace in Havana on March 22. Castro acknowledged that racism existed in Cuba, and he appealed to all Cubans to eliminate racism in order to build a "new *patria*."[81] Responding to this momentous occasion, Argüelles asserted, "From [the nineteenth-century wars] of '68 and '95, up until the glorious triumph of the Revolution on January 1, 1959, Blacks have always been present as soldiers of freedom, as decent and honorable citizens."[82] Argüelles's article more widely reveals her belief that the Revolution could potentially realize the goals of the independence movement that the republican government had failed to achieve.

Argüelles determined that Blacks had faith in the new government because Castro "so valiantly and publicly condemned the segregation of Black Cubans within the workplace." She considered the recently announced agrarian reform program to be the nation's "great hope," that it would alleviate the concerns of Black men and women including the "grave problem of unemployment that confronted the nation."[83] She optimistically suggested that the reform would help facilitate Blacks' entry into employment from which they had been excluded such as in government agencies. These new opportunities would allow Black men and women "more opportunities to sustain themselves honorably." Speaking to all women on behalf of the community of African descent, she concluded, "We hope that the Revolution will resolve the issue of racial discrimination. In the meantime, we fight so that soon, very soon, racism will exist as nothing more than a bad memory for the great Cuban family."[84]

Unlike elite and upwardly mobile Black women from the turn of the twentieth century, individuals like Argüelles did not enact citizenship primarily within Black civic organizations, though many likely remained active in such associations during the initial years of the Revolution. Rather, they performed citizenship through state-organized youth parties and the national women's group, the Federación de Mujeres Cubanas (FMC, Federation of Cuban Women). In this sense, Argüelles's observations point to the multiple avenues, discursive and organizational, through which the new government interpolated Black Cubans in the revolutionary project. Argüelles, as a leader who had largely remained silent on racial issues during the 1940s and 1950s, took the opportunity to speak on behalf of African descendants. She did so through the women's column of the newspaper, which furthered her work in political spaces that paralleled those headed by men. There she spoke to the experiences of all Black citizens rather than Black women only. In other words, by affirming the vision of racial justice articulated by the new government, she helped shape a narrative that confronted racial divisions while affirming gender binaries.

• • •

Attending to the strategies African-descended women communists employed prompts a more nuanced understanding of patriarchal dynamics and Black activism beyond race-based political organizing. Labor and communist organizations mobilized a greater number of African descendants than elite civic clubs had. They addressed material issues affecting the broader population of color and validated the leadership of women across racial lines. At the same time, Black women who joined the URC rarely addressed anti-Black racism in their public discussions. Perhaps women of all races privately encountered pressure from male leaders to avoid issues of racial injustice. Communist women of African descent may have prioritized labor exploitation and government corruption as critical to addressing the social disparities confronted by poor families of African descent.

It is also possible that Black women leaders worried about alienating their white counterparts, as they presented a unified image of womanhood or viewed their race-neutral message as a strategy for enacting racelessness. After 1940, few communist women of any race centered the experiences of Black women in their social inequities, marking a departure from the strategies they employed in the 1930s.

The campaign that Black women of the Communist Party helped carry out on behalf of legal and economic reforms broadens our understanding of women's political organizing after 1940. The historian Michelle Chase has argued that the FDMC established a framework for women's political participation that the revolutionary government appropriated after 1959.[85] The government established the FMC to unify existing women's groups as revolutionary leaders consolidated their political power. It then dissolved existing organizations. The FMC, similar to the FMDC, advocated for women's social reforms that benefited women and children, including health care programs. FMC members supported literacy campaigns and agrarian reforms; they promoted women's movement from the domestic realm into the workforce. Chase observes, "Most of the women who took up prominent positions in the FMC were longtime activists of the Marxist Left who had risen to leadership positions first in 1959 and 1960."[86] Thus the government relied on women who had been politically active from the late 1940s onward.

Examining the FDMC and FMC from the standpoint of Sánchez and Argüelles expands Chase's framework to show that the strategies of this contingent of radical women activists emerged during the late 1930s. It reveals how communist women of all races evolved in their thinking about citizenship. Women of the Communist Party built an influential base that articulated women's political position as workers rather than mothers. This framework allowed for them to address broader issues of government accountability on behalf of laborers. African-descended women's involvement from the 1939 Third National Women's Congress indicates that during the 1940s, many radical women activists turned away from an intersectional critique that centered race. Further, the women's congress of 1949 demonstrates that male leaders continued to marginalize most women from leadership in the broader party under the rubric of separate "women's issues," a practice the revolutionary government continued a decade later by establishing the FMC.

Epilogue

In 1923, as a growing veterans movement joined calls for national regeneration, the Santiago de Cuba councilor José Palomino initiated a campaign to exhume the remains of Mariana Grajales Cuello in Kingston, Jamaica. He sought to return the African-descended mother of Antonio Maceo Grajales, one of the nation's "most distinguished and heroic liberators" to her homeland.[1] That April, Santiago de Cuba residents crowded the city streets to witness her funeral procession to the Santa Ifigenia cemetery. Buildings displayed black drapes and hung flags at half mast. Individuals in attendance offered a prayer of love for Grajales and her family. They sang "a hymn of hope for the definitive redemption of the country that they liberated."[2] Public officials' letters in the press suggest that her return generated optimism in the face of economic crisis and government corruption.[3]

The memorialization of Mariana Grajales was a rare instance in which citizens of a multiracial nation embraced a woman of African descent as its symbolic mother. Historians, politicians, and activists interpreted her life story for nationalist narratives. Grajales became legendary for her sacrifices for the Cuban nation; in addition to risking her own safety as a nurse for the Liberation Army, she compelled her eleven sons to endanger their lives as soldiers; her husband and all but one of her sons died during the wars for independence from Spain. She later went into exile in Kingston, where she continued to organize on behalf of the anticolonial struggle. Newspapers wrote of her heroism, and her prominence rose to mythical status. Filtered throughout these narratives are her visions of freedom, as a Cuban woman staunchly opposed to Spanish colonial rule, a free person of color who taught her children about slave rebellions and the revolutionary African-descended poet Plácido, and an abolitionist who visited the jail that once held *cimarrones* (maroons) to remind herself of the brutality of slavery. Her appeal as a maternal figure best exemplifies the construction of the *mambisa* (revolutionary woman) during the wars for independence.[4]

During the republican era that followed independence, many Cubans interpreted the narrative of Grajales in ways that reflected gendered ideas of citizenship. Public commemorations venerated her as the mother of Liberation Army General Antonio Maceo. Black, mainstream, and feminist publications profiled Grajales as well as her contemporaries María Cabrales and Rosa La Bayamesa alongside white women patriots.[5] Such profiles reinforced women's domestic femininity as activists sought women's suffrage and political representation. Feminist publications celebrated Grajales as an exemplar of women's moral leadership of the nation. Elite Black civic activists recounted Grajales's efforts to defeat Spanish colonialism as evidence of their long history of contributing to nation-building. Elite Black women of Oriente Province established organizations in her name. Their efforts memorialized Black women patriots during a period of democratic reform that left most women on the margins of political institutions.[6]

While many Cubans invoked the life of Mariana Grajales to uphold the nationalist principles of racial egalitarianism, practices of racial stereotyping undermined their efforts. Elite whites depicted privileged white women as the model of modern femininity. They portrayed women of African descent as uncivilized *brujas*, sex workers, and hypersexual *mulatas*. Even as writers and visual artists celebrated African contributions to Cuban culture in the 1920s, they incorporated Black men and women into the national imaginary primarily through folklore.[7] Privileged whites persisted in using racial stereotypes to justify the exclusion of African descendants from elite social spaces, private schools, and employment. In this regard, Grajales served as an exception to racial ideologies that otherwise characterized Black Cuban women as inferior. Even as standards of citizenship evolved in ways that afforded women of African descent greater access to the political system, they confronted ongoing discrimination due to their race and gender.

The contradiction between celebrating Mariana Grajales and discriminating against African-descended women living in contemporary society continued after the outbreak of the revolution in 1952. In 1958, Fidel Castro recast the heroine's narrative to serve his revolutionary goals when he created the Mariana Grajales platoon. The revolutionary government used Grajales's image to inspire Cuban citizens to carry out its 1961 literacy campaign, but it targeted poor Black women, many of whom had labored as sex workers, for moral reform during the same period.[8] It named airports and parks after Grajales while portraying citizens of African descent as beneficiaries of the state.[9] The government also renamed schools and hospitals after Grajales, with more women of all races entering as professionals due to changing gender norms and increased access to universities. Yet many Black women remained in impoverished neighborhoods. Further, many women of African descent complained of racially offensive jokes from their white coworkers and other forms of marginalization in the workplace. Black men and women encountered negative stereotypes of Cubans of African descent in television and the press.[10]

The revolutionary government's programs to eradicate social disparities shifted how Black women activists might respond to racial and gender discrimination. In an era of anticolonial and civil rights movements, dominant visions of history became the domain of the state. State organizations like the Federación de Mujeres Cubanas facilitated women's political ambitions.[11] Government efforts to consolidate nationalist narratives led to the erosion of traditional pathways for challenging anti-Black racism; indeed, the government closed most presses and shut down Black civic clubs. Leaders certainly recognized the heroism of revolutionaries from the nineteenth century and the 1950s, but they overlooked the activities of most activists from the 1940s communist movement. As such, the political system that unfolded after 1958 again compelled women of African descent to remain silent on issues of discrimination in order to buttress the nationalist project of racelessness.

Black women artists employed creative citizenship practices within this context. Among them, Sara Gómez became the first woman filmmaker to work for the Instituto Cubano del Arte e Industria Cinematográficos (Cuban Institute of Cinematographic Art and Industry). Gómez produced a series of short documentary films, notably Iré a Santiago (1964), Excursión a Vueltabajo (1965) and Guanabacoa: Crónica de mi familia (1966). Her feature film De cierta manera (Of a certain manner), released posthumously in 1977, portrays a love story between a white teacher and a Black bus driver. The film called attention to clashes between Cubans of different racial, class, and gender backgrounds; it implied that true change could occur only by dismantling social hierarchies.[12] Similarly, the writers Georgina Herrera and Nancy Morejón navigated racelessness discourses by examining women of Cuba's African past. Herrera's poem "Ibu Sedi" venerates Afro-Cuban culture through its portrayal of the daughter of the orisha Yemaya, and "Primera vez ante un espejo" (First time in front of a mirror) expresses racial pride. Morejón's famous works "Mujer negra" (Black woman) and "Amo a mi amo" (I love my master) also created complex images of Black womanhood that emphasize Cuba's history of interracial intimacy and promote racial dignity.[13] The filmmaker Gloria Rolando documented the Black past through more than a dozen films on Afro-Caribbean history.[14] Collectively, these women have used art to challenge the limitations of racelessness discourses; they affirm Black women's contributions and familial history from slavery to the present.

In the twenty-first century, Black women activist-intellectuals have used digital media platforms and community groups to confront the contradictions between Cuban narratives of equality and the persistence of social discrimination. These political voices are transnational, Afro-diasporic, and for many, feminist. Sandra Abd'Allah-Alvarez Ramírez, in her blog *Negra cubana tiene que ser*, analyzes sexuality and gendered racial dynamics on the island. She published the Directorio de Afro-Cubanas online to archive the contributions of African-descended women to the nation's history. Separately, Daisy Rubiera Castillo and Inés María Martiatu Terry's 2011 edited volume, *Afrocubanas: Historia, pensamiento y prácticas culturales* (Afro-Cuban women: History, thought, and cultural practices), highlights the civic engagement of Black women who established an informal collective named Afrocubanas in response to economic crises of the early twentieth-first century. *Afrocubanas* includes primary texts by African-descended women from the late colonial period through the early 2000s as well as theoretical pieces on gender and racial dynamics that center Black women's experiences. The collective's public work facilitates discussions of Black women's experiences with disparaging media stereotypes, racial profiling by police, their naturally coarse hair textures, disparities in health outcomes and food access, and Black women's economic initiatives.[15] Afrocubanas members do not necessarily call for a radical reform of the political structure; rather, they seek to realize the revolutionary goals on behalf of women of African descent. In doing so, their work extends the legacy of Mariana Grajales as part of a centuries-long, complex trajectory of Black women's social thought, community activism, and cultural production while they imagine a future that validates their full humanity.

. . .

In April 2018, as Raúl Castro prepared to end his family's leadership that had spanned more than fifty-nine years, Cubans elected two Black women to serve as vice presidents alongside incoming president Miguel Díaz Canel Bermúdez. The first vice president, Inés María Chapman Waugh of Holguín, forged a path to national politics through her membership in state political organizations, the Partido Comunista de Cuba, Central de Trabajadores de Cuba, Comités de Defensa de la Revolución, and Federación de Mujeres Cubanas. The second vice president, Beatriz Johnson Urrutia, previously served as president of the Asamblea Nacional de Poder Popular en Santiago de Cuba. While their professional attainments exemplify the socioeconomic mobility attained by many persons of African descent under the Revolution, their political participation underpins their contributions to the revolutionary project. Castro celebrated the women's election as a marker of social progress, as Cubans elected the women "not only for being Black, but for their virtues and qualities."[16] Yet beyond celebrations, how might their political leadership transform the circumstances of African-descended women? What opportunities might Chapman Waugh and Johnson Urrutia have to publicly address the forms of sexism and anti-Black racism critiqued by the Afrocubanas collective? Is it possible that expectations of racial silence will lead them to endorse race-neutral policies and programs?

In this work I have presented a framework for pondering these questions. I historicize the ways African-descended women have interpreted dominant standards of citizenship to suit their aspirations for socioeconomic advancement. I trace the political strategies employed by Black women activists who entered into movements for racial equality, women's rights, labor reform, and national sovereignty. I provide case studies to examine the interrelation of racial discourses and patriarchal power in Latin America, the Caribbean, and African diaspora more broadly. And while centering the contributions of women of African descent to forging a modern Cuban democracy, I underscore the ways women's embrace of patriarchy ultimately helped sustain their marginalization from political and institutional leadership. These lessons, retained and passed on by Black women artists and activist-intellectuals, offer a blueprint for the present and future.

Notes

Introduction

1. Her 1925 poetry collection *"Arpegios íntimos" y poesías* and her 1927 text *Ufanías: Juicios y consideraciones acerca de "Arpegios íntimos" y poesías*, which includes letters heralding the former, illustrates her engagement with the literary world. Dawn Duke analyzes the writings of Dámasa Jova in *Literary Passion, Ideological Commitment*.

2. On the Machado presidency and popular resistance, see Luis E. Aguilar, *Cuba 1933*; Samuel Farber, *Revolution and Reaction in Cuba*; Fabio Grobart, "El movimiento obrero cubano entre 1925 a 1933"; Fernando Martínez Heredia, *La revolución cubana del 30*; Louis A. Pérez, *Cuba under the Platt Amendment*; Lionel Soto, *La revolución del 33*; José Tabares del Real, *La revolución del 30*; Robert Whitney, *State and Revolution in Cuba*.

3. María Dámasa Jova, "A todos y en particular a mis compañeras, amigas y simpatizadores," postulada con el número 1 por el Partido CND en las elecciones para delegados a la Asamblea Constituyente, Santa Clara, 1939, 1–5, Biblioteca Provincial "Martí" Villa Clara, Santa Clara.

4. Louis A. Pérez describes how pro-independence intellectuals articulated a redemption narrative during the late nineteenth century (*Structure of Cuban History*, 75).

5. Dámasa Jova, "A todos y en particular a mis compañeras."

6. Dámasa Jova, "A todos y en particular a mis compañeras."

7. Dámasa Jova, "A todos y en particular a mis compañeras."

8. Dámasa Jova, "A todos y en particular a mis compañeras."

9. Dawn Duke, *Literary Passion, Ideological Commitment*, 79.

10. See the studies cited in endnote 2 as well as Aline Helg, *Our Rightful Share*; Jorge I. Domínguez, *Cuba: Order and Revolution*; Jorge Ibarra, *Prologue to Revolution*; Alejandro de la Fuente, *Nation for All*; Alejandra Bronfman, *Measures of Equality*; Lillian Guerra, *Myth of José Martí*; Melina Pappademos, *Black Political Activism*.

11. Helg, *Our Rightful Share*, 20.

12. Gail Bederman, *Manliness and Civilization*; Eileen J. Suárez Findlay, *Imposing Decency*; Evelyn Brooks Higginbotham, "African-American Women's History" and *Remaking Respectability*. Also see Juanita de Barros, *Reproducing the British Caribbean*; Nicole C. Bourbonnais, *Birth Control in the Decolonizing Caribbean*; Gladys M. Jiménez-Muñoz, "Carmen Maria Colon Pellot"; Anne S. Macpherson, "Doing Comparative (Gender) History"; Katherine Paugh, *Politics of Reproduction*.

13. Bonnie Lucero, *Revolutionary Masculinity and Racial Inequality*; Karen Morrison, *Cuba's Racial Crucible*.

14. Keisha Blain, *Set the World on Fire*; Dayo Gore, *Radicalism at the Crossroads*; Erik McDuffie, *Sojourning for Freedom*; Imaobong D. Umoren, *Race Women Internationalists*.

15. Theories centering on African-descended women in the Cuban imagination are set forth in Melissa Blanco Borell, *She Is Cuba*; Alison Fraunhar, *Mulata Nation*; Sarah Franklin, *Women and Slavery in Nineteenth-Century Colonial Cuba*; Vera Kutzinski, *Sugar's Secrets*; Jill Lane, *Blackface Cuba*; Luz Mena, "Stretching the Limits of Gendered Spaces."

16. De la Fuente, *Nation for All*, 169.

17. Pappademos, *Black Political Activism*, 195.

18. Historians of elite and upwardly mobile communities of African descent have examined in detail the gendered strategies for racial advancement that emerged after emancipation. See Paulina Alberto, *Terms of Inclusion*; Kim Butler, *Freedoms Given, Freedoms Won*; Kevin K. Gaines, *Uplifting the Race*; Michele Mitchell, *Righteous Propagation* and "Silences Broken, Silences Kept": Mimi Sheller, *Democracy after Slavery*; Martin Anthony Summers, *Manliness and Its Discontents*.

19. Ula Taylor, *Promise of Patriarchy*.

20. Allison Berg, *Mothering the Race*; Brittney Cooper, *Beyond Respectability*; Treva Lindsey, *Colored No More*.

21. Tina Campt, *Image Matters*; Jasmine Nichole Cobb, *Picture Freedom*; David Levering Lewis and Deborah Willis, *A Small Nation of People*; Richard J. Powell, *Cutting a Figure*; Caroline Goeser, *Picturing the New Negro*; Susannah Walker, *Style and Status*; Maurice O. Wallace and Shawn Michelle Smith, *Pictures and Progress*; Deborah Willis, *Picturing Us* and *Posing Beauty*; Deborah Willis and Barbara Krauthamer, *Envisioning Emancipation*.

22. I thank Alexandra Gelbard for sharing her forthcoming work on Cuban Congo communities and African diaspora consciousness. Also see Bronfman, *Measures of Equality*, 97; Kristine Juncker, *Afro-Cuban Religious Arts*; Stephan Palmié, *Wizards and Scientists*; Reinaldo Román, *Governing Spirits*, 75–80.

23. Studies of the Cuban women's movement include Michelle Chase, *Revolution within the Revolution*; Catherine Davies, "National Feminism in Cuba"; Julio César González Pagés, *En busca de un espacio*; Esperanza Méndez Oliva and Santiago Alemán Santana, *Villareñas camino a la emancipación*; K. Lynn Stoner, *From the House to the Streets*. For the history of Latin American women's activism, see Susan K. Besse, *Restructuring Patriarchy*; Donna J. Guy, *Troubled Meeting of Sex, Gender* and *Women Build the Welfare State*; Asunción Lavrin, *Women, Feminism, and Social Change*; Francesca Miller, *Latin American Women and the Search for Social Justice*.

24. Stoner, *From the House to the Streets*. Studies of the "cult of domesticity" or the "cult of true womanhood" include Kay Boardman, "Ideology of Domesticity"; Nancy Cott, *Bonds of Womanhood*; Shirley J. Lee, "Black Women and the Cult of True Womanhood"; Venetria K. Patton, *Women in Chains*, especially her chapter "The Cult of True Womanhood and Its Revisions."

25. Manuel Ramírez Chicharro, "Beyond Suffrage," "Más allá del sufragismo," and "El activismo social y político de las mujeres."

26. Chase, *Revolution within the Revolution*, 86.

27. See Susan K. Besse's *Restructuring Patriarchy* for a comparative perspective.

28. Steven Palmer, José Antonio Piqueras, and Amparo Sánchez Cobos, *State of Ambiguity*.

29. Studies of Black Cuban women include María del Carmen Barcia Zequeira, *Mujeres al margen de la historia*; Duke, *Literary Passion, Ideological Commitment*; Oilda Hevia Lanier and Daisy Rubiera Castillo, *Emergiendo del silencio*; Carmen Victoria Montejo Arrechea, "*Minerva*: A Magazine for Women (and Men) of Color"; Daisy Rubiera Castillo, "Apuntes sobre la mujer negra cubana"; Daisy Rubiera Castillo and Inés María Martiatu Terry, *Afrocubanas: Historia, pensamiento y prácticas culturales*.

30. Pappademos notes, "Black clients often approached Black brokers (politicians, professionals, club administrators, civil servants, businessmen, and so on)—occasionally but not always invoking the bonds of racial fraternity—in order to exchange their votes for the goods and services that the brokers possessed" (*Black Political Activism*, 42).

31. On the Oblate Sisters of Providence, see William Montgomery, "Mission to Cuba and Costa Rica"; Diane Batts Morrow, *Persons of Color and Religious at the Same Time*; Thaddeus Posey, "Praying in the Shadows."

32. See Palmié, *Wizards and Scientists*. Notable exceptions include Rubiera Castillo and Martiatu Terry's *Afrocubanas* and the Afrocubanas collective.

Chapter 1. "Look for Progress in Our Moral Perfection": Racial Regeneration and the Post-Zanjón Black Public Sphere

1. See Earl R. Beck, "Martínez Campos Government of 1879"; Louis A. Pérez, *Cuba: Between Reform and Revolution*, 1–6; Louis A. Pérez, *Cuba between Empires*.

2. Ayala's birth name was María Cristina Fragas. See María del Carmen Barcia Zequeira, *Mujeres al margen de la historia*, 123; Monique-Adelle Callahan, *Between the Lines*, 25.

3. Cristina Ayala, "A mi raza," 126. For a study of Ayala's poetry, see María Alejandra Aguilar Dornelles, "Heroísmo y conciencia racial"; Barcia Zequeira, *Mujeres al margen de la historia*; Monique-Adelle Callahan, *Between the Lines*.

4. Ayala, "A mi raza." Translations are mine unless otherwise indicated.

5. See Tiffany Sippial, *Prostitution, Modernity*.

6. Francisco Moreno, *Cuba y su gente*. Also see Francisco Moreno, *El país de chocolate*; Beatriz Calvo Peña, "Prensa, política y prostitución."

7. Ayala, "A mi raza (To My Race)." Also see Cristina Ayala, *Ofrendas mayabequinas*.

8. My analysis of the national and Black public spheres draws on the work of Jürgen Habermas (*Structural Transformation of the Public Sphere*) and Elsa Barkley Brown ("Negotiating and Transforming the Public Sphere"). Also see Benedict Anderson, *Imagined Communities*; Houston A. Baker Jr. "Critical Memory and the Black Public Sphere"; Nancy Fraser, "Rethinking the Public Sphere"; C. K. Doreski, *Writing America Black*.

9. Pedro Deschamps Chapeaux, *El negro en el periodismo cubano*.

10. See Deschamps Chapeaux, *El negro en el periodismo cubano*; Aline Helg, *Our*

Rightful Share; David Sartorius, *Ever Faithful*; Rebecca J. Scott, *Slave Emancipation in Cuba*, 268–278; Karen Morrison, *Cuba's Racial Crucible*, 160–189.

11. The racial regeneration perspectives articulated by elite Black Cubans reflected broader conversations taking place among Latin American social scientists during the 1880s (Sippial, *Prostitution, Modernity*, 112–147; Nancy Leys Stepan, *Hour of Eugenics*, 36).

12. Studies that focus on racial advancement ideals among Cubans of African descent during the late nineteenth century include Helg, *Our Rightful Share*; Frank Guridy, *Forging Diaspora*; Morrison, *Cuba's Racial Crucible*, Marveta Ryan, "Seeking Acceptance."

13. Matt Childs, "'Sewing' Civilization"; Luis Martínez-Fernández, "Life in a 'Male City'"; Luz Mena, "Stretching the Limits of Gendered Spaces."

14. Cecilia, "Carta abierta a mi amigo el caballero Don Miguel Gualba y a las jovenes de Cienfuegos," *La Fraternidad*, March 30, 1888.

15. Ada Ferrer, *Insurgent Cuba*.

16. Cited in Rebecca J. Scott, *Slave Emancipation in Cuba*, 127.

17. Arthur F. Corwin, *Spain and the Abolition of Slavery in Cuba*; Joan Casanovas, *Bread, or Bullets!*; Miriam Herrera Jerez and Mario Castillo Santana, *Contested Community*; Kathleen M. Lopez, *Chinese Cubans*.

18. Helg, *Our Rightful Share*, 43.

19. Cecilia, "Carta abierta a mi amigo."

20. Sartorius, *Ever Faithful*, 150–151; R. Scott, *Slave Emancipation in Cuba*, 227–28.

21. David Sartorius notes that the colonial government called for religious tolerance but passed legislation banning non-Catholic practices (*Ever Faithful*, 168).

22. Manuel Sanguily (*Frente a la dominación española*, 173–175), cited in Helg, *Our Rightful Share*, 46–47.

23. For an examination of how civilization principles shaped civic culture, see Louis A. Pérez, *Intimations of Modernity*.

24. Helg, *Our Rightful Share*, 23–54.

25. Rodolfo de Lagardére, *Blancos y negros*. Notable works by Black intellectuals also include José Pla's *La raza de color* and Rafael Serra y Montalvo's *Para blancos y negros*.

26. See, for instance, Paulina Alberto, *Terms of Inclusion*; Kim Butler, *Freedoms Given, Freedoms Won*; Kevin K. Gaines, *Uplifting the Race*; Mimi Sheller, *Democracy after Slavery*.

27. E. T. Elvira, "Notas Quincenales," *Minerva*, December 15, 1888, 6–7.

28. Martha K. Cobb, "Martín Morúa Delgado"; Pedro Deschamps Chapeaux, *Rafael Serra y Montalvo*; Leopoldo Horrego Estuch, *Juan Gualberto Gómez* and *Martín Morúa Delgado*.

29. Among historians who have examined honor in Latin America and the Caribbean, see Sueann Caulfield, *In Defense of Honor*; Sueann Caulfield, Sarah C. Chambers, Lara Putnam, *Honor, Status, and Law in Modern Latin America*; Sherry Johnson, "Señoras en sus clases no ordinarias"; Sonya Lipsett-Rivera and Lyman L. Johnson, *Faces of Honor*; Nicole Von Germeten, *Violent Delights, Violent Ends*.

30. *La Fraternidad*, February 20, 1888, 4; March 30, 1888, 4; April 11, 1888, 4.

31. Phillip Howard, *Changing History*, 143.

32. The historian Melina Pappademos explains that the *directorio* "provided member

organizations with high visibility and distinction, access to education and social networks, and a platform to demonstrate Black cultural refinement, and it represented the colony's most powerful sector of African-descended Cubans" (*Black Political Activism*, 73).

33. For overviews of the directory see Oilda Havier Lanier, *El Directorio Central de las Sociedades Negras de Cuba*; Helg, *Our Rightful Share*, 35–43; R. Scott, *Slave Emancipation in Cuba*.

34. *La Igualdad*, February 16, 1893; Helg, *Our Rightful Share*, 31; Scott, *Slave Emancipation in Cuba*, 271.

35. Elite Blacks' responses to how the colonial government sought to regulate *cabildos* is detailed in Martha Silvia Escalona, *Los cabildos de africanos*, 73; Nathaniel Samuel Murrell, *Afro-Caribbean Religions*, 104.

36. David H. Brown writes that Abakuá lodges in Cuban port cities "grew exponentially during the last third of the century, as proletarianization changed the face of the urbanizing workforce in the teeming ports of these cities, where the Abakuá Society came to control stevedore, transportation, and local manufacturing labor between the 1870s and 1942" (*Light Inside*, 14). Also see Rafael López Valdés, "La sociedad secreta abakuá."

37. D. Brown, *Light Inside*; Howard, *Changing History*; Kristine Juncker, *Afro-Cuban Religious Arts*; Stephan Palmié, *Wizards and Scientists*; Reinaldo L. Román, *Governing Spirits*.

38. Martínez-Fernández, "Life in a 'Male City.'"

39. K. Lynn Stoner (*From the House to the Streets*) and Teresa Prados-Torreira (*Mambisas*) have described the ways many women ventured beyond the household for the first time to sacrifice themselves for the independence cause. Women worked as cooks, spies, nurses, seamstresses, fundraisers, and occasionally soldiers. See also V. E. Rodríguez de Cuesta, *Patriotas cubanas*. Studies of Black women who participated in the wars for independence include James Henderson, "Mariana Grajales"; Jose Luciano Franco, "Mariana and Maceo"; Jean Stubbs, "Social and Political Motherhood of Cuba."

40. Pérez, *Imitations of Modernity*, 12.

41. Pérez, *Imitations of Modernity*. Bonnie Lucero also theorizes the connections between gender and civilization discourses in "Civilization before Citizenship."

42. Sarah Franklin, *Women and Slavery in Nineteenth-Century Colonial Cuba*.

43. Mena, "Stretching the Limits of Gendered Spaces."

44. Childs, "'Sewing' Civilization"; Martínez-Fernández, "Life in a 'Male City"; Mena, "Stretching the Limits of Gendered Spaces."

45. David H. Brown, *Santería Enthroned*, 34, 53; Henry B. Lovejoy, *Prieto*, 89; Paul Niell, *Urban Space as Heritage in Late Colonial Cuba*, 54; Miguel Willie Ramos, "La División de la Habana."

46. Aisha Finch, *Rethinking Slave Rebellion in Cuba*; Pilar Egüez Guevara, "Dangerous Encounters, Ambiguous Frontiers"; Fernando Ortiz, *Los negros curros*.

47. Barcia Zequeira, *Mujeres al margen de la historia*, 120.

48. Bonnie Lucero notes that women comprised the majority of free persons of color by the mid-nineteenth century (*Cuban City, Segregated*, 108).

49. Karen Y. Morrison, "White Fathers and Slave Mothers" and "'Whitening' Revisited."

50. The historian Karen Morrison explains that *mulato* and mestizo elites constituted a small but significant population who were freeborn and often enjoyed their white fathers' "wealth and connections while maintaining strong links to the Afro-Cuban community" (*Cuba's Racial Crucible*, 170). Also see Verena Martinez-Alier, *Marriage, Class, and Colour*; Michelle Reid, *The Year of the Lash*; Matthew Pettway, *Cuban Literature in the Age of Black Insurrection*.

51. Verena Stolcke (Martínez-Alier), *Marriage, Class, and Colour in Nineteenth-Century Cuba*. Also see Karen Y. Morrison, "Creating an Alternative Kinship"; Morrison "White Fathers and Slave Mothers."

52. Morrison, *Cuba's Racial Crucible*, 168.

53. Morrison, *Cuba's Racial Crucible*, 121.

54. Miriam DeCosta-Willis writes that Ayala gave poetry readings and published in more than twenty newspapers during this period. See *Daughters of the Diaspora*, 30–31.

55. Barcia Zequeira, *Mujeres al margen de la historia*, 117.

56. R. Scott, *Slave Emancipation in Cuba*, 264.

57. Susan Greenbaum, *More than Black*; Jesse Hoffnung-Garskof, *Racial Migrations*; Nancy Raquel Mirabal, *Suspect Freedoms*; Gerald Poyo, *With All, and for the Good of All*.

58. Clark, "Labor Conditions in Cuba"; Helg, *Our Rightful Share*, 26; Jean Stubbs, "Tobacco on the Periphery," 69–70; US War Department, *Report on the Census, 1899*, 462–463.

59. The destruction of plantations during the wars made property more affordable in regions such as central Cuba. Many African descendants remained on the properties of their former masters; others took advantage of the 1870s resettlement program that allocated for small plots of land in designated areas. See Michael Zueske, "Two Stories of Gender and Slave Emancipation," 192; Ferrer, *Insurgent Cuba*, 73, 100–104; Rebecca J. Scott and Michael Zueske, "Property in Writing," 10; Imilcy Balboa Navarro, *Los brazos necesarios*, 49–54; Lucero, "Racial Geographies, Imperial Transitions."

60. Lucero, *Cuban City, Segregated*, 108.

61. Cluster and Hernández, *History of Havana*, 153.

62. Casanovas, *Bread, or Bullets!*, 134.

63. "Expediente sobre el reglamento proyecto en la sociedad de socorro mutuo titulado 'La Caridad,' fundado por las pardas Ramona Lomovida y Flora Bonell en Las Villas," June 25, 1879, legajo 97, no. 4424, Gobierno General, Archivo Nacional de Cuba, Havana (hereafter cited as ANC).

64. Adelaida Ponce de León, "Discurso," *El Pueblo* (Matanzas), June 13, 1880; also cited in Howard, *Changing History*, 159.

65. E. T. Elvira, "Notas Quincenales," *Minerva*, February 15, 1889.

66. *La Familia*, May 15, 1884, cited in Deschamps Chapeaux, *El negro en el periodismo cubano*, 49.

67. Deschamps Chapeaux, *El negro en el periodismo cubano*, 49; Howard, *Changing History*, 158.

68. Deschamps Chapeaux, *El negro en el periodismo cubano*, 49; Howard, *Changing History*, 158.

69. See Sartorius, *Ever Faithful*, 147–148.

70. *Minerva*, October 15, 1888, 5.

71. Barcia Zequeira finds that of 312 women who promoted the magazine, 94 were from Havana Province, 41 from Matanzas, 105 from Las Villas, and 72 from the United States, 58 of these from Key West and 14 from New York City (*Mujeres al margen de la historia*, 118).

72. For an analysis of how *Minerva* challenged racism and sexism after emancipation, see Carmen Victoria Montejo Arrechea, "*Minerva*: A Magazine for Women (and Men) of Color."

73. Jaime Martí-Miquel, "La mujer en la vida social" *Minerva*, April 30, 1889, 1–2.

74. Laura Clarens, "La mujer y la academia," *Minerva* 30 May 1889: 4–5. Also see Felipa Basilio, "La mujer ante la razón," *Minerva*, May 30, 1889, 1–2.

75. On the "blood codes" and Black Cuban women's calls for education, see Montejo Arrechea, "*Minerva*: A Magazine for Women (and Men) of Color," 39.

76. África C. Céspedes, "A Cuba," *Minerva*, March 16, 1889, 2–4.

77. Á. Céspedes, "A Cuba."

78. E. T. Elvira, "Notas Quincenales," *Minerva*, December 7, 1889, 7; April 30, 1889, 8; July 19, 1889, 7–8.

79. Elvira, "Notas Quincenales," *Minerva*, December 7, 1889, 7.

80. Stolcke, *Marriage, Class, and Colour.*

81. Morrison, *Cuba's Racial Crucible*, xviii–xix. Also see Stolcke, *Marriage, Class, and Color.*

82. Morrison, *Cuba's Racial Crucible*, 160–189.

83. Landaluze's works romanticized subjects but were interpreted as authentic representations of Cuban life by many of his contemporaries. He depicted women of African descent who birthed children lighter in skin complexion with each generation. On his work, see Antonio Bachiller y Morales and Victor Patricio de Landaluze, *Colección de artículos*; Kwame Dixon and John Burdick, "Visions of a Nineteenth-Century Cuba"; E. Carmen Ramos, "Painter of Cuban Life."

84. Vera Kutzinski argues in her foundational study, *Sugar's Secrets*, that the *mulata* has been regarded as a "symbolic container" for race, gender, and sexuality simultaneously informing power relations in Cuba's colonial and postcolonial society. Also see Suzanne Bost, *Mulattas and Mestizas*; Gema R. Guevara, "Inexacting Whiteness"; Mena, "Stretching the Limits of Gendered Spaces."

85. Jill Lane, *Blackface Cuba*. Also see Barcia Zequeira, *Mujeres al margen de la historia*; Sippial, *Prostitution, Modernity.*

86. Benjamin de Céspedes, *La prostitución en la Ciudad de la Habana.*

87. "Una carta y un libro," *La Fraternidad*, December 10, 1888.

88. Cited in Sippial, *Prostitution, Modernity*, 91.

89. África Céspedes, "Reflexionemos," *Minerva*, February 28, 1889.

90. ORP, "La familia," *Minerva*, December 30, 1888. Also cited in Deschamps Chapeaux, *El negro en el periodismo cubano*, 86.

91. ORP, "La familia. Elvira supports similar values the following month in "Notas Quincenales," *Minerva*, January 26, 1889.

92. Michael Zueske cites a case in which the *parda* Francisca Bulí of central Cuba "used her will to ask the man with whom she had lived without marriage for many years to recognize their children as his, so that they did not grow up 'without another

surname'" ("Two Stories of Gender and Slave Emancipation," 187). Also see María de los Reyes Castillo Bueno, *Reyita*, 18, 173.

93. See Eileen J. Suárez Findlay, *Imposing Decency*, 33–37, 105.

94. Elvira, "Notas Quincenales," *Minerva*, January 26, 1889.

95. "P???p [illegible] notorio," *La Fraternidad*, May 13, 1889.

96. V. Kop y Torres, "La felicidad del hogar," *Minerva*, January 26, 1889, 3.

97. Carlota T., "De Santiago de Cuba," *La Fraternidad*, March 2, 1889.

98. Martín Morúa Delgado, "La mujer y sus derechos: Conferencia," *Minerva*, February 15, 1889, 2–4.

99. *Minerva* published Martín Morúa Delgado's speech "La mujer y sus derechos" as a series (February 15, 1889, 2–4; February 28, 1889, 1–2; March 16, 1889, 1–2; April 30, 1889, 2–4).

100. María Storni, "Carta," *Minerva*, November 30, 1888, 3.

101. Storni, "Carta," 3–5. For a discussion of women's education in the late nineteenth century, see Barcia Zequeira, *Mujeres al margen de la historia*. Lucrecia González writes about it in "La instrucción," *Minerva*, January 26, 1889.

102. "Mosaicos," *La Fraternidad*, September 10, 1888; "Importante acto," *La Fraternidad*, May 13, 1889.

103. "Colegio de Señoritas," *La Igualdad*, February 24, 1894; Raquel Alicia Otheguy, "Education as a Political Tool," 6.

104. Sartorius, *Ever Faithful*, 145–146.

105. Cited in Deschamps Chapeaux, *El negro en el periodismo cubano*, 68.

106. Otheguy, "Education as a Political Tool." Also see Raquel Otheguy, "Es de suponer que los maestros sean de la misma clase," 174–192.

107. Marial Iglesias Utset, *Cultural History of Cuba*, 70, 82; Pérez, *Cuba between Empires*, 197–203.

Chapter 2. Writing Black Political Networks during the Early Republic

1. Melina Pappademos, *Black Political Activism*, 69–70.

2. Louis A. Pérez, *Cuba under the Platt Amendment*.

3. Lillian Guerra, *Myth of José Martí*, 201.

4. See Aline Helg, *Our Rightful Share*; Rebecca J. Scott, *Slave Emancipation in Cuba*.

5. Alejandra Bronfman, *Measures of Equality*; Alejandro de la Fuente, *Nation for All*; Helg, *Our Rightful Share*; Melina Pappademos, *Black Political Activism*.

6. Melina Pappademos refers to these men as "Black brokers" (*Black Political Activism*, 42).

7. Gómez practiced what the historian Alejandra Bronfman characterizes as "civil citizenship," a vision of "political integration for Cubans of color as a process involving education and the acquisition of civic virtue" (*Measures of Equality*, 68–69).

8. For a description of the movement, see R. Scott, *Slave Emancipation in Cuba*, 255–278.

9. In 1895 he led an uprising against Spanish forces in Matanzas. Although the movement failed, Gómez's leadership contributed to support from Afro-Cubans, who constituted 50 percent of the region's insurgents, during subsequent uprisings (Helg, *Our Rightful Share*, 58, 82).

10. Helg, *Our Rightful Share*, 121.

11. On the life of Gómez, see Angelina Edreira de Caballero, *Vida y obra de Juan Gualberto Gómez*; Juan Alberto Gómez, *Por Cuba libre*; Rafael Marquina, *Juan Gualberto Gómez en sí*; Jesús Saborín Fornaris, *Juan Gualberto Gómez*.

12. Hevia Lanier, "Introducción a la selección de documentos," in Leopoldo Horrego Estuch, *Juan Gualberto Gómez, un gran inconforme*, 211.

13. On Gómez as a caudillo, see Pappademos, *Black Political Activism*, 75.

14. Many Afro-Cuban women employed the terms *la raza* (the race), *la raza negra* (the Black race), or *la raza de color* (the colored race) in their letters.

15. Pappademos, *Black Political Activism*, 77.

16. Pappademos, *Black Political Activism*, 63–91. Also see de la Fuente, *Nation for All*, 128–31; Gillian McGillivray, *Blazing Cane*, 86–144; Thomas Orum, "Politics of Color."

17. In Leonardo Horrego Estuch, *Juan Gualberto Gómez, un gran inconforme*, 283.

18. Louis A. Pérez, *Cuba: Between Reform and Revolution*, 161–164.

19. Rafael Serra y Montalvo, *Redención* (1903), cited in Bronfman, *Measures of Equality*, 74; Pedro Deschamps Chapeaux, *Rafael Serra y Montalvo*, 161.

20. Serra y Montalvo raised these issues in the newspapers *Redención* and his *El Nuevo Criollo* as well as in numerous essays, collected into the volumes *Ensayos políticos, sociales y económicos*, and *Para blancos y negros*.

21. De la Fuente, *Nation for All*, 67.

22. Helg, *Our Rightful Share*, 117–139; Enid Lynette Logan, "Conspirators, Pawns, Patriots, and Brothers"; Pappademos, *Black Political Activists*.

23. Helg, *Our Rightful Share*, 4–5.

24. The PIC manifesto is cited in Serafín Portuondo Linares, *Los Independientes de Color*, 37.

25. Portuondo Linares, *Los Independientes de Color*, 39–41.

26. Maikel Colón Pichardo, ¿*Es fácil ser hombre y difícil ser negro?*; Consuelo Naranjo Orovio, "Blanco sobre negro."

27. Cited in Helg, "Afro-Cuban Protest," 109–110.

28. Helg, *Our Rightful Share*, 157.

29. Pérez explains, "Educational patterns were at once cause and effect of the low occupational status of women" (*Cuba: Between Reform and Revolution*, 158).

30. De la Fuente, *Nation for All*, 138–141.

31. Cuba, *Censo de la República de Cuba, 1907*.

32. Helg, *Our Rightful Share*, 157.

33. Cuba, *Censo de la República de Cuba, 1907*.

34. Pérez, *Cuba: Between Reform and Revolution*, 179.

35. De la Fuente, *Nation for All*, 117.

36. De la Fuente, *Nation for All*, 46.

37. Aviva Chomsky, "Barbados or Canada?"; de la Fuente, *Nation for All*, 101.

38. De la Fuente, *Nation for All*, 122.

39. De la Fuente, *Nation for All*, 102.

40. De la Fuente, *Nation for All*, 102.

41. Pérez, *Cuba: Between Reform and Revolution*, 149–157.

42. Studies of Caribbean migrant workers in Cuba include Matthew Casey, *Empire's*

Guestworkers; Chomsky, "Barbados or Canada?"; Alejandro de la Fuente, "Two Dangers, One Solution"; Jana K. Lipman, *Guantánamo*; Kathleen Lopez, *Chinese Cubans*; Jorge L. Giovannetti-Torres, *Black British Migrants in Cuba*.

43. "El problema," *El Nuevo Criollo*, October 29, 1904.

44. US War Department, *Report on the Census 1899*, 361–362; Cuba, *Censo de la República de Cuba 1907*, 465–466. For an overview of race and literacy rates during the Republican Era, see de la Fuente, *A Nation for All*, 142.

45. De la Fuente notes that the number of Afro-Cuban teachers remained below 5 percent through the 1920s (*Nation for All*, 144).

46. Carmela López Garrido to Juan Gualberto Gómez, March 27, 1908, legajo 29, expediente 2163, Fondo Adquisiciones, Archivo Nacional de Cuba (ANC).

47. María Amparo Callara to Juan Gualberto Gómez, February 1912, legajo 13, expediente 666, Fondo Adquisiciones, ANC.

48. Callara to Gómez, ANC.

49. Thomas C. Holt, *Problem of Freedom*; Philip A. Howard, *Black Labor, White Sugar*; April J. Mayes, *Mulatto Republic*; Lara Putnam, *Radical Moves*.

50. Una cubana holguinera, "Una carta," *Previsión*, October 30, 1908. Rebecca Scott explains, "The newspaper *Previsión* appears to have circulated fairly widely, promoting demands for reform and a discourse of racial pride" (*Degrees of Freedom*, 232).

51. Una cubana holguinera, "Una carta."

52. Una cubana holguinera, "Una carta."

53. Studies that discuss the PIC press include Silvio Castro Fernández, *La masacre de los Independientes*, 43–59; Helg, *Our Rightful Share*, 146–156, and "Afro-Cuban Protest"; Portuondo Linares, *Los Independientes de Color*; R. Scott, *Degrees of Freedom*; Alexander Sotelo-Eastman, "Neglected Narratives of Cuba's Partido Independiente de Color." Also see Gloria Rolando's documentaries *1912: Voces para un silencio* and *Las raíces de mi corazón*.

54. Julia Argüelles de García, *Previsión*, 1910.

55. Carmen Piedra, "A los hombres de color," *Previsión*, March 5, 1910.

56. Piedra, "A los hombres de color."

57. Cited in Helg, *Our Rightful Share*, 158.

58. Cecilia Lara, "Carta," *Previsión*, February 20, 1910. Also cited in Helg, *Our Rightful Share*, 151.

59. Piedra, "A los hombres de color."

60. Piedra, "A los hombres de color."

61. Helg, *Our Rightful Share*, 53.

62. Helg, *Our Rightful Share*, 164.

63. Piedra, "A los hombres de color."

64. Eulalia Morales, "Señoritas, señoras y caballeros," *Previsión*, March 26, 1910.

65. Morales, "Señoritas, señoras y caballeros."

66. Morales, "Señoritas, señoras y caballeros." On Black Cuban women's use of writing as a political strategy, see Dawn Duke, *Literary Passion, Ideological Commitment*; Takkara Brunson, "'Writing' Black Cuban Womanhood." My analysis of the connections between writing, gender performance, and racial resistance also draws on the scholarship of African American women's writings. This scholarship includes Hazel Carby, *Recon-*

structing Womanhood; Ann duCille, "Occult of True Black Womanhood"; Michelle N. Garfield, "Literary Societies"; Anna Storm, "Quinine Pills and Race Progress"; Andreá N. Williams, "Recovering Black Women Writers in Periodical Archives."

67. Morales, "Señoritas, señoras y caballeros."

68. "De Santiago de Cuba," *Previsión*, February 15, 1910. The article summarizes activities of the Damas Protectoras del Partido.

69. Rosa Brioso, "Una carta," *Previsión*, February 15, 1910.

70. Brioso, "Una carta."

71. Brioso, "Una carta."

72. Rosa Brioso, "Iran los negros a Palacio," *Previsión*, February 20, 1910.

73. Brioso, "Iran los negros a Palacio."

74. Brioso, "Iran los negros a Palacio."

75. See Helg, *Our Rightful Share*, 189–191; Pappademos, *Black Political Activism*, 56; Rebecca J. Scott, *Degrees of Freedom*, 235–252.

76. Aline Helg documents the PIC's rise to political prominence in "Afro-Cuban Protest: The Partido Independiente de Color, 1908–1912" *Cuban Studies* 21 (1991): 101–121. Also see Helg, *Our Rightful Share*.

77. The 1912 PIC protest and violent government repression are detailed in Helg, *Our Rightful Share*, 193–226.

78. María de los Ángeles Meriño Fuentes makes a similar argument (*Una vuelta necesaria*, 113).

79. See Damaris A. Torres Elers, "Santiagueras en el alzamiento de 1912"; Guerra, *Myth of José Martí*; Meriño Fuentes, *Una vuelta necesaria*.

80. Such accounts may be found in María de los Reyes Castillo Bueno, *Reyita*.

81. Cited in Guerra, *Myth of José Martí*, 240.

82. Cited in Castro Fernández, *La masacre de los Independientes*, 98; and Meriño Fuentes, *Una vuelta necesaria*, 115–116.

83. The newspaper stated that Caballo possessed "bundles of clothing, various papers, a prayer that contained part of a 'credo calado,' and a bag of food" (Pedro Castro Monterrey, Sandra Estévez Rivero, and Olga Portuondo Zúñiga, *Por la identidad del negro cubano*, 191).

84. Meriño Fuentes, *Una vuelta necesaria*, 117.

85. "El despertar," *Diario de la Marina*, May 23, 1912.

86. Manuel Domingo Hernández and Julio Hernández to Juan Gualberto Gómez, May 25, 1912, legajo 4071, expediente 53, Fondo Adquisiciones, ANC.

87. Aline Helg, "Black Men, Racial Stereotyping"; Helg, *Our Rightful Share*, 193–226.

88. Helg, "Black Men, Racial Stereotyping."

89. Bronfman, *Measures of Equality*, 37–66; Helg, "Black Men, Racial Stereotyping," 193–226.

90. See Rafael Conte and José M. Campany's *Guerra de razas* for a contemporary account of the events that took place at La Maya.

91. Helg, *Our Rightful Share*, 228.

92. De la Fuente, *A Nation for All*, 78–81; Guridy, "Racial Knowledge in Cuba," 106–168.

93. De la Fuente, *A Nation for All*, 78.

94. De la Fuente, *A Nation for All*, 90.

95. Ana María Álvarez Martínez to Juan Gualberto Gómez, August 1915 legajo 10, expediente 292, Fondo Adquisiciones, ANC. For an examination of Afro-Cubans who attended historically Tuskegee and other Black schools in the United States, see Frank Guridy's *Forging Diaspora*.

96. Alvarez Martínez to Gómez, ANC.

97. Rita Baldoquín to Juan Gualberto Gómez, October 18, 1919, legajo 11, expediente 445, Fondo Adquisiciones, ANC. Baldoquín's letter is published in Horrego Estuch, *Juan Gualberto Gómez, un gran inconforme*.

98. Baldoquín to Gómez, ANC.

99. Baldoquín to Gómez, ANC.

100. Robert Whitney, *State and Revolution in Cuba*, 34.

101. Gabriela Oliva Viuda de Sausa to Juan Gualberto Gómez, legajo 2688, expediente 35, Fondo Adquisiciones, ANC.

102. Oliva to Gómez, ANC.

103. Pérez, *Cuba: Between Reform and Revolution*, 159.

104. Helg, *Our Rightful Share*, 92–97.

105. Castillo Bueno, *Reyita*, 41.

106. Pérez, *Cuba: Between Reform and Revolution*, 171; Pérez, *Cuba under the Platt Amendment*, 224.

107. Louis Pérez defines *colecturías* as "collectorships that conferred on each owner the privilege of selling sixteen tickets for each of the three monthly drawings. Each ticket was purchased at discounted costs from the lottery administration and resold to the public at inflated prices" (*Cuba: Between Reform and Revolution*, 165).

108. Maria Smith to Juan Gualberto Gómez, August 8, 1921, legajo 46, expediente 3611, Fondo Adquisiciones, ANC.

109. Ana Sánchez Viuda de Martínez to Juan Gualberto Gómez, June 19, 1921 legajo 46, expediente 3599, Fondo Adquisiciones, ANC.

110. Inocencia Silveira to Juan Gualberto Gómez, January 7, 1924, legajo 44, expediente 3476, Fondo Adquisiciones, ANC.

111. Lillian Guerra discusses the 1906 and 1917 revolts in *Myth of José Martí*, 170–191, 234–248.

112. Inocencia Silveira to Juan Gualberto Gómez, January 7, 1924, legajo 44, expediente 3476, Fondo Adquisiciones, ANC.

113. Inocencia Silveira to Juan Gualberto Gómez, April 24, 1924 legajo 46, expediente 3599, Fondo Adquisiciones, ANC.

114. Steven Hewitt, "Veterans' Movements and the Early Republican State"; Jorge Ibarra, *Prologue to Revolution*, 66; Pérez, *Cuba under the Platt Amendment*, 214–256; Whitney, *State and Revolution in Cuba*.

115. Pedro Padrón, *La mujer trabajadora*.

Chapter 3. Leadership of Recognized Character: Comportment and the Politics of Elite Black Social Life

1. Marial Iglesias Utset, *Cultural History of Cuba*, 3.

2. This cultural process is the subject of Marial Iglesias Utset's *Cultural History of Cuba*.

3. The US administration in Cuba further developed the city's water system, electric streetlights, telephones, natural gas, and garbage collection. It paved roadways and replaced the horse-drawn tram in the budding neighborhood of Vedado with the electric streetcar (Iglesias Utset, *Cultural History of Cuba*, 18–25; Antoni Kapcia, *Havana*; Louis A. Pérez, *Cuba under the Platt Amendment* and *Cuba and the United States*).

4. Louis A. Pérez, *On Becoming Cuban*, 96–164.

5. *La Antorcha* article cited in "Dos cartas decorosas," *El Nuevo Criollo*, January 21, 1905; Leopoldo Horrego Estuch, *Juan Gualberto Gómez*, 153. Also see Alejandro de la Fuente, *Nation for All*, 62; Kim Welch, "Our Hunger Is Our Song," 184.

6. Jose Manuel Poveda, "La razón de una protesta," *Minerva*, March 1912, 7–8; "¿Existe en Cuba la clasificación oficial de razas?" *Minerva*, January 15, 1911, 1.

7. See de la Fuente, *Nation for All*, 78; Frank Guridy, "War on the Negro," 49–73.

8. Alejandra Bronfman, *Measures of Equality*, 17–66; Aline Helg, "Black Men, Racial Stereotyping."

9. Marial Iglesias Utset, *Cultural History of Cuba*.

10. On affect and photography, see Pierre Bourdieu, *Outline of a Theory of Practice*; Linda Martín Alcoff, *Visible Identities*; Mimi Sheller, *Citizenship from Below*; Iris Marion Young, "Throwing Like a Girl."

11. De la Fuente, *A Nation for All*; Frank Guridy, *Forging Diaspora*; Melina Pappademos, *Black Political Activism*.

12. Kirwin R. Shaffer, "Freedom Teaching"; K. Lynn Stoner, *From the House to the Streets* and "Militant Heroines."

13. Henry Louis Gates Jr., "Trope of a New Negro"; David Levering Lewis and Deborah Willis, *Small Nation of People*; Shawn Michelle Smith, *Photography on the Color Line*; Carla Williams and Deborah Willis, *Black Female Body*; Deborah Willis, *Picturing Us*; Deborah Willis and Barbara Krauthamer, *Envisioning Emancipation*.

14. Tina Campt, *Image Matters* and *Listening to Images*; Tao Leigh Goffe, "Albums of Inclusion"; Dixa Ramírez, "Against Type"; Leigh Raiford, "Marcus Garvey in Stereograph"; Lou Smith and Karina Smith, "The Sound of Unknowing"; Julia Kim Wertz, "Fashioning Modernity."

15. Guridy, *Forging Diaspora*; Lara Putnam, *Radical Moves*, 123–152.

16. Deborah Poole, *Vision, Race, and Modernity*, 7–8.

17. Beatriz González-Stephan, "Dark Side of Photography," 29.

18. See Robert Levine, *Images of History*; Jorge Duany, "Portraying the Other"; Krista Thompson, *Eye for the Tropics* and "Evidence of Things Not Photographed"; Esther Gabara, *Errant Modernism*; Marcus Wood, *Black Milk*, especially the chapter "Photography and Slavery in America and Brazil."

19. The images also were published in Serra y Montalvo's 1907 essay collection, *Para blancos y negros*, the fourth volume in his series of political essays.

20. "Consuelo Serra y Heredía," *El Nuevo Criollo*, June 18, 1905, emphasis mine.

21. On affect and photography, see Ariella Azoulay, *Civil Contract of Photography*; Sarah Bassnett, "Archive and Affect in Contemporary Photography"; Elizabeth Edwards, "Anthropology and Photography"; Katja Haustein, *Regarding Lost Time*; Benjamin Smith and Richard Vokes, "Haunting Images."

22. "Consuelo Serra y Heredia."

23. *El Nuevo Criollo*, *Minerva: Revista Universal Ilustrada*, and *Labor Nueva* were published in Havana. *Ecos Juveniles* was published in Santa Clara.

24. Serra published photographic portraits of the families of the *mulato* Senator Martín Morúa Delgado and the African American activist-intellectual Booker T. Washington in his 1907 essay collection, *Para blancos y negros*. These were not published in his newspapers and likely did not circulate as widely. I have found few other images of Black nuclear families from this period.

25. On the use of word and image in crafting a Black political identity, see Anne Elizabeth Carroll, *Word, Image, Text, and the New Negro*.

26. Malcolm Barnard discusses dream objects in *Fashion as Communication*, 6.

27. Caroline Kitch, *Girl on the Magazine Cover*, 3.

28. Studies of the eugenics movement in Latin America include Sarah Arvey, "Sex and the Ordinary Cuban"; Donna J. Guy, "The Pan American Child Congresses"; Aline Helg, "Race in Argentina and Cuba"; Nancy Stepan, *"Hour of Eugenics."*

29. Bronfman, *Measures of Equality*, 117–124.

30. Henri Dumont, "Antropología y patología comparadas de los negros esclavos," translated by Israel Castellanos, edited by Fernando Ortiz, *Revista Bimestre Cubana* 10–11 (1915–1916); Gabino La Rosa Corzo, "Henri Dumont y la imagen antropológica," 175–182.

31. Jasmine Nichole Cobb, *Picture Freedom*, 219.

32. Theories of images of Black Cuban women are discussed in Onelia Chaveco Chaveco, "Propuesta de una mirada incluyente y no sexista"; María Ileana Faguaga Iglesias, "En torno a los estereotipos respecto a la afrocubana"; Inés María Martiatu Terry, "El negrito y la mulata en el vórtice de la nacionalidad"; Aymée Rivera Pérez, "El imaginario femenino negro en Cuba." Each of these essays appears in the anthology *Afrocubanas*, edited by Daisy Rubiera Castillo and Inés María Martiatu Terry. Also see Alison Fraunhar, *Mulata Nation*; Jill Lane, "Smoking Habaneras."

33. Elaine Scarry, *On Beauty and Being Just*, 4.

34. "Srta. Antonia Hernandez," *Labor Nueva*, May 14, 1916, 11.

35. Kitch, *Girl on the Magazine Cover*, 3; Megan E. Williams, "Crisis Cover Girl."

36. Here I heed Tina Campt's call to "theorize how these photographs function as images and as practices of social and cultural enunciation that exceeded their biographical details" (*Image Matters*, 196).

37. "La vida social en todas sus manifestaciones," *Previsión*, March 30, 1910.

38. "Revista de Modas," *La Igualdad*, February 18, 1893.

39. María Antoineta, "Correo de Modas," *Minerva*, September 30, 1910, 10.

40. The visual culture theorist Roland Barthes contends that fashion constitutes part of a normative system of self-representation regulated and recognized by society (*Language of Fashion*, 7).

41. The interpretation of Hernandez's dress is based on my reading of several costume history books: Nancy Bradfield, *Costume in Detail*; Christopher Breward, *Fashion*; James Laver, *Costume and Fashion*; John Peacock, *Fashion since 1900*.

42. Barnard, *Fashion as Communication*, 5.

43. Pamela Gerrish Nunn, "Fine Arts and the Fan." Also see Louis A. Pérez, *Intimations of Modernity*.

44. Back cover, *Minerva*, April 1914. Such advertisements frequently promoted the

services of agents and establishments that sold the products. The April 1915 issue of *Minerva* features an advertisement for the hair products of the African American businesswoman Madame C. J. Walker.

45. *Minerva*, July 1912, 20.

46. Noliwe M. Rooks, *Hair Raising*, 29; Susannah Walker, *Style and Status*, 7–8; Shane White and Graham White, *Stylin'*, 189.

47. López Silvero, "Boda suntuosa," *Minerva*, April 1915, 8–9.

48. López Silvero, "Boda suntuosa."

49. López Silvero, "Boda suntuosa."

50. López Silvero, "Boda suntuosa."

51. López Silvero, "Boda suntuosa."

52. López Silvero, "Boda suntuosa."

53. De la Fuente, *Nation for All*, 165.

54. Lawrence J. Gutman, "Imagining Athens, Remaking Afrocubanidad," 23.

55. Fondo Provincial, leg. 2659, no. 2, Archivo Histórico Provincial de Santiago de Cuba.

56. De la Fuente, *Nation for All*, 170; Frank Guridy, "Racial Knowledge in Cuba," 86; Aline Helg, *Our Rightful Share*, 244.

57. Though they were estimated at 27.7 percent of the island's inhabitants in 1931, non-white Cubans comprised 45.9 percent of the eastern region's urban population and 53.3 percent of the population in Santiago de Cuba (Cuba, *Memorias inéditas del censo de 1931*, 306–315; Guridy, "Racial Knowledge in Cuba," 50–51).

58. Yanira Mesa Jiménez, "Las sociedades 'La Bella Union' y 'El Gran Maceo.'"

59. Eladio Garzón Carrión, "La invasión de Maceo: Una problema social," *Oriente*, May 30, 1923.

60. Garzón Carrión, "La invasión de Maceo."

61. Mesa Jiménez, "Las sociedades 'La Bella Union' y 'El Gran Maceo,'" 5.

62. Mesa Jiménez, "Las sociedades 'La Bella Union' y 'El Gran Maceo,'" 5.

63. Cited in Mesa Jiménez, "Las sociedades 'La Bella Union' y 'El Gran Maceo,'" 5.

64. Pedro Pérez Sarduy, "The Maids," 251. Also see Pedro Pérez Sarduy, *Las criadas de la Habana*.

65. Pérez Sarduy, "The Maids," 253.

66. Pérez Sarduy, "The Maids," 252.

67. Cited in Guridy's "Racial Knowledge in Cuba," 99–101.

68. Miguel Ángel Céspedes, "Origen, tendencias y finalidad del Club Atenas," *Atenas: Revista Mensual Ilustrada de Afirmación Cubana, Órgano Oficial del Club Atenas* 1, no. 1 (December 1920): 8, cited in Melina Pappademos, "Alchemist of a Race," 105–106.

69. Juan Gualberto Gómez, "Minerva," *Minerva*, September 15, 1910, 2–3.

70. Gómez, "Minerva," 2–3.

71. Julián González, "El futuro de la mujer intellectual," *Labor Nueva*, June 18, 1916, 8.

72. María Risquet de Márquez, "Impresiones y comentarios," *Minerva*, November 1, 1910.

73. Cited in the records of the Centro Cultural Martín Morúa Delgado, Fondo Provincial, legajo 2458, no. 8, Archivo Histórico Provincial de Santiago de Cuba.

74. Asociación Patriótica de Damas Amiradoras de Moncada, legajo 2624, expediente 7, Registro de Asociaciones, ANC.

Chapter 4. Feminism and the Transformation
of Black Women's Social Thought

1. Manuel Ramírez Chicharro, "El activismo social y político de las mujeres durante la República de Cuba," 144–147; K. Lynn Stoner, *From the House to the Streets*, 54–57. Stoner cites *Aspiraciones* as the earliest feminist magazine. Although not an explicitly feminist magazine, the Trinidad women's publication *La Mariposa* discussed feminism during the early 1900s.

2. Discussions of Cuban women's charity organizations include Manuel Ramírez Chicharro, "El activismo social y político de las mujeres durante la República de Cuba" and *Más allá del sufragismo*, 337–354; Stoner, *From the House to the Streets*, 54–77.

3. Cuban women's literary activism is documented in the series by Úrsula Coimbra Valverde, "La mujer en la poesía cubana, I," in *El Nuevo Criollo* (October 15, 1904, November 12 and 19, 1904). Catherine Davies characterizes women's writings of 1900–1935 as "predominately oppositional" (*A Place in the Sun?*, 35).

4. Salie Derome, "Sr. Director de El Nuevo Criollo," *El Nuevo Criollo*, December 10, 1904.

5. Melina Pappademos, *Black Political Activism*, 42.

6. Takkara Brunson, "'Writing' Black Womanhood."

7. Coimbra de Valverde, "La mujer en la poesía cubana, I"; "¡Salve *Minerva*!," *Minerva*, October 15, 1911, 15; "Párrafos del alma," *Minerva*, March 15, 1912, 12; "Nostalgia," *Minerva*, July 30, 1912, 14.

8. María G. Sánchez, "Ante 'Labor Nueva,'" *Labor Nueva*, August 20, 1915, 6.

9. Studies of women's public health activism include Nicole C. Bourbonnais, *Birth Control in the Decolonizing Caribbean*; Juanita de Barros, *Reproducing the British Caribbean*; Donna J. Guy, *The Troubled Meeting of Sex, Gender*; Okezi Otovo, *Progressive Mothers, Better Babies*; Katherine Paugh, *The Politics of Reproduction*.

10. For studies of Black women's evolving perspectives on racial and gender issues during the period, see Dawn Duke, *Literary Passion, Ideological Commitment*; Karen Morrison, "Afro-Latin American Women Writers"; Valentina Salinas Carvacho, "El pensamiento social de las mujeres negras."

11. Alejandro de la Fuente, *A Nation for All*, 177.

12. Marc McLeod, "We Cubans Are Obligated Like Cats"; Daniel Rodriguez, "'To Fight These Powerful Trusts'"; Kelly Urban, "The 'Black Plague' in a Racial Democracy."

13. Robin Moore, *Nationalizing Blackness*.

14. De la Fuente, *A Nation for All*, 178.

15. See Richard Graham, *Idea of Race in Latin America*; Nancy Stepan, *"Hour of Eugenics."*

16. On the subject of Blackness and the construction of Cuba's national identity, see Melissa Blanco Borelli, *She Is Cuba*; Alison Fraunhar, *Mulata Nation*; Kutzinski, *Sugar Secrets*; Moore, *Nationalizing Blackness*.

17. *Carteles* covers of the 1920s through the 1950s featured such images. These and other covers are discussed in Fraunhar, *Mulata Nation*, 106–149.

18. Robert Whitney, *State and Revolution in Cuba*.

19. Frank Guridy, "War on the Negro," 49–73.

20. Stoner, *From the House to the Streets*, 34–35. Also see Julio César González Pagés, *En busca de un espacio*; Liset López Francisco, "El movimiento feminista cubano."

21. K. Lynn Stoner, "On Men Reforming the Rights of Men" and *From the House to the Streets*.

22. Asunción Lavrin, *Women, Feminism, and Social Change*, 4.

23. Notable exceptions include April Mayes, "Why Dominican Feminism Moved to the Right"; Eileen J. Suárez Findlay, *Imposing Decency*.

24. Jill Lane, *Blackface Cuba*, 208–223; Carmen Victoria Montejo Arrechea, "*Minerva*: A Magazine for Women (and Men) of Color," 33–48.

25. La redacción, "En marcha," *Minerva*, September 15, 1910, 1–2.

26. On the history of women who wrote for both phases of *Minerva*, see María del Carmen Barcia Zequeira, "Mujeres en torno a *Minerva*," 77–92; Brunson, "'Writing' Black Womanhood," 480–500; Duke, *Literary Passion, Ideological Commitment*, 99–100; Montejo Arrechea, "*Minerva*: A Magazine for Women (and Men) of Color," 33–48.

27. Consuelo David Calvet, "¡Adelante Minerva!" *Minerva*, March 15, 1911, 8.

28. María del Carmen Barcia Zequeira, *Capas populares*, 139.

29. La redacción, "En marcha."

30. Sabina Fernández, "Club Feminista 'Minerva,'" *Minerva*, January 15, 1911.

31. Louis A. Pérez, *On Becoming Cuban*, 166–98; Guridy, *Forging Diaspora*, 151–194.

32. La Infanta Eulalia, "El feminismo," *Minerva*, February 1, 1912, 12–13.

33. Jasón Miseret, "La razón de feminismo," *Minerva*, October 1, 1913. Also see Victor Hugo's "El derecho de la mujer," *Minerva*, January 15, 1914.

34. Carmelina Serracent, "La influencia de la mujer en el porvenir de la sociedad," *Minerva*, November 1, 1910.

35. On the history of the Oblate Sisters of Providence, see Diane Batts Morrow, *Persons of Color and Religious at the Same Time*.

36. Lucrecia Loret de Mola, "La ilustración," *Minerva*, April 15, 1912.

37. De la Fuente, *A Nation for All*, 155.

38. Enid Lynette Logan, "The 1899 Cuban Marriage Law Controversy."

39. Karen Y. Morrison, "Afro-Latin American Women Writers," 88–117, and *Cuba's Racial Crucible*, 180.

40. Carmelina Serracent, "El divorcio," *Minerva*, March 30, 1911, 7.

41. Serracent, "El divorcio."

42. Anonymous, "¡Divorciémonos!" *Minerva*, April 15, 1914, 7–8.

43. De la Fuente, *A Nation for All*, 166–167.

44. De la Fuente, *A Nation for All*, 167–168; Pappademos, *Black Political Activism*, 161–165.

45. Morrison, *Cuba's Racial Crucible*, 181.

46. Both studies are cited in de la Fuente, *A Nation for All*, 45–46.

47. Tristán, "Tres puntos," *La Prensa*, August 16, 1915.

48. Caridad Chacón de Guillén, "Mi opinión," *La Prensa*, September 30, 1915.

49. Chacón de Guillén, "Mi opinión."

50. Indiana, "Reflecciones femeninas," *La Prensa*, August 31, 1915.

51. Indiana to Tristán, "Palpitaciones de la raza de color," *La Prensa*, September 11, 1915.

52. N. Lesnar, "Palabras de mujer," *La Prensa*, August 10, 1915.

53. Ana Hidalgo Vidal, "¿Es mejor no me aneallo?" *La Prensa*, November 10, 1915.

54. María G. Sánchez, "Accionemos," *Labor Nueva*, September 10, 1916, 10.

55. In De la Fuente, *A Nation for All*, 160.

56. De la Fuente, *A Nation for All*, 106.

57. De la Fuente, *A Nation for All*, 122–123.

58. Inocencia Silveira, "Lo que somos," *Diario de la Marina*, February 10, 1929.

59. Consuelo Serra de G. Veranes, "Nuestro valores étnicos," *Diario de la Marina*, January 27, 1929.

60. Gustavo Urrutia, "Consuelo Serra," *Diario de la Marina*, December 1, 1929.

61. "Takes Course While on 'Little Vacation': Dr. Consuelo Serra de G. de Veranes of Cuba is Founder of School and Professor," *New York Amsterdam News*, July 25, 1936.

62. "Hermanas Oblatas," *Adelante* 1936.

63. Consuelo Serra, interview by Nicolás Guillén, "Señorita Consuelo Serra," *Diario de la Marina*, December 1, 1929, 5.

64. Consuelo Serra, "Intimidades," *Diario de la Marina*, June 1, 1930.

65. Calixta María Hernández de Cervantes, "Ana Echegoyen de Cañizares," *Adelante*, February 1938, 13.

66. Ana Echegoyen de Cañizares, "Para la mujer: Del cultivo de las cualidades específicas de la mujer, dependerá en gran parte, el futuro de la humanidad," *Adelante*, September 1935, 16–18.

67. Their writings include Ana Echegoyen de Cañizares's essays "Para la mujer," *Adelante*, September 1935 and October 1935, and "Los intereses fundamentals del matrimonio," *Adelante*, November 1935; and Consuelo Serra de G. Veranes's essays "Valor de la espiritualidad en la educación," *Adelante*, September 1935, and "La educación y los problemas sociales," *Adelante*, October 1935.

68. Asociación Cultural Femenina, legajo 111, nos. 23246–23248, Fondo Asociaciones, ANC.

69. Asociación Cultural Femenina, ANC.

70. Guridy, *Forging Diaspora*, 151–194; Devyn Spence Benson, *Antiracism in Cuba*, 153.

71. "Se inaugura hoy el local de la ass. Cultural femenina." *Noticias de Hoy*, May 24, 1938; "Ass. Cultural Femenina," *Noticias de Hoy*, May 30, 1938.

72. See Guridy, *Forging Diaspora*, 151–194.

73. Unión Nacional de Mujeres, legajo 16, expediente 159, Fondo Donativos y Remisiones, ANC.

74. Gerardo del Valle, "La negra cubana," *Diario de la Marina*, November 2, 1930.

75. Del Valle, "La negra cubana."

76. Del Valle, "La negra cubana."

77. Del Valle, "La negra cubana."

78. Catalina Pozo Gato, "La negra cubana y la cultura: Para el escritor Gerardo del Valle, en indagación," *Diario de la Marina*, November 30, 1930.

79. Pozo Gato, "La negra cubana y la cultura."

80. Pozo Gato, "La negra cubana y la cultura."

81. Pozo Gato, "La negra cubana y la cultura."

82. Pozo Gato, "La negra cubana y la cultura."

83. Cloris Tejo, "En torno a la Convención de Sociedades Negras." *Adelante*, June 1938, 5. Tejo similarly speaks to the issues confronted by poor Black Cuban women, in "Legislación social," *Adelante*, October 1938, 9–20.

84. Tejo, "En torno a la Convención de Sociedades Negras."

85. Tejo, "En torno a la Convención de Sociedades Negras."

86. Tejo, "En torno a la Convención de Sociedades Negras."

87. Maria Teresa Ramirez, "Mujeres de ayer y de hoy," *Boletín Oficial del Club Atenas*, September 1930, 26–27.

88. Calixta María Hernández de Cervantes, "Tópicos femeninos," *Diario de la Marina*, July 28, 1929.

89. Hernández, "Tópicos femeninos." Cloris Tejo expressed a similar position ("Orientación femenina," *Adelante*, May 1937).

90. Tete Ramírez Medina, "La marcha de una raza," *El Mundo*, August 9, 1931.

91. Gilberto Ante Jiménez, "Feminismo y endocrinología," *Atenas*, August–September 1931. A writer in the mid-1950s, Angel C. Arce, discusses sexuality in his monthly magazine *Sexología: Mensuario Revista Paramédica* and "El problema sexual y social de Cuba: El hombre ignorante sexual," *Alerta*, February 9, 1956.

92. Echegoyen de Canizares, "Para la mujer," *Adelante*, November 1935.

93. Sarah R. Arvey, "Sex and the Ordinary Cuban," 98.

94. Calixta María Hernández de Cervantes, "Feminismo," *Adelante*, November 1935.

95. Calixta María Hernández de Cervantes, "Feminismo: La mujer y la política," *Adelante*, September 1935.

96. Hernández de Cervantes, "Feminismo: La mujer y la política."

97. Hernández de Cervantes, "Feminismo: La mujer y la política."

98. Manuel Machado, "El voto femenino," *Adelante*, July 1935.

99. Gustavo Urrutia, "Mujeres nuevas," *Diario de la Marina*, February 15, 1933.

100. In Urrutia, "Mujeres nuevas."

101. Catalina Pozo Gato, "El PUN y la mujer negra," *Noticias de Hoy*, August 3, 1939.

102. Pozo Gato, "El PUN y la mujer negra."

Chapter 5. Racial Politics in the National Women's Movement

1. The records of the Comité de Sufragio Femenino, Partido Popular Feminista, and Partido Nacional Feminista can be found in no. 6, caja box 622, Fondo Donativos y Remisiones, ANC; legajo 400, expediente 11886, Fondo Registro de Asociaciones, ANC.

2. Pilar Morlón de Menéndez, "El Primer Congreso Nacional de Mujeres," Discurso leído en la sesión de aperture el 1 de abril de 1923, *Revista Bimestre Cubana* 18, no. 2 (1923), 123.

3. "Las despaliladoras en el Congreso de Mujeres," *Diario de la Marina*, April 3, 1925, 4.

4. Federación Nacional de Asociaciones Femeninas, "Reglamento del Segundo Congreso Nacional de Mujeres," in *Memoria del Segundo Congreso Nacional de Mujeres*, Havana, 1925, 15.

5. Pedro Luis Padrón, *La mujer trabajadora*, 22–23.

6. Padrón, *La mujer trabajadora*, 22–23.

7. Inocencia Valdés, "El trabajo femenino en la industria tabacalera," in *Memoria del Segundo Congreso Nacional de Mujeres*, 194–196.

8. Valdés, "El trabajo femenino en la industria tabacalera."

9. Federación Nacional de Asociaciones Femeninas, "Conclusiones," in *Memoria del Segundo Congreso Nacional de Mujeres*, 646–648.

10. María Julia de Lara, "Lucha contra las enfermedades," 373.

11. "Las sesiones del Congreso de Mujeres," *El Mundo*, April 19, 1925, 12.

12. K. Lynn Stoner, *From the House to the Streets*, 69. This debate is recounted in "Segundo Congreso Nacional," *Diario de la Marina*, April 1, 1925, 8; "Las sesiones del Congreso de Mujeres," *El Mundo*, April 19, 1925, 12.

13. In Julio César González Pagés, *En busca de un espacio*, 86.

14. Led by the Black female labor leaders Eudosia Lara and Inocencia Valdés, women's tobacco stemmers unions helped to mobilize thousands of Black women who demanded higher wages, maternity regulations, and improved working conditions (González Pagés, *En busca de un espacio*, 86).

15. I thank Ariel Mae Lambe for introducing me to the activism of Rosa Pastora Leclerc. For more information on Leclerc's political activism, see Niall Binns, "La matanza de los inocentes"; Ariel Mae Lambe, *No Barrier Can Contain It*, 124–126, 212.

16. Ofelia Domínguez Navarro, interview, n.d., 3/54.1/1–8, Fondo General, Archivo del Instituto de Historia, Havana (AIH).

17. Legajo 298, expediente 8622, Fondo Registro de Asociaciones, ANC.

18. Stoner, *From the House to the Streets*, 116.

19. Ofelia Domínguez Navarro, "Rosa Pastora Leclerc en el campo político," n.d., Fondo General, AIH.

20. Stoner, *From the House to the Streets*, 75; see 116–126 for an overview of women's activism in the anti-Machado movement.

21. Stoner, *From the House to the Streets*, 123.

22. Stoner, *From the House to the Streets*, 123–126; Luis E. Aguilar, *Cuba 1933*.

23. Stoner, *From the House to the Streets*, 112.

24. Amauri Gutiérrez Coto, "Izquierda cubana y republicanismo español," 85.

25. Frank Guridy, "War on the Negro," 68.

26. Raúl Suárez Mendoza, "A la mujer cubana," *Ahora*, October 20, 1933 (quote); Raúl Suárez Mendoza, "La mujer piñarena y sus clubs femeninos," *Ahora*, October 21, 1933.

27. Stoner, *From the House to the Streets*, 162.

28. Alejandro de la Fuente, *A Nation for All*, 210–258.

29. Maria Nuñez, "Postura de la mujer cubana frente al Congreso Femenino que se celebrará en la Habana," *Diario de Cuba*, March 12, 1939.

30. Catalina Causse Viuda de Mercer, "Congreso Femenino," *Diario de Cuba*, March 29, 1939.

31. María Patrocinado Garbey Aguila's leadership is documented in the records of the Centro Cultural Martín Morúa Delgado, legajo 2455, expediente 10, Registro de Asociaciones, Archivo Histórico Provincial de Santiago de Cuba.

32. María Patrocinado Garbey Águila, "Una opinión sobre el Congreso Femenino," *Diario de Cuba*, March 12, 1939.

33. Garbey Águila, "Una opinión sobre el Congreso Femenino."

34. "Asamblea femenino auspiciada por la F. de Sociedades Negras," *Noticias de Hoy*, March 11, 1939.

35. Garbey Águila, "Una opinión sobre el Congreso Femenino."

36. Garbey Águila, "Una opinión sobre el Congreso Femenino."

37. "Gran actividad de la mujer oriental para el Congreso," *Noticias de Hoy*, April 7, 1939.

38. "La mujer en general y la mujer negra en particular," *Noticias de Hoy*, February 18, 1939.

39. "La mujer en general y la mujer negra en particular."

40. "La mujer en general y la mujer negra en particular."

41. "La mujer en general y la mujer negra en particular."

42. Pastora Causede de Atiés, "Congreso Femenino," *Oriente*, April 5, 1939. She was responding to assertions two months earlier in "La mujer en general y la negra en particular."

43. Causede de Atiés, "Congreso Femenino."

44. Causede de Atiés, "Congreso Femenino."

45. Causede de Atiés, "Congreso Femenino."

46. "Brillante inauguración del congreso femenino," *Noticias de Hoy*, April 20, 1939.

47. "Brillante inauguración del congreso femenino."

48. In "Renuncia como delegada la sra. Berta Arocena," *Noticias de Hoy*, April 20, 1939, 10.

49. Berta Arocena, "Mi renuncia," *Noticias de Hoy*, April 21, 1939, 10.

50. In "Labora el Congreso Femenino," *Noticias de Hoy*, April 20, 1939, 1, 12.

51. María Dámasa Jova Baró, "Ponencia presentada en el III Congreso Nacional de Mujeres," Havana, 1939, cited in Esperanza Méndez Oliva, *El estirpe de Mariana en la Villas*.

52. Dámasa Jova, cited in Méndez Oliva, *El estirpe de Mariana*.

53. Dámasa Jova, cited in Méndez Oliva, *El estirpe de Mariana*.

54. Dámasa Jova, cited in Méndez Oliva, *El estirpe de Mariana*.

55. Dámasa Jova, cited in Méndez Oliva, *El estirpe de Mariana*.

56. The historian Esperanza Méndez Oliva contends that Dámasa Jova's groundbreaking address demanded respect for the intellectual perspectives of Black women, and it challenged white women to act on any cause affecting Cuban women regardless of their race and color (*El estirpe de Mariana en la Villas*).

57. "Conclusiones" presented at the end of the conference references a speech given by Serafina Causse (10.6/76, Fondo General, AIH).

58. "Demanda el Congreso Femenino una campaña activa contra la corrupción de menores," *Noticias de Hoy*, April 22, 1939, 1, 20.

59. "Conclusiones," AIH.

60. "Conclusiones," AIH.

61. "Conclusiones," AIH.

62. "Efectua un magnífico acto el C. contra la discriminación," *Noticias de Hoy*, March 19, 1939.

63. This exchange between Mariblanca Sabás Alomá and Angel César Pinto Albiol is

documented in Mariblanca Sabas Alomá, "Negras en el congreso de mujeres," in *Negras en el congreso de mujeres*, ed. Pinto Albiol and Angel César (Havana, 1939), which can be found in reel 2 of Lynn Stoner, *The Women's Movement in Cuba, 1898–1958: The Stoner Collection on Cuban Feminism*.

64. Sabas Alomá, "Negras en el congreso de mujeres." For a brief biography on César Pinto Albiol, see Devyn Spence Benson, *Antiracism in Cuba*, 89.

65. Sabas Alomá, "Negras en el congreso de mujeres."

66. Inocencia Valdés, interview, "La entrevista de hoy: Inocencia Valdés," *Noticias de Hoy*, July 7, 1938.

67. Emma Pérez, "Mi verdad y la vuestra: Mujeres y elecciones," *Noticias de Hoy*, November 15, 1939.

68. Emma Pérez, "Mi verdad y la vuestra."

69. Cited in Pérez, "Mi verdad y la vuestra."

70. Emma Pérez, "Mi verdad y la vuestra: Única mujer constituyente," *Noticias de Hoy*, November 19, 1939.

71. "Gran éxito obtiene el acto organizado por el C. Femenino," *Noticias de Hoy*, December 15, 1939.

Chapter 6. The Limits of Democratic Citizenship in the New Constitutional Era

1. Thomas M. Leonard and John F. Bratzel, *Latin America during World War II*.

2. Rawn James Jr., *The Double V*; Cheryl Mullenbach, *Double Victory*.

3. Cited in "Intensifican las Sociedades Negras de Las Villas sus labores contra el Nazi-Fascismo," *Noticias de Hoy*, January 28, 1943, 1, 8.

4. Cited in Sánchez Mastrapa, "Informe ante la Comisión de los Derechos de la Mujer," in "El II Congreso Internacional de Mujeres" (1949), 24.9/92, Archivo del Instituto de Historia.

5. Studies of the 1940 Constitution include Graciela Cruz-Taura, "Women's Rights and the Cuban Constitution of 1940"; Julio César Guanche, "La Constitución de 1940: Una reinterpretación"; Ana Suárez Díaz, *Retrospección crítica de la asamblea constituyente de 1940*.

6. Manuel Ramírez Chicharro, "Beyond Suffrage."

7. Johanna I. Moya Fábregas, "The Cuban Woman's Revolutionary Experience," 62. Also see Julio César González Pagés, *En busca de un espacio*; Stoner, *From the House to the Streets*; Carrie Hamilton, *Sexual Revolutions in Cuba*, 23–50.

8. On the career and legacies of Fernando Ortiz, see Mauricio A. Font and Alfonso W. Quiroz, *Cuban Counterpoints*.

9. During her trips to New York City, Echegoyen attended the events of the Club Cubano Interamericano, an Afro-Caribbean social organization. Nancy Raquel Mirabal examines the club in *Suspect Freedoms* (193–226).

10. "Ojos y olbos," *Amanecer*, January 1953.

11. "Ojos y olbos," emphasis mine.

12. *Memoria de los trabajos realizados por la Quinta Convención Provincial de So-*

ciedades de Camagüey en la Sociedad, 1947, Registro de Sociedades, Archivo Histórico Provincial de Camagüey.

13. Juana Oliva Bulnes, "En torno al momento política," *Nuevos Rumbos*, December 1946.

14. A.M.Z., "Dos magníficos actos de la 'Asociación Cultural Femenina,'" *Nuevos Rumbos*, September-October 1946, 11.

15. "Sociales. Festividad de la Cultura Femenina," *El Mundo*, February 8, 1948.

16. "Ponche de inauguración del 'Thesalia Club,'" *Nuevos Rumbos*, July 1946, 15.

17. Gobierno Provincial, legajo 2623, no. 13, Archivo Histórico Provincial de Santiago de Cuba.

18. Gobierno Provincial, legajo 2463, no. 1, Archivo Histórico Provincial de Santiago de Cuba.

19. Gobierno Provincial, leg. 2460, no. 4, Archivo Histórico Provincial de Santiago de Cuba.

20. On the African American organization, see Joyce Ann Hanson, *Mary McLeod Bethune and Black Women's Political Activism*; Rebecca Tuuri, *Strategic Sisterhood*.

21. Frank Guridy examines Black Cuban and African American relations during the 1930s in *Forging Diaspora*, 152–194.

22. Sue Bailey Thurman, "The Seminar in Cuba," *Aframerican Women's Journal* (Summer–Fall 1940): 4.

23. Hanson, *Mary McLeod Bethune and Black Women's Political Activism*.

24. Cited in Thurman, "Seminar in Cuba," 4.

25. Cited in Thurman, "Seminar in Cuba," 4.

26. Ana Echegoyen de Cañizares, "Cuban Social Life and the Negro Woman," *Aframerican Woman's Journal*, Summer/Fall 1940, 9–11.

27. Echegoyen de Cañizares, "Cuban Social Life and the Negro Woman."

28. Echegoyen de Cañizares, "Cuban Social Life and the Negro Woman." On discourses of racial intermixing in Cuba, see Gema R. Guevara, "Inexacting Whiteness"; Karen Y. Morrison, "'Whitening' Revisited."

29. Echegoyen de Cañizares, "Cuban Social Life and the Negro Woman." In the memoir *Reyita*, María de los Reyes Castillo Bueno cites an example of the dynamics between Black women and white men that individuals like Echegoyen may have critiqued, in particular, cases in which white men chose not to marry the Black women with whom they had children. Castillo Bueno reveals that she decided to have children with a white man in order to *adelentarse la raza* (advance the race). Her daughter Daisy Rubiera Castillo, who cowrote the memoir with her mother, later discovered that her father had never legally married her mother.

30. Echegoyen de Cañizares, "Cuban Social Life and the Negro Woman."

31. Echegoyen de Cañizares, "Cuban Social Life and the Negro Woman." Echegoyen's discussion of Cuban racial formations resembled analyses by the intellectual Fernando Ortiz. In fact, both Echegoyen and Bethune served as members of Ortiz's Sociedad de Estudios Afrocubanos, founded in 1936. The organization published the journal *Phylon* to promote the study of African culture, literature, and religions in Cuba. An example of Ortiz's writings on race during the period is "The Relations between Blacks and Whites in Cuba," *Phylon* 5, no. 1 (1st quarter, 1944): 15–29.

32. Celia Planos to Mary McLeod Bethune, January 1950, Bethune Papers, Bethune-Cookman College Collection, National Archives for Black Women's History, Washington, DC.

33. Planos to Bethune, January 1950.

34. Planos to Bethune, January 1950.

35. Planos to Bethune, January 1950.

36. Planos to Bethune, January 1950.

37. Henry Grillo to McLeod Bethune, November 25, 1950, Mary McLeod Bethune Papers, Bethune-Cookman College Collection, National Archives for Black Women's History, Washington, DC.

38. Anita Casavantes Bradford, *The Revolution Is for the Children*, 35.

39. Ted A. Henken, Miriam Celaya, and Dimas Castellanos, *Cuba*, 232. Also see Alfonso W. Quiroz, "Martí in Cuban Schools."

40. Consuelo Serra, interview, "American-Training Cuban Woman Leads Fight on Segregation," *Atlanta Daily World*, August 20, 1941, 3.

41. Serra, interview.

42. See, for instance, the critiques by the communist activist Juan Marinello in *La cuestión racial en la constitución* and "La constitución cubana y la enseñanza privada," *Confederación de Trabajadores de Cuba* 6 (July 1945).

43. Casavantes Bradford, *The Revolution Is for the Children*, 34–37.

44. See Alejandro de la Fuente, *A Nation for All*, 138–148.

45. Xiomara Calderón Arteaga and Alejandro L. Fernández Calderón, *Haydee Arteaga*.

46. Luis Javier Pentón Herrera, "La dra. Ana Echegoyen de Cañizares."

47. Walter S. Monroe, Ana Echegoyen de Cañizares, and Calixto Suárez Gómez, *Enciclopedia de educación científica*.

48. George S. Schuyler, "Racial Integration Works in Cuba's Army," *Pittsburgh Courier*, July 17, 1948, 1.

49. Cuba, *República de Cuba, censo de 1943*, 1112; de la Fuente, *A Nation for All*, 144.

50. Cuba, *República de Cuba, censo de 1943*, 1112. Manuel Ramírez Chicharro also details ongoing racial disparities among Cuban women in education and the labor force in "Doblemente sometidas."

51. Sarah Franklin, *Women and Slavery*, 71–101.

52. Cuba, *Constitución de la República de Cuba*, 1940.

53. Graciella Cruz-Taura, "Women's Rights and the Cuban Constitution of 1940," 123.

54. Cruz-Taura, "Women's Rights and the Cuban Constitution of 1940," 123–124.

55. "Visitan domésticos al dr. Carlos Azcarate," *Noticias de Hoy*, August 9, 1946.

56. Anasa Hicks, "Hierarchies at Home," 155–161.

57. *Memoria de los trabajos realizados por la Quinta Convención Provincial de Sociedades de Camagüey en la Union Fraternal, June 14–15, 1947*, Biblioteca Provincial de Camagüey.

58. *Memoria de los trabajos realizados por la Quinta Convención*.

59. *Memoria de los trabajos realizados por la Quinta Convención*.

60. *Memoria de los trabajos realizados por la Quinta Convención*.

61. *Memoria de los trabajos realizados por la Quinta Convención*.

62. De la Fuente, *A Nation for All*, 221.

63. In "Contra la discriminación racial," *Prensa Libre*, December 13, 1951.

64. "¡Ya fueron lanzadas a la calle las muchachitas negras que comenzaron a trabajar el pasado mes de diciembre en las grandes tiendas comerciales de la capital!" *Noticias de Hoy*, January 1, 1952, 1, 6.

65. "¡Ya fueron lanzadas a la calle las muchachitas negras."

66. Mesa Ejecutiva de la Federación Nacional de Sociedades Cubanas, "Declaraciones de la Federación Nacional de Sociedades en torno al problema de las muchachas negras desplazadas," *Orientación Social*, December 1951, 4.

67. Mesa Ejecutiva, "Declaraciones de la Federación, 4.

68. Mesa Ejecutiva, "Declaraciones de la Federación Nacional."

69. Mesa Ejecutiva, "Declaraciones de la Federación Nacional."

70. "Discriminación y segregación," *Orientación Social*, September 1954, 16.

71. "Discriminación y segregación."

72. "Declaración Universal de los Derechos del Hombre," *Orientación Social*, August 1951, 13–14.

73. "Declaración Universal de los Derechos del Hombre"; "Editorial. Los derechos humanos," *Orientación Social*, December 1955, 1.

74. "Federaciones y sociedades," *Orientación Social*, May 1953, 5.

Chapter 7. "A Heroic and Revolutionary Undertaking": African-Descended Women of the Communist Movement

1. Robert J. Alexander, *A History of Organized Labor in Cuba*; Frank Argote-Freyre, *Fulgencio Batista*; Robert Whitney, *State and Revolution in Cuba*.

2. Devyn Spence Benson, *Antiracism in Cuba*; Alejandro de la Fuente, *A Nation for All*; Whitney, *State and Revolution in Cuba*.

3. Michelle Chase, *Revolution within the Revolution*, 105–115; Steve Cushion, "Working-class Heroine"; Nicole Murray, "Socialism and Feminism."

4. Joan Casanovas, *Bread, or Bullets!*, 196.

5. Pedro Luis Padrón, *La mujer trabajadora*; Jean Stubbs, *Tobacco on the Periphery*.

6. Maria P. Garbey, "Sobre el trabajo de la mujer."

7. On the evolution of class rule during Republican Era, see Whitney, *State and Revolution in Cuba*.

8. Esperanza Sánchez Mastrapa, interview by Romilio A. Portuondo Calá, "Esperanza Sánchez Mastrapa: Una mujer negra en el Congreso," *Noticias de Hoy*, October 8, 1944.

9. Bertha Darder Babé, "Unión Radical de Mujeres expone sus criterios sobre la situación que confronta el país" (Havana: Unión Radical de Mujeres, 1931), Fondo General, Archivo del Instituto de Historia, Havana (AIH); Bertha Darder Babé, "Unión Radical de mujeres expresa su oposición para el gobierno del Presidente Bru" (Havana: Unión Radical de Mujeres, 1937), Fondo General, AIH.

10. De la Fuente, *A Nation for All*, 225.

11. Louis A. Pérez, *Cuba: Between Reform and Revolution*, 211.

12. Benson, *Antiracism in Cuba*, 85, 87; de la Fuente, *Nation for All*, 222.

13. Alexander, *A History of Organized Labor in Cuba*, 115.

14. De la Fuente, *A Nation for All*, 228.

15. Alejandro de la Fuente, *A Nation for All*, 221.

16. Esperanza Sánchez Mastrapa, "Las orientales de pié," *Noticias de Hoy*, March 27, 1940.

17. Sánchez Mastrapa, "Las orientales de pié."

18. Sánchez Mastrapa, "Las orientales de pié."

19. Sánchez Mastrapa, "Las orientales de pié."

20. Sánchez Mastrapa, "Las orientales de pié."

21. Sánchez Mastrapa, interview by Portuondo Calá.

22. Sánchez Mastrapa, interview by Portuondo Calá.

23. Sánchez Mastrapa, interview by Portuondo Calá.

24. Sánchez Mastrapa, interview by Portuondo Calá.

25. Olga Coffigny Leonard, "Mujeres parlamentarias cubanas."

26. For an overview of race and the labor market during the 1940s, see de la Fuente, A Nation for All, 153.

27. Cuba, *República de Cuba, censo de 1943*. Also see Anasa Hicks, "Hierarchies at Home."

28. "Activa y entusiasta joven socialista," *Noticias de Hoy*, July 20, 1947; Laurentino Rodríguez, "Aurora Santiago, única mujer en Cuba agente de periódicos, reparte cada día doscientos ejemplares," *Noticias de Hoy*, February 15, 1944.

29. Baldomero Exposito Rodríguez et al., *Apuntes del movimiento de los trabajadores de la educación*, 74–80.

30. "Un homenaje a dos mujeres," *Hoy*, October 6, 1939.

31. Consuelo Silveira, "Nuestras tareas y el 8 de marzo," *Noticias de Hoy*, March 8, 1940.

32. Silveira, "Nuestras tareas y el 8 de marzo."

33. Pérez, *Cuba: Between Reform and Revolution*, 215–16.

34. "Llamamiento a todas las amas de casa para una acción unida contra los especuladores," *Noticias de Hoy*, March 5, 1943.

35. Consuelo Silveira, keynote speech, in "Una asamblea de mujeres velará por el cumplimiento de las leyes contra la especulación y el agio," *Noticias de Hoy*, December 29, 1942, 1, 8.

36. Silveira, keynote speech.

37. Silveira, keynote speech.

38. Silveira, keynote speech.

39. "La mujer frente a la guerra," *Noticias de Hoy*, October 13, 1942.

40. "Se anuncia una gran campaña de 'amas de casa,'" *Noticias de Hoy*, January 5, 1943.

41. "Son retenidos los donativos de maternidad," *Noticias de Hoy*, October 4, 1941.

42. "Son retenidos los donativos de maternidad."

43. "Son retenidos los donativos de maternidad."

44. "Son retenidos los donativos de maternidad."

45. "Solicitan aumentos las despalilladoras," *Noticias de Hoy*, April 1, 1943.

46. "Solicitan aumentos las despalilladoras."

47. "Obtienen las despalilladoras de toda la República aumento de 25% en sus jornales," *Noticias de Hoy*, April 18, 1943; "Declaraciones sobre el aumento de salarios a despalilladoras," *Noticias de Hoy*, April 20, 1943.

48. De la Fuente, *A Nation for All*, 222–243; Jorge Domínguez, *Cuba: Order and Revolution*, 100–103.

49. Pérez, *Between Reform and Revolution*, 211.

50. De la Fuente, *A Nation for All*, 253.

51. Alexander, *A History of Organized Labor in Cuba*, 105–132.

52. "Llamamiento de María Argüelles," *Hoy*, June 1, 1948.

53. "Llamamiento de María Argüelles."

54. "¿Como votaron las mujeres?," *Noticias de Hoy*, June 6, 1948.

55. "¿Como votaron las mujeres?"

56. "¿Como votaron las mujeres?"

57. "¿Como votaron las mujeres?"

58. "La voz de protesta de la mujer cubana," *Hoy*, June 24, 1948.

59. "La voz de protesta de la mujer cubana."

60. "Llamamiento de la FDMC," *Mujeres Cubanas*, February 1951, 7.

61. "Llamamiento de la FDMC," 7.

62. "Llamamiento de la FDMC," 7.

63. Chase, *Revolution within the Revolution*, 111.

64. An example is Zoila Castellanos Ferrer, "Una realidad desgarradora, *Mujeres Cubanas*, April 1951, 9.

65. "Una carta," *Mujeres Cubanas*, January 1951.

66. "Una carta."

67. Esperanza Sánchez Mastrapa, "Informe ante la Comisión de los Derechos de la Mujer," in *El II Congreso Internacional de Mujeres*, 1949, record book 24.9/92, AIH.

68. Sánchez Mastrapa. "Informe ante la Comisión."

69. Sánchez Mastrapa, "Informe ante la Comisión."

70. The Black communist activist and FDMC member Zoila Castellanos occasionally addressed racial disparities in her writings for the organization's magazine, *Mujeres Cubanas*.

71. Sánchez Mastrapa, "Informe ante la Comisión," emphasis mine.

72. Sánchez Mastrapa, "Informe ante la Comisión."

73. I have found no evidence that the two women ever met. The intersectional approach of Sánchez and Jones, as activists who joined international movements, resembles the framework theorized by Imaobong Umoren in *Race Women Internationalists*. Also see Carole Boyce Davies, *Left of Karl Marx*; Erik S. McDuffie, *Sojourning for Freedom*.

74. "Expulsada de la FDMC por sus actuaciones Esperanza Sánchez," *Mujeres Cubanas*, November 1950, 11. Her expulsion is detailed in "Resolución de la C.E.N. del P.S.P. sobre el caso de Esperanza Sánchez Mastrapa," *Fundamentos: Revista Mensual*, October 1950, 961–963.

75. "Expulsada de la FDMC."

76. Blas Roca, "Sobre la traición de Esperanza Sánchez y la gran vigilancia revolucionaria," *Fundamentos*, November 1950, 1019.

77. "La defección de Esperanza," *Oriente*, September 1, 1950.

78. CIA, "Activities of the PSP," April 7, 1954, CIA-RDP80–00810A003900480009–8, CREST Database, General CIA Records.

79. CIA, "Activities of the PSP."

80. María Argüelles, "El avance de la revolución y la lucha contra la discriminación racial," *Noticias de Hoy*, August 2, 1959, 4.

81. De la Fuente, *A Nation for All*, 261.

82. Argüelles, "El avance de la revolución."

83. Argüelles, "El avance de la revolución."

84. Argüelles, "El avance de la revolución."

85. Chase, *Revolution within the Revolution*, 114.

86. Chase, *Revolution within the Revolution*, 123.

Epilogue

1. García, "Han sido encontrados, en el Cementerio licio de Kingston, los restos de Mariana Grajales, madre de los Maceo," *El Cubano Libre*, April 2, 1923, 1. Newspapers note that the exhumation took place with the support of Grajales's daughter, Dominga Maceo.

2. "Un acto de imponente patriotism y del sentimiento del pueblo santiaguense fué el sepelio de los restos de la madre de los heróicos Maceos," *El Cubano Libre*, April 25, 1923, 1, 8.

3. Rafael Herrera Elías, "Alrededor de los restos de la madre de los Maceos," *El Cubano Libre*, May 7, 1923; José Medina Duchesne, "Alrededor de los restos de la madre de los Maceos," *El Cubano Libre*, May 12, 1923; Jacob A.P.M. Andrade, "Alrededor de los restos de la madre de los Maceos," *El Cubano Libre*, May 15, 1923; Pedro E. Betancourt, "Alrededor de los restos de la madre de los Maceos," *El Cubano Libre*, May 29, 1923.

4. For more on the life and legacy of Grajales, see Rachel Elaine Archer, "Society, Cultures, and Heroes"; Jose Luciano Franco, "Mariana and Maceo"; James Henderson, "Mariana Grajales"; Jean Stubbs, "Social and Political Motherhood of Cuba."

5. Stubbs, "Social and Political Motherhood of Cuba."

6. Nancy Priscilla Naro, *Blacks, Coloureds, and National Identity*, 97.

7. On the incorporation of Black Cubans into the national imaginary, see Robin Moore, *Nationalizing Blackness*.

8. Devyn Spence Benson, *Antiracism in Cuba*, 238–247; Lillian Guerra, *Visions of Power*, 96; Carrie Hamilton, *Sexual Revolutions in Cuba*, 51–74.

9. Devyn Spence Benson documents how revolutionary imagery implied the government was to be credited for what Black Cubans received (*Antiracism in Cuba*, 30–71). Examples of buildings and parks named after Grajales are the Mariana Grajales Airport and Mariana Grajales Revolution Square in Guantánamo, the gynecology and obstetrics hospitals of Santa Clara and Santiago de Cuba, and the Faculty of Medical Sciences in Holguín.

10. Carrie Hamilton discusses the complexities of Black women's experiences after 1959 in *Sexual Revolutions in Cuba*, 64, 86–90, 209–213.

11. See Benigno Aguirre, "Women in the Cuban Bureaucracies"; Chase, *Revolution within the Revolution*; Lois M. Smith and Alfred Padula, *Sex and Revolution*.

12. Benson, *Antiracism in Cuba*, 231–248.

13. Armando González-Pérez, "Mother Africa and Cultural Memory"; Miriam De-Costa-Willis, *Daughters of the Diaspora*.

14. Gloria Rolando's films include *1912, Voces para un silencio, capítulos 1–3*; *Diálogo con mi abuela*; *Los hijos de Baragua*; and *Nosotros y el jazz*.

15. Benson examines the Afrocubanas collective in *Antiracism in Cuba*, 243–248.

16. Raul Castro is quoted in Raquel Reichard, "These Two Black Women Just Became Cuba's Vice Presidents—And It's Monumental," *We Are Mitu*, April 26, 2018, https://fierce.wearemitu.com/politics/cuba-two-Black-women-break-barriers-countrys-new-vice-presidents/; Frances Robles and Azam Ahmed, "More Black Officials in Power in Cuba as Leadership Changes," *New York Times*, April 22, 2018.

Bibliography

Archives and Libraries

CUBA

Biblioteca Provincial de Guantánamo, Guantánamo
Biblioteca Provincial "Martí" Villa Clara, Santa Clara, Cuba
Fondo Adquisiciones, Archivo Nacional de Cuba, Havana (ANC)
Fondo Asociaciones, Archivo Nacional de Cuba, Havana (ANC)
Fondo Registro de Asociaciones, Archivo Histórico Municipal de Trinidad, Trinidad, Cuba
Fondo Gobierno Provincial, Archivo Histórico Provincial de Santiago de Cuba, Santiago de Cuba
Fondo Donativos y Remisiones, Archivo Nacional de Cuba, Havana (ANC)
Fondo General, Archivo del Instituto de Historia de Cuba, Havana (AIC)
Fondo Vilaseca, Archivo del Instituto de Historia de Cuba, Havana (AIC)
Gobierno General, Archivo Nacional de Cuba, Havana (ANC)
Instituto Literatura y Lingüística, Havana
Registro de Asociaciones, Archivo Histórico Provincial de Camagüey, Camagüey
Registro de Asociaciones, Archivo Histórico Provincial de Cienfuegos, Cienfuegos
Registro de Asociaciones, Archivo Histórico Provincial de Santiago de Cuba, Santiago de Cuba
Sala Cubana, Biblioteca Nacional José Martí, Havana

UNITED STATES

Bethune, Mary McLeod Papers, Bethune-Cookman College Collection, National Council of Negro Women Papers, National Archives for Black Women's History, Washington, DC.
Cuban Heritage Collection (CHC), University of Miami Libraries, Coral Gables, FL.
General CIA Records, CREST (CIA Records Search Tool): 25-Year Program Archive, College Park, MD, https://www.cia.gov/readingroom/collection/crest-25-year-program-archive.
Schomburg Center for Research in Black Culture, New York Public Library, New York, NY.

Secondary Sources

Abreu García, Leidy. "Matrimonio interracial: Legislación, familia y senso en la Habana colonial (1776–1881)." *Familia y Género* 8 (January–July 2012).

Adderly, Rosanne Marion. *"New Negroes from Africa": Slave Trade, Abolition, and Free African Settlement in the Nineteenth-Century Caribbean.* Bloomington: Indiana University Press, 2006.

Aguilar, Luis E. *Cuba 1933: Prologue to Revolution.* Ithaca, NY: Cornell University Press, 1972.

Aguilar Dornelles, María Alejandra. "Heroísmo y conciencia racial en la obra de poeta afrocubana Cristina Ayala." *Meridional: Revista Chilena de Estudios Latinoamericanos,* no. 7 (October 2016): 179–202.

Aguirre, Benigno E. "Women in the Cuban Bureaucracies: 1968–1974." *Journal of Comparative Family Studies* 7, no. 1 (Spring 1976): 23–40.

Alberto, Paulina. *Terms of Inclusion: Black Intellectuals in Twentieth-Century Brazil.* Chapel Hill: University of North Carolina Press, 2011.

Alexander, M. Jacqui. *Pedagogies of Crossing: Meditations on Feminism, Sexual Politics, Memory, and the Sacred.* Durham, NC: Duke University Press, 2005.

Alexander, Robert J. *A History of Organized Labor in Cuba.* Westport, CT: Praeger, 2002.

Allen, Jafari. *¡Venceremos? The Erotics of Black Self-Making in Cuba.* Durham, NC: Duke University Press, 2011.

Alonso, Gladys, and Ernesto Chávez Álvarez. *Memorias inéditas del censo de 1931.* Havana: Ciencias Sociales, 1978.

Altnik, Henrice. "'We Are Equal to Men in Ability to Do Anything!' African Jamaican Women and Citizenship in the Interwar Years." In *Women's Activism: Global Perspectives from the 1890s to the Present,* edited by Francisca de Haan, Margaret Allen, June Purvis, and Krassimira Daskolova, 77–89. New York: Routledge, 2013.

Alvarez, Sonia E., and Kia Lilly Caldwell. "Promoting Feminist *Amefricanidade*: Bridging Black Feminist Cultures and Politics in the Americas." *Meridians: Feminism, Race, Transnationalism* 14, no. 1 (2017): v–xi.

Ameringer, Charles D. *The Cuban Democratic Experience: The Auténtico Years, 1944–1952.* Gainesville: University Press of Florida, 2000.

Amparo Alves, Jaime. *The Anti-Black City: Police Terror and Black Urban Life in Brazil.* Minneapolis: University of Minnesota Press, 2018.

Anderson, Benedict. *Imagined Communities: Reflections on the Origin and Spread of Nationalism.* London: Verso, 2003.

Anderson, James D. *The Education of Black Folks in the South, 1860–1935.* Chapel Hill: University of North Carolina Press, 1988.

Andrews, George Reid. *Afro-Latin America 1800–2000.* New York: Oxford University Press, 2004.

———. *Blackness in the White Nation: A History of Afro-Uruguay.* Chapel Hill: University of North Carolina Press, 2010.

Applebaum, Nancy, Peter Wade and Karin Alejandra Rosemblatt, eds. *Race and Nation in Latin America.* Chapel Hill: University of North Carolina Press, 1997.

Archer, Rachel Elaine. "Society, Cultures, and Heroes: Depictions of Cuban Heroine

Mariana Grajales Cuello, 1893–2000." Albuquerque: Latin American Institute, University of New Mexico, 2001.

Argote-Freyre, Frank. *Fulgencio Batista: The Making of a Dictator.* 2 vols. New Brunswick, NJ: Rutgers University Press, 2006.

———. *Fulgencio Batista: From Revolutionary to Strongman.* New Brunswick, NJ: Rutgers University Press, 2006.

Arnedo-Gómez, Miguel. *Uniting Blacks in a Raceless Nation: Blackness, Afro-Cuban Culture, and Mestizaje in the Prose and Poetry of Nicolás Guillén.* Lewisburg, PA: Bucknell University Press, 2016.

Arvey, Sarah R. "Making the Immoral Moral: Consensual Unions and Birth Status in Cuban Law and Everyday Practice, 1940–1958." *Hispanic American Historical Review* 90:4 (2010): 627–659.

———. "Sex and the Ordinary Cuban: Cuban Physicians, Eugenics, and Marital Sexuality, 1933–1958." *Journal of the History of Sexuality* 21, no. 1 (January 2012): 93–120.

Ayala, César. *American Sugar Kingdom: The Plantation Economy of the Spanish Caribbean, 1898–1934.* Chapel Hill: University of North Carolina Press, 1999.

Ayala, Cristina. "A mi raza (To My Race)." Translated by Monique-Adelle Callahan. *Obsidian: Literature in the African Diaspora* 13, no. 1 (Spring/Summer 2012): 126–127.

———. *Ofrendas mayabequinas: Recopilación de poesías publicadas en distintos periódicos de esta y otras provincias.* Güines, Cuba: Tosco Heralda, 1926.

Ayorinde, Christine. *Afro-Cuban Religiosity Revolution, and National Identity.* Gainesville: University of Florida Press, 2004.

Azoulay, Ariella. *The Civil Contract of Photography.* New York: Zone, 2008.

Bachiller y Morales, Antonio, and Victor Patricio de Landaluze. *Colección de artículos: Tipos y costumbres de la isla de Cuba.* Havana: M. de Villa, 1881.

Baker, Houston A. Jr. "Critical Memory and the Black Public Sphere." *Public Culture* 7 (1994): 7–33.

Balboa Navarro, Imilcy. *Los brazos necesarios: Inmigración, colonización y trabajo libre in Cuba, 1878–1898.* Valencia, Spain: Centro Francisco Tomas y Valiente de la Universidad Nacional de la Educación a Distancia, 2000.

Baldwin, Davarian L. *Chicago's New Negroes: Modernity, the Great Migration, and Black Urban Life.* Chapel Hill: University of North Carolina Press, 2007.

Barcia Zequeira, María del Carmen. *Capas populares y modernidad en Cuba (1878–1930).* Havana: Ciencias Sociales, 2009.

———. *Mujeres al margen de la historia.* Havana: Ciencias Sociales, 2009.

Barnard, Malcolm. *Fashion as Communication.* London: Routledge, 1996.

Barros, Juanita de. *Reproducing the British Caribbean: Sex, Gender, and Population Politics after Slavery.* Chapel Hill: University of North Carolina Press, 2014.

Barthes, Roland. *Camera Lucida: Reflections on Photography.* Translated by Richard Howard. New York: Farrar, Straus, and Giroux, 2010.

———. *The Language of Fashion.* Oxford, England: Berg, 2004.

Bassnett, Sarah. "Archive and Affect in Contemporary Photography." *Photography and Culture* 2, no. 3 (2009): 241–251.

Beals, Carleton. *The Crime of Cuba.* Philadelphia: Lippincott, 1933.

Beck, Earl R. "The Martínez Campos Government of 1879: Spain's Last Chance in Cuba." *Hispanic American Historical Review* 56, no. 2 (1976): 268–289.

Bederman, Gail. *Manliness and Civilization: A History of Gender and Race in the United States, 1880–1917*. Chicago: University of Chicago Press, 1995.

Benítez-Rojo, Antonio. *The Repeating Island: The Caribbean and the Postmodern Perspective*. Translated by James Maraniss. 2nd ed. Durham, NC: Duke University Press, 1996.

Benjamin, Walter. *Selected Writings*. Vol. 4: *1938–1940*. Cambridge, MA: Harvard University Press, 2003.

Benson, Devyn Spence. *Antiracism in Cuba: The Unfinished Revolution*. Chapel Hill: University of North Carolina Press, 2016.

Berg, Allison. *Mothering the Race: Women's Narratives of Reproduction, 1890–1930*. Chicago: University of Illinois Press, 2002.

Berland, Oscar. "The Emergence of the Communist Perspective on the 'Negro Question' in America: 1919–1931: Part One." *Science and Society* 63, no. 4 (1999): 411–432.

———. "The Emergence of the Communist Perspective on the 'Negro Question' in America: 1919–1931: Part Two." *Science and Society* 64, no. 2 (2000): 194–217.

Besse, Susan K. *Restructuring Patriarchy: The Modernization of Gender Inequality in Brazil, 1914–1940*. Chapel Hill: University of North Carolina Press, 1996.

Besson, Jean. "Reputation and Respectability Reconsidered: A New Perspective on Afro-Caribbean Peasant Women." In *Women and Change in the Caribbean: A Pan-Caribbean Perspective*, edited by Janet Momsen, 15–37. Kingston, Jamaica: Ian Randle, 1993.

Binns, Niall. "La matanza de los inocentes: Intelectuales cubanas en defensa del niño español." *Anuario Colombiano de Historia Social y de la Cultura* (July–December 2011): 83–110.

Biottin, Jennifer Anne. *Colonial Metropolis: The Urban Grounds of Anti-Imperialism and Feminism in Interwar Paris*. Lincoln: University of Nebraska Press, 2010.

Blain, Keisha N. *Set the World on Fire: Black Nationalist Women and the Global Struggle for Freedom*. Philadelphia: University of Pennsylvania Press, 2017.

Blanco Borelli, Melissa. *She Is Cuba: A Genealogy of the Mulata Body*. Oxford, England: Oxford University Press, 2016.

Blum, Ann Shelby. *Domestic Economies: Family, Work, and Welfare in Mexico City, 1884–1943*. Lincoln: University of Nebraska Press, 2009.

Boardman, Kay. "The Ideology of Domesticity: The Regulation of the Household Economy in Victorian Women's Magazines." *Victorian Periodicals Review* 33, no. 2 (Summer 2000): 150–164.

Boris, Eileen. "The Power of Motherhood: Black and White Activist Women Redefine the 'Political.'" In *Mothers of a New World: Maternalist Politics and the Origins of Welfare States*, edited by Seth Koven and Sonya Michel, 213–245. New York: Routledge, 1993.

Bost, Suzanne. *Mulattas and Mestizas: Representing Mixed Identities in the Americas, 1850–2000*. Athens: University of Georgia Press, 2005.

Bourbonnais, Nicole C. *Birth Control in the Decolonizing Caribbean: Reproductive Politics and Practice on Four Islands, 1930–1970*. Cambridge, England: Cambridge University Press, 2016.

Bourdieu, Pierre. *Outline of a Theory of Practice*. Cambridge, England: Cambridge University Press, 1977.

Bradfield, Nancy. *Costume in Detail: Women's Dress, 1730–1930*. London: Harrap, 1981.

Brereton, Bridget. "Family Strategies, Gender, and the Shift to Wage Labor in the British Caribbean." In *Gender and Slave Emancipation in the Atlantic World*, edited by Pamela Scully and Diana Paton, 143–161. Durham, NC: Duke University Press, 2005.

———. "General Problems and Issues in Studying the History of Women." In *Gender in Caribbean Development*, edited by Patricia Mohammed and Catherine Shepherd, 123–141. Kingston, Jamaica: Canoe, 1999.

Breward, Christopher. *Fashion*. Manchester, England: Manchester University Press, 1995.

Briggs, Laura. *Reproducing Empire: Race, Sex, Science, and U.S. Imperialism in Puerto Rico*. Berkeley: University of California Press, 2002.

Brock, Lisa, and Digna Castañeda Fuertes, eds. *Between Race and Empire: African Americans and Cubans before the Cuban Revolution*. Philadelphia: Temple University Press, 1998.

Bronfman, Alejandra. "The Allure of Technology: Photographs, Statistics, and the Elusive Female Criminal in 1930s Cuba." *Gender and History* Vol. 19 No. 1 (April 2007): 60–77.

———. *Isles of Noise: Sonic Media in the Caribbean*. Chapel Hill: University of North Carolina Press, 2016.

———. *Measures of Equality: Social Science, Race, and Citizenship in Cuba, 1902–1940*. Chapel Hill: University of North Carolina Press, 2004.

Brown, David H. *The Light Inside: Abakua Society Arts and Cuban Cultural History*. Washington: Smithsonian Books, 2003.

———. *Santería Enthroned: Art, Ritual, and Innovation in an Afro-Cuban Religion*. Chicago: University of Chicago Press, 2003.

Brown, Elsa Barkley. "Negotiating and Transforming the Public Sphere: African American Political Life in the Transition from Slavery to Freedom." *Public Culture* 7 (1994): 267–302.

Brown, Nikki. *Private Politics and Public Voices: Black Women's Activism from World War I to the New Deal*. Bloomington: Indiana University Press, 2006.

Browne, Simone. *Dark Matters: On the Surveillance of Blackness*. Durham, NC: Duke University Press, 2015.

Brunson, Takkara. "Eusebia Cosme and Black Womanhood on the Transatlantic Stage." *Meridians: Feminism, Race, Transnationalism* 15, no. 2 (2017): 389–411.

———. "'In the General Interest of All Conscious Women': Race, Class, and the Cuban Women's Movement, 1923–1939." *Cuban Studies* 46 (2018): 159–182.

———. "Women, Gender, and the Partido Independiente de Color." In *Breaking the Chains, Making the Nation: The Black Cuban Fight for Freedom and Equality, 1812–1912*, edited by Fannie T. Rushing and Aisha Finch, 272–288. Baton Rouge: Louisiana State University Press, 2019.

———. "'Writing' Black Womanhood in the Early Cuban Republic, 1904–1916." *Gender and History* 28, no. 2 (August 2016): 480–500.

Butler, Kim. *Freedoms Given, Freedoms Won: Afro-Brazilians in Post-Abolition São Paolo and Salvador*. New Brunswick, NJ: Rutgers University Press, 1998.

———. "From Black History to Diasporan History: Brazilian Abolition in Afro-Atlantic Context." *African Studies Review* 43 (2001): 125–139.

Calderón Arteaga, Xiomara, and Alejandro L. Fernández Calderón. *Haydee Arteaga: Raiz siempre viva; biografía de una mujer centenaria.* Havana: Bologna, 2018.

Callahan, Monique-Adelle. *Between the Lines: Literary Transnationalism and African American Politics.* Oxford, England: Oxford University Press, 2011.

———. "Race and Redemption in 19th Century 'American' Poetry across the Americas: Frances Harper's 'Deliverance' and Cristina Ayala's 'Redención.'" *Negritud: Revista de Estudios Afro-Latinoamericanos,* no. 1 (2008): 44–63.

Calvo Peñaz, Beatriz. "Prensa, política y prostitución en La Habana finisecular: El caso de *La Cebolla* y la 'polémica de las meretrices.'" *Cuban Studies* 36 (2005): 23–49.

Campt, Tina. *Image Matters: Archive, Photography, and the African Diaspora in Europe.* Durham, NC: Duke University Press, 2012.

———. *Listening to Images.* Durham, NC: Duke University Press, 2017.

Candelario, Ginetta E. B. *Black behind the Ears: Dominican Racial Identity from Museums to Beauty Shops.* Durham, NC: Duke University Press, 2007.

Carby, Hazel. *Reconstructing Womanhood: The Emergence of the Afro-American Novelist.* Oxford, England: Oxford University Press, 1989.

Carr, Barry. "Identity, Class, and Nation: Black Immigrant Workers, Cuban Communism, and the Sugar Industry, 1925–1934." *Hispanic American Historical Review* 78, no. 1 (February 1995): 83–116.

———. "'Omnipotent and Omnipresent'? Labor Shortages, Worker Mobility, and Employer Control in the Cuban Sugar Industry, 1910–1934." In *Identity and Struggle at the Margins of the Nation-State: The Laboring Peoples of Central America and the Hispanic Caribbean,* edited by Aviva Chomsky and Aldo Aluria-Santiago, 260–291. Durham, NC: Duke University Press, 1998.

Carroll, Anne Elizabeth. *Word, Image, Text, and the New Negro: Representation and Identity in the Harlem Renaissance.* Bloomington: University of Indiana Press, 2007.

Casanovas, Joan. *Bread, or Bullets! Urban Labor and Spanish Colonialism in Cuba, 1850–1898.* Pittsburgh, PA: University of Pittsburgh Press, 1998.

Casavantes Bradford, Anita. *The Revolution Is for the Children: The Politics of Childhood in Havana and Miami, 1959–1962.* Chapel Hill: University of North Carolina Press, 2014.

Casey, Matthew. *Empire's Guestworkers: Haitian Migrants in Cuba during the Age of U.S. Occupation.* Cambridge, England: Cambridge University Press, 2017.

———. "Sugar, Empire, and Revolution in Eastern Cuba: The Guantánamo Sugar Company Records in the Cuban Heritage Collection." *Caribbean Studies* 42, no. 2 (Fall 2015): 121–151.

Castellanos, Israel. *Medicina legal y criminología afro-cubanas.* Havana: Librería e Imprenta La Moderna Poesía, 1937.

Castellanos, Jorge, and Isabel Castellanos. *Cultura Afrocubana.* Vol. 2: *El negro en Cuba, 1845–1959.* Miami: Universal, 1990.

Castilho, Celso Thomas. *Slave Emancipation and Transformations in Brazilian Political Citizenship.* Pittsburgh, PA: University of Pittsburgh Press, 2016.

Castillo Bueno, María de los Reyes, with Daisy Rubiera Castillo. *Reyita: The Life of a*

Black Cuban Woman in the Twentieth Century. Translation by Anne McLean. Durham, NC: Duke University Press, 2000.

Castro Fernández, Silvio. *La masacre de los Independientes de Color en 1912.* Havana: Ciencias Sociales, 2002.

Castro Monterrey, Pedro, Sandra Estévez Rivero, and Olga Portuondo Zúñiga. *Por la identidad del negro Cubano.* Santiago de Cuba: Caserón, 2011.

Caulfield, Sueann. "The History of Gender in the Historiography of Latin America." *Hispanic American Historical Review* 81 (2001): 449–490.

———. *In Defense of Honor: Sexual Morality, Modernity, and Nation in Early Twentieth-Century Brazil.* Durham, NC: Duke University Press, 2000.

Caulfield, Sueann, Sarah C. Chambers, and Lara Putnam, eds. *Honor, Status, and Law in Modern Latin America.* Durham, NC: Duke University Press, 2005.

Céspedes, Benjamin de. *La prostitución en la Ciudad de la Habana.* Havana: Establecimiento Tipográfico O'Reilly, 1888.

Chapman, Erin D. *Prove It on Me: New Negroes, Sex, and Popular Culture in the 1920s.* New York: Oxford University Press, 2012.

Chase, Michelle. *Revolution within the Revolution: Women and Gender Politics in Cuba, 1952–1962.* Chapel Hill: University of North Carolina Press, 2015.

Chatelain, Marcia. *South Side Girls: Growing Up in the Great Migration.* Durham, NC: Duke University Press, 2015.

Chaveco Chaveco, Onelia. "Propuesta de una mirada incluyente y no sexista." In *Afrocubanas: Historia, pensamineto y prácticas* culturales, edited by Daisy Rubiera Castillo and Inés María Martiatu Terry, 163–169. Havana: Ciencias Sociales, 2011.

Childs, Matt. *The 1812 Aponte Rebellion in Cuba and the Struggle against Atlantic Slavery.* Chapel Hill: University of North Carolina Press, 2006.

———. "'Sewing' Civilization: Cuban Female Education in the Context of Africanization, 1800–1860." *The Americas* 54, no. 1 (July 1997): 83–107.

Chomsky, Aviva. "Afro-Jamaican Traditions and Labor Organizing on United Fruit Company Plantations in Costa Rica, 1910." *Journal of Social History* 29, no. 4 (Summer 1995): 837–855.

———. "'Barbados or Canada?' Race, Immigration, and Nation in Early Twentieth-Century Cuba." *Hispanic American Historical Review* 80, no. 3 (2000): 415–462.

———. *Linked Labor Histories: New England, Colombia, and the Making of a Global Working Class.* Durham, NC: Duke University Press, 2008.

———. *West Indian Workers and the United Fruit Company in Costa Rica, 1870–1940.* Baton Rouge: Louisiana State University Press, 1996.

Clark, Victor. "Labor Conditions in Cuba." *Bulletin of the Department of Labor* 41 (July 1902): 663–793.

Cluster, Dick, and Rafael Hernández. *The History of Havana.* New York: Palgrave Macmillan, 2006.

Cobb, Jasmine Nichole. *Picture Freedom: Remaking Black Visuality in the Early Nineteenth Century.* New York: New York University Press, 2015.

Cobb, Martha K. *Harlem, Haiti, and Havana: A Comparative Critical Study of Langston Hughes, Jacques Romain, and Nicolás Guillén.* Washington, DC: Three Continents, 1979.

———. "Martín Morúa Delgado: Black Profile in Spanish America." *Negro History Bulletin* 36 (January 1973): 523–541.

Coffigny Leonard, Olga. "Mujeres parlamentarias cubanas (1936–1958)." *Temas* 55 (July–September 2008): 185–198.

Collins, Patricia Hill. *Black Feminist Thought: Knowledge, Consciousness, and the Politics of Empowerment*. 2nd ed. New York: Routledge, 2000.

Colón Pichardo, Maikel. ¿*Es fácil ser hombre y difícil ser negro? Masculinidad y estereotipos raciales en Cuba (1898–1912)*. Havana: Abril, 2015.

———. "Racismo y feminism en Cuba: Dos mitades y una misma naranja? Claves históricas para su estudio." *Boletín Americanista* 67, no. 72 (2016): 179–198.

———. "Sábanas blancas en mi balcón, negra mi condición: Hacia una (re)evaluación de narrativas cubanas decimonónicas sobre género, 'raza' y nación en las páginas de *Minerva*." *Mitologías Hoy: Revista de Pensamiento, Crítica y Estudios Literarios Latinoamericanos* 13 (June 2016): 39–56.

Conte, Rafael, and José M. Campany. *Guerra de razas: Negros contra blancos en* Cuba. Havana: Militar de a Pérez, 1912.

Cooper, Brittney. *Beyond Respectability: The Intellectual Thought of Race Women*. Chicago: University of Illinois Press, 2017.

Cordoví Núñez, Yoel. *Magisterio y nacionalismo en las escuelas públicas de Cuba (1899–1920)*. Havana: Ciencias Sociales, 2012.

Corwin, Arthur F. *Spain and the Abolition of Slavery in Cuba, 1817–1886*. Austin: University of Texas Press, 1967.

Cott, Nancy. *The Bonds of Womanhood: "Woman's Sphere" in New England, 1780–1835*. New Haven, CT: Yale University Press, 1997.

Cowling, Camillia. *Conceiving Freedom: Women of Color, Gender, and the Abolition of Slavery in Havana and Rio de Janeiro*. Chapel Hill: University of North Carolina Press, 2013.

———. "Negotiating Freedom: Women of Colour and the Transition to Free Labour in Cuba, 1870–1886." *Slavery and Abolition: A Journal of Slave and Post-Slave Studies* 26, no. 3 (December 2005): 377–391.

Crenshaw, Kimberlé. "Demarginalizing the Intersection of Race and Sex: A Black Feminist Critique of Antidiscrimination Doctrine, Feminist Theory, and Antiracist Politics." *University of Chicago Legal Forum* 1 (1989): 139–167.

———. "Mapping the Margins: Intersectionality, Identity Politics, and Violence against Women of Color." In *The Public Nature of Private Violence*, edited by Martha Albertson Fineman and Roxanne Mykitiuk, 93–118. New York: Routledge, 1994.

Cruz-Taura, Graciela. "Women's Rights and the Cuban Constitution of 1940." *Cuban Studies* 24 (1994): 123–140.

Cruz-Janzen, Marta. "Latinegras: Desired Women—Undesirable Mothers, Daughters, Sisters, and Wives." *Frontiers: A Journal of Women's Studies* 22, no. 3 (2001): 168–183.

Cuba. *Censo de la República de Cuba bajo la administración provisional de los Estado Unidos, 1907*. Washington, DC: Oficina del Censo de los Estados Unidos, 1908.

———. *Constitución de la República de Cuba*. Havana: Imp. y Encuadernación, 1902.

———. *Constitución de la República de Cuba*. Edited by Jesús Montero. Havana: Berea, 1940.

Cuba, Dirección General del Censo. *República de Cuba, censo de 1943*. Havana: P. Fernández, 1943.

———. *Censos de población, viviendas y electoral, 1953*. Havana: Dirección General del Censo, 1953.

Cuba, Oficina Nacional del Censo. *Censo de la República de Cuba, año de 1919*. Havana: Oficina Nacional del Censo, 1922.

Cuba de la Cruz, Armando. *Holguín 1898–1920: De la colonia a la República*. Holguín, Cuba: Holguín, 2006.

Cumming, Valerie. *Gloves*. New York: Drama, 1982.

Cushion, Steve. "A Working-Class Heroine Is Also Something To Be: The Untold Story of Cuban Railway Workers and the Struggle against Batista." *MaComére* 12, no. 2 (Fall 2010).

Dámasa Jova, María. *"Arpegios íntimos" y poesías*. Santa Clara, Cuba: El Arte, 1925.

———. *Ufanías: Juicios y consideraciones acerca de "Arpegios íntimos" y poesías*. Santa Clara, Cuba: A. Clapera, 1927.

Davies, Carole Boyce. *Left of Karl Marx: The Political Life of Black Communist Claudia Jones*. Durham, NC: Duke University Press, 2007.

Davies, Catherine. "National Feminism in Cuba: The Elaboration of a Counter-Discourse, 1900–1935." *Modern Language Review* 91, no. 1 (January 1996): 107–123.

———. *A Place in the Sun? Women Writers in Twentieth-Century Cuba*. London: Zed, 1997.

Davila, Jerry. *Diploma of Whiteness: Race and Social Policy in Brazil, 1917–1945*. Durham, NC: Duke University Press, 2003.

DeCosta-Willis, Miriam, ed. *Daughters of the Diaspora: Afra-Hispanic Writers*. Kingston, Jamaica: Ian Randle, 2003.

de la Fuente, Alejandro. *A Nation for All: Race, Inequality, and Politics in Twentieth-Century Cuba*. Chapel Hill: University of North Carolina Press, 2001.

———. "Slaves and the Creation of Legal Rights in Cuba: Coartación and Papel." *Hispanic American Historical Review* 87, no. 4 (2007): 659–692.

———. "Two Dangers, One Solution: Immigration, Race, and Labor in Cuba, 1900–1930." *International Labor and Working-Class History* no. 51 (Spring 1997): 30–49.

de la Torre, Mildred. *Conflictos y cultura política: Cuba, 1878–1898*. Havana: Política, 2006.

Derby, Lauren H. *The Dictator's Seduction: Politics and the Popular Imagination in the Era of Trujillo*. Durham, NC: Duke University Press, 2003.

Deschamps Chapeaux, Pedro. *El negro en el periodismo cubano: Ensayo bibliográfico*. Havana: Revolución, 1963.

———. *El negro en la economía habanera del siglo XIX*. Havana: Unión de Escritores y Artistas de Cuba, 1971.

———. *Los batallones de pardos y morenos libres*. Havana: Instituto Cubano del Libro, 1970.

———. *Rafael Serra y Montalvo, obrero incansable de nuestra independencia*. Havana: Unión de Escritores y Artistas de Cuba, 1975.

Deschamps Chapeaux, Pedro, and Juan Pérez de la Riva. *Contribución a la historia de la gente sin historia*. Havana: Ciencias Sociales, 1974.

Díaz Castañón, María del Pilar, ed. Éditos *inéditos: Documentos olvidados de la historia de Cuba*. Havana: Ciencias Sociales, 2005.

———. *Perfiles de la nación II*. Havana: Ciencias Sociales, 2006.

Dixon, Kwame, and John Burdick. "Visions of a Nineteenth-Century Cuba: Images of Blacks in the Work of Victor Patricio de Landaluze." In *Comparative Perspectives on Afro-Latin America*, 114–132. Gainesville: University Press of Florida, 2012.

Domínguez, Jorge. *Cuba: Order and Revolution*. Cambridge, MA: Belknap, 1978.

Dore, Elizabeth, and Maxine Molyneux, eds. *Hidden Histories of Gender and the State in Latin America*. Durham, NC: Duke University Press, 2000.

Doreski, C. K. *Writing America Black: Race Rhetoric in the Public Sphere*. Cambridge, England: Cambridge University Press, 1998.

Dorsey, Joseph C. "Identity, Rebellion, and Social Justice among Chinese Contract Workers in Nineteenth-Century Cuba." *Latin American Perspectives* 31, no. 3 (2004): 18–47.

Duany, Jorge. "Portraying the Other: Puerto Rican Images in Two American Photographic Collections." *Discourse* 23, no. 1 (Winter 2001): 119–153.

duCille, Ann. "The Occult of True Black Womanhood: Critical Demeanor and Black Feminist Studies." *Signs: Journal of Women in Culture and* Society 19, no. 3 (Spring 1994): 591–629.

Duke, Dawn. *Literary Passion, Ideological Commitment: Toward a Legacy of Afro-Cuban and Afro-Brazilian Women Writers*. Lewisburg, PA: Bucknell University Press, 2008.

Duncan, Natanya. "Henrietta Vinton Davis: The Lady of the Race." *Journal of New York History* 95, no. 4 (Fall 2014): 558–583.

———. "Laura Kofey and the Reverse Atlantic Experience." In *The American South and the Atlantic* World, edited by Brian Ward, 218–237. Gainesville: University of Florida Press, 2013.

Echegoyen de Cañizares, Ana. *Mi libro: Libro pre-primario*. Havana: Cultural, 1946.

Echegoyen de Cañizares, Ana, and Calixto Suárez Gómez. *El continente de la esperanza: Unidad de trabajo*. Oficina de Cooperación Intelectual, Unión Panamericana, 1947.

Edreira de Caballero, Angelina. *Vida y obra de Juan Gualberto Gómez: Seis lecciones en su centenario, cursillo de divulgación*. 2nd ed. Havana: R. Méndez, 1973.

Edwards, Brent Hayes. *The Practice of Diaspora: Literature, Translation, and the Rise of Black Internationalism*. Cambridge, MA: Harvard University Press, 2003.

———. "The Uses of Diaspora." *Social Text* 19, no. 1 (2001): 45–73.

Edwards, Elizabeth. "Anthropology and Photography: A Long History of Knowledge and Affect." *Photographies* 3, no. 3 (2015): 235–252.

Egüez Guevara, Pilar. "Dangerous Encounters, Ambiguous Frontiers: Dance, Sex, and Intimacy in Nineteenth-Century Cuba." *New West Indian Guide* 90 (2016): 225–256.

———. "Manuales de urbanidad y discursos sobre el ornato en Cuba en el siglo XIX: Hacia un gobierno de los sentidos, el cuerpo y la ciudad." *Latin American Research Review* 4, no. 53 (2018): 785–798.

———. "Sabor Colonial: Crafting Savory Bodies through Cuban Music and Dance." *Cuban Studies* 45 (2017): 199–226.

Escalona, Martha Silvia. *Los cabildos de africanos y sus descendientes en Matanzas: Siglo xix y primera decada del xx*. Matanzas, Cuba: Matanzas, 2008.

Estevez Rivero, Sandra, Pedro Castro Monterrey, and Olga Portuondo Zúñiga, eds. *Por la identidad del negro cubano*. Santiago de Cuba: Caseron, 2011.

Expósito Rodríguez, Baldomero, Lidia Dávila Montes, and Alejandrino Borroto Mora. *Apuntes del movimiento de los trabajadores de la educación, 1889–1961*. Havana: Ciencias Sociales, 1985.

Fábregas, Johanna I. Moya. "The Cuban Woman's Revolutionary Experience: Patriarchal Culture and the State's Gender Ideology, 1950–1976." *Journal of Women's History* 22 (Spring 2010): 61–84.

Faguaga Iglesias, María Ileana. "En torno a los estereotipos respecto a la afrocubana." In *Afrocubanas: Historia, pensamineto y prácticas* culturales, edited by Daisy Rubiera Castillo and Inés María Martiatu Terry, 150–162. Havana: Ciencias Sociales, 2011.

Farber, Samuel. *Revolution and Reaction in Cuba: From Machado to Castro, 1933–1960*. Middleton, CT: Wesleyan University Press, 1976.

Federación Nacional de Asociaciones Femeninas. "Reglamento del Segundo Congreso Nacional de Mujeres." Memoria del Segundo Congreso Nacional de Mujeres. Havana, 1925.

Fermoselle, Rafael. *Política y color en Cuba: La guerrita de 1912*. Montevideo, Uruguay: Colibrí, 1998.

Fernandez Robaina, Tomás. *Bibliografía de temas afrocubanos*. Havana: Ciencias Sociales, 1994.

———. *El negro en Cuba, 1902–1958: Apuntes para la historia de la lucha contra la discriminación racial*. Havana: Ciencias Sociales, 1990.

———. "Mujeres negras hablan de su problemática genérica, racial, y social." *Caminos: Revista Cubana de Pensamiento Sociotelógico* (2012): 102–104.

Ferrer, Ada. "Cuba, 1898: Rethinking Race, Nation, and Empire." *Radical History Review* 73 (1999): 22–46.

———. *Insurgent Cuba: Race, Nation, and Revolution, 1868–1898*. Chapel Hill: University of North Carolina Press, 1999.

Fields, Barbara Jeanne. "Slavery, Race, and Ideology in the United States of America." *New Left Review* 181 (1990): 95–118.

Finch, Aisha. *Rethinking Slave Rebellion in Cuba: La Escalera and the Insurgencies of 1841–1844*. Chapel Hill: University of North Carolina Press, 2015.

Findlay, Eileen J. Suárez. *Imposing Decency: The Politics of Sexuality and Race in Puerto Rico, 1870–1902*. Durham, NC: Duke University Press, 2000.

Fischer, Brodwyn. *A Poverty of Rights: Citizenship and Inequality in Twentieth-Century Brazil*. Stanford, CA: Stanford University Press, 2008.

Flacón, Sylvanna M. "The Particularism of Human Rights for Latin American Women of African Descent." *Feminist Formations* 28, no. 1 (Spring 2016): 190–204.

Fleetwood, Nicole. *Troubling Vision: Performance, Visuality, and Blackness*. Chicago: University of Chicago Press, 2011.

Foner, Philip S. *Antonio Maceo: The "Bronze Titan" of Cuba's Struggles for Independence*. New York: Monthly Review Press, 1977.

———. *Organized Labor and the Black Worker, 1619–1973*. New York: Praeger, 1974.

———. *The Spanish-Cuban-American War and the Birth of U.S. Imperialism*. New York: Monthly Review Press, 1972.

Font, Mauricio Agusto, and Alfonso W. Quiroz, eds. *The Cuban Republic and José Martí: Reception and Use of a National Symbol.* Oxford, England: Lexington, 2006.

———. *Cuban Counterpoints: The Legacy of Fernando Ortiz.* Lanham, MD: Lexington, 2005.

Ford, Tanisha C. *Liberated Threads: Black Women, Style, and the Global Politics of Soul.* Chapel Hill: University of North Carolina Press, 2015.

Ford-Smith, Honor. "Una Marson: Black Nationalist and Feminist Writer." *Caribbean Quarterly* 34, no. 3/4 (September/December 1988): 22–37.

———. "Unruly Virtues of the Spectacular: Performing Engendered Nationalisms in the UNIA in Jamaica." *Interventions* 6, no. 1 (2004): 18–44.

Franco, José Luciano. "Mariana and Maceo." In *AfroCuba: An Anthology of Cuban Writing on Race, Politics, and Culture,* edited by Pedro Pérez Sarduy and Jean Stubbs, 47–54. Melbourne: Center for Cuban Studies, Ocean, 1993.

Franklin, Sarah. *Women and Slavery in Nineteenth-Century Colonial Cuba.* Rochester, NY: University of Rochester Press, 2012.

Fraser, Nancy. "Rethinking the Public Sphere: A Contribution to a Critique of Actually Existing Democracy." In *Habermas and the Public Sphere: A Contribution to a Critique of Actually Existing Democracy,* edited by Craig Calhoun, 109–142. Cambridge, MA: MIT Press, 1992.

Fraunhar, Alison. *Mulata Nation: Visualizing Race and Gender in Cuba.* Jackson: University Press of Mississippi, 2018.

French, Joan. "Colonial Policy towards Women after the 1938 Uprising: The Case of Jamaica." *Caribbean Quarterly* 34, no. 3/4 (September/December 1988): 38–61.

Fuentes, Marissa J. *Dispossessed Lives: Enslaved Women, Violence, and the Archive.* Philadelphia: University of Pennsylvania Press, 2016.

Gabara, Esther. *Errant Modernism: The Ethos of Photography in Mexico and Brazil.* Durham, NC: Duke University Press, 2008.

Gaines, Kevin. *Uplifting the Race: Black Leadership, Politics, and Culture in the Twentieth Century.* Chapel Hill: University of North Carolina Press, 1996.

Galván, Raul C. "Nineteenth-Century Cuban Transnationals: Sugar, Revolution, and Citizenship." PhD diss., University of Wisconsin-Milwaukee, 2011.

Garbey, Maria P. "Sobre el trabajo de la mujer." In *Boletín del Congreso Nacional Obrero: Memoria de los trabajos presentados al Congreso Nacional Obrero.* Havana: La Universal, 1915.

García, Guadalupe. *Beyond the Walled City: Colonial Exclusion in Havana.* Berkeley: University of California Press, 2015.

García-Peña, Lorgia. *The Border of Dominicanidad: Race, Nation, and Archives of Contradiction.* Durham, NC: Duke University Press, 2016.

Garfield, Michelle N. "Literary Societies: The World of Self-Improvement and Racial Uplift." In *Black Women's Intellectual Traditions: Speaking Their Minds,* edited by Kristin Waters and Carol B. Conaway, 113–128. Hanover, MA: University Press of New England, 2007.

Gates, Henry Louis Jr. "The Trope of a New Negro and the Reconstruction of the Image of the Black." *Representations* 24 (Fall 1998): 129–155.

Giddings, Paula J. *When and Where I Enter: The Impact of Black Women on Race and Sex in America*. New York: William Morrow, 1984.

Gill, Tiffany M. *Beauty Shop Politics: African American Women's Activism in the Beauty Industry*. Urbana: University of Illinois Press, 2010.

Gilmore, Glenda. *Gender and Jim Crow: Women and the Politics of White Supremacy in North Carolina, 1896–1920*. Chapel Hill: University of North Carolina Press, 1996.

Gilroy, Paul. *The Black Atlantic: Modernity and Double Consciousness*. Cambridge, MA: Harvard University Press, 1993.

Giovannetti-Torres, Jorge. *Black British Migrants in Cuba: Race, Labor, and Empire in the Twentieth Century Caribbean, 1898–1948*. Cambridge, England: Cambridge University Press, 2018.

Goeser, Caroline. *Picturing the New Negro: Harlem Renaissance Print Culture and Modern Black Identity*. Lawrence: University Press of Kansas, 1997.

Goett, Jennifer. *Black Autonomy: Race, Gender, and Afro-Nicaraguan Activism*. Stanford, CA: Stanford University Press, 2016.

Goffe, Tao Leigh. "Albums of Inclusion: The Photographic Poetics of Caribbean Chinese Visual Kinship." *Small Axe* (2018): 35–56.

Gómez, Juan Alberto. *Por Cuba libre: Homenaje de la Ciudad de la Habana al gran cubano en el centenario de su nacimiento*. Havana: Oficina del Historiador de la Ciudad, 1954.

González, Mario, and K. Lynn Stoner. *Minerva: Revista quincenal dedicada a la mujer de color*. Havana: Instituto de Historia de Cuba, 1998.

González, Reynaldo. *La Fiesta de los Tiburones*. 3rd ed. Havana: Ciencias Sociales, 2001.

González Pagés, Julio César. *En busca de un espacio: Historia de mujeres en Cuba*. Havana: Ciencias Sociales, 2003.

González-Pérez, Armando. "Mother Africa and Cultural Memory." In *Feminine Voices in Contemporary Afro-Cuban poetry/Voces femeninas en la poesía afrocubana contemporánea*, edited by Armando González-Pérez. Philadelphia: La Gota de Agua, 2006.

González-Stephan, Beatriz. "The Dark Side of Photography: Techno-Aesthetics, Bodies, and the Residues of Coloniality in Nineteenth-Century Latin America." *Discourse* 38, no. 1 (Winter 2016): 22–45.

Gordon, Linda. "Black and White Visions of Welfare: Women's Welfare Activism, 1890–1945." In *"We Specialize in the Wholly Impossible": A Reader in Black Women's History*, edited by Darlene Clark Hine, Wilma King, and Linda Reed, 449–486. Brooklyn, NY: Carlson, 1995.

Gore, Dayo F. *Radicalism at the Crossroads: African American Women Activists in the Cold War*. New York: New York University Press, 2011.

Graham, Richard, ed. *The Idea of Race in Latin America, 1870–1940*. Austin: University of Texas Press, 1990.

Graham, Sandra Lauderdale. *House and Street: The Domestic World of Servants and Masters in Nineteenth-Century Rio de Janeiro*. Cambridge, England: Cambridge University Press, 1988.

Greenbaum, Susan. *More than Black: Afro-Cubans in Tampa, Florida*. Gainesville: University Press of Florida, 2002.

Greenblatt, Stephen. *Renaissance Self-Fashioning: From More to Shakespeare*. Chicago: University of Chicago Press, 1983, 2005.

Gregg, Veronica M. "'How with This Rage Shall Beauty Hold a Plea': The Writings of Miss Amy Beckford Bailey as Moral Education in the Era of Jamaican Nation Building." *Small Axe* 11, no. 2 (June 2007): 16–23.

Grobart, Fabio. "El movimiento obrero cubano entre 1925 a 1933." *Pensamineto Crítico* 39 (1970): 72–84.

Guanche, Julio César. "La Constitución de 1940: Una reinterpretación." *Cuban Studies* 45 (2017): 66–88.

Guerra, Lillian. *The Myth of José Martí: Conflicting Nationalism in Early Twentieth-Century Cuba*. Chapel Hill: University of North Carolina Press, 2005.

———. *Visions of Power in Cuba: Revolution, Redemption, and Resistance, 1959–1971*. Chapel Hill: University of North Carolina Press, 2012.

Guevara, Gema R. "Inexacting Whiteness: Blanqueamineto as a Gender-Specific Trope in the Nineteenth Century." *Cuban Studies* 36 (2005): 105–128.

Guridy, Frank. "Feeling Diaspora in Harlem and Havana." *Social Text* 27 (Spring 2009): 83–114.

———. *Forging Diaspora: Afro-Cubans and African Americans in a World of Empire and Jim Crow*. Chapel Hill: University of North Carolina Press, 2010.

———. "Racial Knowledge in Cuba: The Production of a Social Fact." PhD diss., University of Michigan, 2002.

———. "'War on the Negro': Race and the Revolution of 1933." *Cuban Studies* 40 (2009): 49–73.

Gutiérrez Coto, Amauri. "Izquierda cubana y republicanismo español." In *El Atlántico como frontera: Mediaciones culturales entre Cuba y España*, edited by Damaris Puñales Alpízar, 69–90. Madrid: Verbum, 2014.

Gutman, Lawrence J. "Imagining Athens, Remaking Afrocubanidad: Club Atenas and the Politics of Afro-Cuban Incorporation." Master's thesis, University of Texas at Austin, 2003.

Guy, Donna J. "The Pan American Child Congresses, 1916–1942: Pan Americanism, Child Reform, and the Welfare State in Latin America." *Journal of Family History* 23, no. 3 (1993): 272–291.

———. *The Troubled Meeting of Sex, Gender, Public Health, and Progress in Latin America*. Lincoln: University of Nebraska Press, 2000.

———. *Women Build the Welfare State: Performing Charity and Creating Rights in Argentina, 1880–1955*. Durham, NC: Duke University Press, 2009.

Habermas, Jürgen. *The Structural Transformation of the Public Sphere: An Inquiry into a Category of Bourgeois Society*. Cambridge, MA: MIT Press, 1991.

Hamilton, Carrie. *Sexual Revolutions in Cuba: Passion, Politics, and Memory*. Chapel Hill: University of North Carolina Press, 2012.

Hanson, Joyce Ann. *Mary McLeod Bethune and Black Women's Political Activism*. Columbia: University of Missouri Press, 2003.

Haustein, Katja. *Regarding Lost Time: Photography, Identity, and Affect in Proust, Benjamin, and Barthes*. New York: Routledge, 2017.

Helg, Aline. "Afro-Cuban Protest: The Partido Independiente de Color, 1908–1912." *Cuban Studies* 21 (1991): 101–121.

———. "Black Men, Racial Stereotyping, and Violence in the U.S. South and Cuba at the Turn of the Century." *Comparative Studies in Society and History* 42, no. 3 (July 2000): 576–604.

———. *Our Rightful Share: The Afro-Cuban Struggle for Equality, 1886–1912.* Chapel Hill: University of North Carolina Press, 1995.

———. "Race and Mobilization in Colonial and Early Independent Cuba: A Comparative Perspective." *Ethnohistory* 44, no. 1 (Winter 1997): 53–74.

———. "Race in Argentina and Cuba, 1880–1930: Theory, Policies, and Popular Reaction." In *The Idea of Race in Latin America, 1870–1940*, edited by Thomas E. Skidmore, Aline Helg, and Alan Knight, 37–70. Austin: University of Texas Press, 1990.

Henderson, James. "Mariana Grajales: Black Progenitress of Cuban Independence." *Journal of Negro History* 63, no. 2 (April 1978): 135–148.

Henderson, Kaitlyn D. "Black Activism in the Red Party: Black Politics and the Cuban Communist Party, 1925–1962." Ph.D. diss., Tulane University, 2018.

Henken, Ted A., Miriam Celaya, and Dimas Castellanos. *Cuba.* Santa Barbara, CA: ABC-CLIO, 2013.

Herrera Jerez, Miriam, and Mario Castillo Santana. *Contested Community: Identities, Spaces, and Hierarchies of the Chinese in the Cuban Republic.* Leiden, Netherlands: Brill, 2017.

Hevia Lanier, Oilda. *El Directorio Central de las Sociedades Negras de Cuba, 1886–1894.* Havana: Ciencias Sociales, 1996.

———. "Introducción a la selección de documentos." In *Juan Gualberto Gómez, un gran inconforme*, by Leonardo Horrego Estuch, 205–214. Havana: Ciencias Sociales, 2004.

Hevia Lanier, Oilda, and Daisy Rubiera Castillo. *Emergiendo del silencio: mujeres negras en la historia de Cuba.* Havana: Ciencias Sociales, 2016.

Hewitt, Nancy A. *Southern Discomfort: Women's Activism in Tampa, Florida, 1880s–1920s.* Urbana: University of Illinois Press, 2001.

Hewitt, Steven. "The Veterans' Movements and the Early Republican State in Cuba." *Bulletin of Latin American Research* 34, no. 3 (2015): 356–369.

Hicks, Anasa. "Hierarchies at Home: A History of Domestic Service in Cuba from Abolition to Revolution." Ph.D. diss., New York University, 2017.

Hidalgo de la Paz, Ibrahím. *Cuba 1895–1898, contradicciónes y disoluciónes.* Havana: Centro de Estudios Martianos, 1999.

Higginbotham, Evelyn Brooks. "African-American Women's History and the Metalanguage of Race." *Signs: Journal of Women in Culture and Society* 17, no. 2 (1992): 251–274.

———. *Righteous Discontent: The Women's Movement in the Black Baptist Church, 1880–1920.* Cambridge, MA: Harvard University Press, 1993.

Hirsch, Marianne. *Family Frames: Photography, Narrative, and Postmemory.* Cambridge, MA: Harvard University Press, 1997.

Hoemel, Robert, B. "Sugar and Social Change in Oriente, Cuba, 1898–1946." *Journal of Latin American Studies* 8 (1976): 215–249.

Hoffnung-Garskof, Jesse. *Racial Migrations: New York City and the Revolutionary Politics of the Spanish Caribbean, 1850–1902*. Princeton, NJ: Princeton University Press, 2019.

Hoganson, Kristin. *Fighting for American Manhood: How Gender Politics Provoked the Spanish-American and Philippine-American Wars*. New Haven, CT: Yale University Press, 2000.

Holt, Thomas C. *The Problem of Freedom: Race, Labor, and Politics in Jamaica and Britain, 1832–1938*. Baltimore, MD: Johns Hopkins University Press, 1991.

hooks, bell. *Black Looks: Race and Representation*. Boston: South End, 1992.

———. *Feminist Theory: From Margin to Center*. Boston: South End, 1984.

———. *Yearning: Race, Gender, and Cultural Politics*. Boston: South End, 1990.

Horrego Estuch, Leopoldo. *Juan Gualberto Gómez, un gran inconforme*. Havana: Ciencias Sociales, 2004.

———. *Martín Morúa Delgado*. Santa Clara: Universidad Central de la Villas, 1957.

Howard, Phillip A. *Black Labor, White Sugar: Caribbean Braceros and Their Struggle for Power in the Cuban Sugar Industry*. Baton Rouge: Louisiana State University Press, 2015.

———. *Changing History: Afro-Cuban Cabildos and Societies of Color in the Nineteenth Century*. Baton Rouge: Louisiana State University Press, 1998.

Hunter, Tera W. *To 'Joy My Freedom: Black Women's Lives and Labors after the Civil War*. Cambridge, MA: Harvard University Press, 1997.

Ibarra, Jorge. *Prologue to Revolution: Cuba, 1898–1958*. Boulder, CO: Lynne Reinner, 1998.

Iglesias Utset, Marial. *A Cultural History of Cuba during the U.S. Occupation, 1898–1902*. Chapel Hill: University of North Carolina Press, 2011.

James, Rawn Jr. *The Double V: How Wars, Protest, and Harry Truman Desegregated America's Military*. New York: Bloomsbury, 2013.

James, Winston. *Holding Aloft the Banner of Ethiopia: Caribbean Radicalism in Early Twentieth-Century America*. London: Verso, 1998.

Jiménez-Muñoz, Gladys M. "Carmen Maria Colon Pellot: On 'Womanhood' and 'Race' in Puerto Rico during the Interwar Period." *New Centennial Review* 3, no. 3 (2003): 71–91.

Johnson, Sherry. "'Señoras en sus clases no ordinarias': Enemy Collaborators or Courageous Defenders of the Family?" *Cuban Studies* 34 (2003): 11–37.

Jones, Claudia. "An End to the Neglect of the Problems of the Negro Woman." *Political Affairs* (June 1949): 28–29.

Juncker, Kristine. *Afro-Cuban Religious Arts: Popular Expressions of Cultural Inheritance in Espiritismo and Santería*. Gainesville: University Press of Florida, 2014.

Kapcia, Antoni. *Havana: The Making of Cuban Culture*. Oxford, England: Berg, 2004.

Kelley, Robin D. G. *Freedom Dreams: The Black Radical Imagination*. Boston: Beacon, 2002.

———. *Race Rebels: Culture, Politics, and the Black Working Class*. New York: Free Press, 1994.

Kitch, Carolyn. *The Girl on the Magazine Cover: The Origins of Visual Stereotypes in American Mass Media*. Chapel Hill: University of North Carolina Press, 2009.

Knight, Franklin. *Slave Society in Cuba during the Nineteenth Century.* Madison: University of Wisconsin Press, 1970.

Kutzinski, Vera. *Sugar's Secrets: Race and the Erotics of Cuban Nationalism.* Charlottesville: University of Virginia Press, 1993.

Lagardére, Rodolfo de. *Blancos y negros.* Havana: Imp. La Universal, 1889.

Lambe, Ariel Mae. *No Barrier Can Contain It: Cuban Antifascism and the Spanish Civil War.* Chapel Hill: University of North Carolina Press, 2019.

Landers, Jane. *Atlantic Creoles in the Age of Revolutions.* Cambridge, MA: Harvard University Press, 2011.

Lane, Jill. *Blackface Cuba, 1840–1895.* Philadelphia: University of Pennsylvania Press, 2005.

———. "Smoking Habaneras, or A Cuban Struggle with Racial Demons." *Social Text* 28, no. 3 (Fall 2010): 11–37.

La Rosa Corzo, Gabino. "Henri Dumont y la imagen antropológica del esclavo africano en Cuba." In *Historia y memoria: Sociedad, cultura y vida cotidiana en Cuba, 1878–1917,* 175–182. Havana: Centro de Investigación y Desarrollo de la Cultura Cubana Juan Marinello, 2003.

Laver, James. *Costume and Fashion: A Concise History.* New York: Thames and Hudson, 2002.

Lavrin, Asunción. *Women, Feminism, and Social Change in Argentina, Chile, and Uruguay, 1890–1940.* Lincoln: University of Nebraska Press, 1995.

Lazo, Rodrigo. *Writing to Cuba: Filibustering and Cuban Exiles in the United States.* Chapel Hill: University of North Carolina Press, 2005.

Lee, Shirley J. "Black Women and the Cult of True Womanhood." In *Black Women Abolitionists: A Study in Activism, 1828–1860,* 40–59. Knoxville: University of Tennessee Press, 1992.

Leonard, Thomas M., and John F. Bratzel, eds. *Latin America during World War II.* Lanham, MD: Rowman and Littlefield, 2006.

Levine, Robert. *Images of History: Nineteenth and Twentieth Century Latin American Photographs as Documents.* Durham, NC: Duke University Press, 1990.

Lewis, David Levering, and Deborah Willis. *A Small Nation of People: W.E.B. DuBois and African American Portraits of Progress.* New York: Amistad, Harper Collins, 2003.

Lightfoot, Natasha. *Troubling Freedom: Antigua and the Aftermath of British Emancipation.* Durham, NC: Duke University Press, 2015.

Lindsey, Treva. *Colored No More: Reinventing Black Womanhood in Washington, D.C.* Chicago: University of Illinois Press, 2017.

Lipman, Jana. *Guantánamo: A Working-Class History between Empire and Revolution.* Berkeley: University of California Press, 2008.

Lipsett-Rivera, Sonya, and Lyman L. Johnson, eds. *The Faces of Honor: Sex, Shame, and Violence in Colonial Latin America.* Albuquerque: University of New Mexico Press, 1998.

Logan, Enid Lynette. "The 1899 Cuban Marriage Law Controversy: Church, State, and Empire in the Crucible of the Nation." *Journal of Social History* 42 (2008): 469–494.

———. "Conspirators, Pawns, Patriots, and Brothers: Race and Politics in Western Cuba

1906–1909." In *Political Power and Social Theory*, edited by Diane E. Davis, 3–51. Leamington Spa, England: Emerald Group, 2001.

———. "Each Sheep with Its Mate: Marking Race and Legitimacy in Cuban Ecclesiastical Archives, 1890–1940." *New West Indian Guide* 84, 1–2(2010): 5–39.

———. "El apóstol y el comandante en jefe: Racial Discourses and Practices in Cuba, 1890–1899." In *The Global Color Line: Racial and Ethnic Inequality and Struggle from a Global Perspective*, vol. 6, edited by Pinar J. Batur-Vanderlippe and Joe Feagin, 195–213. Greenwich, CT: JAI, 1999.

López, Alfred J. *José Martí: A Revolutionary Life*. Austin: University of Texas Press, 2014.

López, Antonio. *Unbecoming Blackness: The Diaspora Cultures of Afro-Cuban America*. New York: New York University Press, 2012.

Lopez, Kathleen. *Chinese Cubans: A Transnational History*. Chapel Hill: University of North Carolina Press, 2013.

López Francisco, Liset. "El movimiento feminista cubano desde las páginas de la revista literaria *Horizontes de Sancti Spíritus* (1935–1939)." *Revista Caribeña de Ciencias Sociales* (January 2017).

López Valdés, Rafael. "La sociedad secreta abakua en un grupo de trabajadores portuarios." In *Componentes africanos en el etnos cubano*, 151–185. Havana: Ciencias Sociales.

Lorde, Audre. *A Burst of Light*. Ithaca, NY: Firebrand, 1988.

Lotz, Lizabeth M. "Leading the Life of a Modern Girl: Representations of Womanhood in Cuban Popular Culture, 1919–1929." PhD diss., University of North Carolina, 2008.

Lovejoy, Henry B. *Prieto: Yorubá Kingship in Colonial Cuba during the Age of Revolutions*. Chapel Hill: University of North Carolina Press, 2018.

Lucero, Bonnie. "Civilization before Citizenship: Education, Racial Order, and the Material Culture of Female Domesticity, Cuba (1899–1902)." *Atlantic Studies: Global Currents* 12, no. 1 (2015): 26–49.

———. *A Cuban City, Segregated: Race and Urbanization in the Nineteenth Century*. Tuscaloosa: University of Alabama Press, 2019.

———. "Racial Geographies, Imperial Transitions: Property Ownership and Race Relations in Cienfuegos, Cuba, 1894–1899." *Journal of Transnational American Studies* 3 (2).

———. *Revolutionary Masculinity and Racial Inequality: Gendering War and Politics in Cuba*. Albuquerque: University of New Mexico Press, 2018.

Macpherson, Anne S. "Doing Comparative (Gender) History." *Small Axe* (2014): 72–86.

———. *From Colony to Nation: Women Activists and the Gendering of Politics in Belize, 1912–1982*. Lincoln: University of Nebraska Press, 2007.

Makalani, Minkah. *In the Cause of Freedom: Black Internationalism from Harlem to London, 1917–1939*. Chapel Hill: University of North Carolina Press, 2011.

Manley, Elizabeth S. "Of Celestinas and Saints, or Deconstructing the Myths of Dominican Womanhood." *Small Axe* (2018): 72–84.

———. *The Paradox of Paternalism: Women and the Politics of Authoritarianism in the Dominican Republic*. Gainesville: University Press of Florida, 2017.

Marien, Mary Warner. *Photography: A Cultural History*. London: Laurence King, 2002.

Marinello, Juan. "La cuestión racial en el trabajo, la inmigración y la cultura." *Criterios de Unión Revolucionaria*, March 10, 1939.

———. *La cuestión racial en la constitución*. Havana, 1940.

Marquina, Rafael. *Juan Gualberto Gómez en sí*. Havana: Instituto Nacional de Cultura, 1956.

Martiatu, Inés María. *Bufo y nación: Interpelaciones desde el presente*. Havana: Letras Cubanas, 2008.

———. "El negrito y la mulata en el vórtice de la nacionalidad." In *Afrocubanas: Historia, pensamineto y prácticas culturales*, edited by Daisy Rubiera Castillo and Inés María Martiatu Terry, 273–298. Havana: Ciencias Sociales, 2011.

Martín Alcoff, Linda. *Visible Identities: Race, Gender, and the Self*. Oxford, England: Oxford University Press, 2005.

Martínez-Fernández, Luis. "Life in a 'Male City': Native and Foreign Elite Women in Nineteenth-Century Havana." *Cuban Studies* 25 (1995): 27–49.

———. "The 'Male City' of Havana: The Coexisting Logics of Colonialism, Slavery, and Patriarchy in Nineteenth-Century Cuba." In *Women and the Colonial Gaze*, edited by Tamara L. Hunt and Micheline R. Lessard, 104–116. Hampshire, England: Palgrave, 2002.

Martínez Heredia, Fernando. *La revolución cubana del 30: Ensayos*. Havana: Ciencias Sociales, 2007.

Martínez-Vergne, Teresita. "Bourgeois Women in the Early Twentieth Century Dominican National Discourse." *New West Indian Guide* 75 (2001): 65–89.

———. *Nation and Citizen in the Dominican Republic, 1880–1916*. Chapel Hill: University of North Carolina Press, 2005.

Mayes, April J. *The Mulatto Republic: Class, Race, and Dominican National Identity*. Gainesville: University Press of Florida, 2014.

———. "Why Dominican Feminism Moved to the Right: Class, Colour, and Women's Activism in the Dominican Republic, 1880s–1940s." *Gender and History* 20, no. 2 (2008): 349–371.

McDuffie, Erik S. *Sojourning for Freedom: Black Women, American Communism, and the Making of Black Left Feminism*. Durham, NC: Duke University Press, 2011.

Mcgee Deutsch, Sandra. "The New School Lecture 'An Army of Women': Communist-Linked Solidarity Movements, Maternalism, and Political Consciousness in 1930s and 1940s Argentina." *The Americas* 75, no. 1 (January 2018): 95–125.

McGillivray, Gillian. "Blazing Cane: Cuban Sugar Communities in Peace and Insurrection, 1898–1939." *Journal of Social History* 31 (Spring 1998): 599–623.

McGraw, Jason. *The Work of Recognition: Caribbean Colombia and the Postemancipation Struggle for Citizenship*. Chapel Hill: University of North Carolina Press, 2014.

McLeod, Marc. "'Sin Dejar de Ser Cubanos': Cuban Blacks and the Challenges of Garveyism in Cuba." *Caribbean Studies* 31, no. 1 (January-June 2003): 75–105.

———. "'We Cubans Are Obligated Like Cats to Have a Clean Face': Malaria, Quarantine, and Race in Neocolonial Cuba, 1898–1940." *The Americas* 67, no. 1 (July 2010): 57–81.

Mena, Luz. "Stretching the Limits of Gendered Spaces: Black and Mulatto Women in 1830s Havana." *Cuban Studies* 36 (2005): 87–104.

Méndez Oliva, Esperanza. *El estirpe de Mariana en la Villas*. Santa Clara, Cuba: Capiro, 2006.

Méndez Oliva, Esperanza, and Santiago Alemán Santana. *Villareñas camino a la emancipación*. Havana: Política, 2008.

Meriño Fuentes, María de los Ángeles. *Una vuelta necesaria a mayo de 1912*. Havana: Ciencias Sociales, 2006.

Mesa Jiménez, Yanira. "Las sociedades 'La Bella Union' y 'El Gran Maceo,' un reto para el racismo de aquella época." Thesis, Escuela Professional de Arte, Villa Clara, 1993–1994.

Miller, Francesca. *Latin American Women and the Search for Social Justice*. Hanover, NH: University Press of New England, 1991.

Miller, Ivor. *Voice of the Leopard: African Secret Societies and Cuba*. Jackson: University Press of Mississippi, 2009.

Mirabal, Nancy Raquel. *Suspect Freedoms: The Racial and Sexual Politics of Cubanidad in New York, 1823–1957*. New York: New York University Press, 2017.

Mitchell, Dolores. "Images of Exotic Women in Turn-of-the-Century Tobacco Art." *Feminist Studies* 18, no. 2 (Summer 1992): 327–350.

Mitchell, Michele. *Righteous Propagation: African Americans and the Politics of Racial Destiny after Reconstruction*. Chapel Hill: University of North Carolina Press, 2004.

——. "Silence Broken, Silences Kept: Gender and Sexuality in African American History." *Gender and History* 11, no. 3 (November 1999): 433–444.

Mitchell, W. J. T. *Picture Theory Essays on Verbal and Visual Representation*. Chicago: University of Chicago Press, 1994.

Monroe, Walter S., Ana Echegoyen de Cañizares, Calixto Suárez Gómez. *Enciclopedia de educación científica*. Havana: Cultural, 1942.

Montejo Arrechea, Carmen Victoria. "*Minerva*: A Magazine for Women (and Men) of Color." In *Between Race and Empire: African-Americans and Cubans before the Cuban Revolution*, edited by Lisa Brock and Digna Castaneda Fuertes, 33–48. Philadelphia: Temple University Press, 1998.

——. *Sociedades de instrucción y recreo de pardos y morenos que existieron en Cuba colonial: Período 1878–1898*. Veracruz, Mexico: Gobierno del Estado de Veracruz, Instituto Veracruzano de Cultura, 1993.

——. *Sociedades negras en Cuba, 1878–1960*. Havana: Ciencias Sociales, 2004.

Montgomery, William. "Mission to Cuba and Costa Rica: The Oblate Sisters of Providence in Latin America, 1900–1970." PhD diss., Catholic University of America, 1997.

Moore, Robin. *Nationalizing Blackness: Afrocubanismo and Artistic Revolution in Havana, 1920–1940*. Pittsburgh, PA: University of Pittsburgh Press, 1997.

Moreno, Francisco. *Cuba y su gente (apuntes para la historia)*. Madrid: Enrique Teodora, 1887.

——. *El país de chocolate (la inmoralidad en Cuba)*. Madrid: Enrique Teodora, 1887.

Morris, Courtney. "Becoming Creole, Becoming Black: Migration, Diasporic Self-Making, and the Many Lives of Madame Maymie Leona Turpeau de Mena." *Women, Gender, and Families of Color* 4, no. 2 (2016): 171–195.

Morrison, Karen Y. "Afro-Latin American Women Writers and the Historical Complexities of Reproducing Race." *Meridians* 14, no. 2 (2016): 88–117.

———. "Creating an Alternative Kinship: Slavery, Freedom, and Nineteenth-Century Afro-Cuban *Hijos Naturales*." *Journal of Social History* (September 2007): 55–80.

———. *Cuba's Racial Crucible: The Sexual Economy of Social Identities, 1750–2000*. Bloomington: Indiana University Press, 2015.

———. "White Fathers and Slave Mothers in Nineteenth-Century Cuba: Defining Family and Social Status." *Slavery and Abolition* 31 (March 2010): 29–55.

———. "'Whitening' Revisited: Nineteenth-Century Cuban Counterpoints." In *Africans to Spanish America: Expanding the Diaspora*, edited by Sherwin Bryant, Rachel O'Toole, and Ben Vinson, 163–185. Champaign: University of Illinois Press, 2012.

Morrow, Diane Batts. *Persons of Color and Religious at the Same Time: The Oblate Sisters of Providence, 1828–1860*. Chapel Hill: University of North Carolina Press, 2002.

Mullenbach, Cheryl. *Double Victory: How African American Women Broke Race and Gender Barriers to Help Win World War II*. Chicago: Chicago Review, 2013.

Muller, Dalia Antonia. *Cuban Émigrés and Independence in the Nineteenth-Century Gulf World*. Chapel Hill: University of North Carolina Press, 2017.

Murray, Nicole. "Socialism and Feminism: Women and the Cuban Revolution, Part I." *Feminist Review* 2 (1979): 57–73.

Murrell, Nathaniel Samuel. *Afro-Caribbean Religions: An Introduction to Their Historical, Cultural, and Sacred Traditions*. Philadelphia: Temple University Press, 2010.

Nadel, Joshua. "Processing Modernity: Social and Cultural Adaptation in Eastern Cuba, 1902–1933." PhD diss., University of North Carolina, 2007.

Naranjo Orovio, Consuelo. "Blanco sobre negro: Debates en torno a la identidad en Cuba, 1900–1920." In *Relatos de nación: La construcción de las identidades nacionales en el mundo hispánico*, edited by Peter Lang, 849–869. Madrid: Iberoamericana, 2005.

Naro, Nancy Priscilla, ed. *Blacks, Coloureds, and National Identity in Nineteenth-Century Latin America*. London: Institute of Latin American Studies, 2003.

Niell, Paul. *Urban Space as Heritage in Late Colonial Cuba: Classicism and Dissonance on the Plaza de Armas of Havana, 1754–1828*. Austin: University of Texas Press, 2015.

Nunn, Pamela Gerrish. "Fine Arts and the Fan, 1860–1930." *Journal of Design History* 17, no. 3 (2004): 251–266.

Olmsted, Victor H., and Henry Gannett. *Cuba: Population, History, and Resources, 1907*. Washington, DC: US Bureau of the Census, 1909.

Ortiz, Fernando. *Los cabildos y la fiesta afrocubanos del Día de Reyes*. Havana: Ciencias Sociales, 1992.

———. *Hampa afro-cubana: Los negros brujos; apuntes para un estudio de etnología criminal*. Madrid: Editorial América: 1917.

———. *Los negros curros*. Havana: Ciencias Sociales, 1986.

Orum, Thomas Tondee. "The Politics of Color: The Racial Dimension of Cuban Politics during the Early Republican Years, 1900–1912." PhD diss., New York University, 1975.

Otheguy, Raquel Alicia. "Education as a Political Tool: El Directorio Central de las Sociedades de la Raza de Color and the Spanish Colonial Government in Cuba, 1880s-

1890s." Paper presented at the Association of Caribbean Historians conference, May 11–16, 2014. Fort-de-France, Martinique.

———. "Es de suponer que los maestros sean de la misma clase." *Cuban Studies* 49 (2020): 174–192.

Otovo, Okezi. *Progressive Mothers, Better Babies: Race, Public Health, and the State in Brazil, 1850–1945*. Austin: University of Texas Press, 2016.

Padrón, Pedro Luis. *La mujer trabajadora*. Havana, 1972.

Palmer, Steven, José Antonio Piqueras, and Amparo Sánchez Cobos. *State of Ambiguity: Civic Life and Culture in Cuba's First Republic*. Durham: Duke University Press, 2014.

Palmié, Stephan. *Wizards and Scientists: Explorations in Afro-Cuban Modernity and Tradition*. Durham, NC: Duke University Press, 2002.

Pappademos, Melina. "Alchemists of a Race: Politics and Culture in Black Cuban Societies, 1899–1959." PhD diss., University of New York, 2004.

———. *Black Political Activism and the Cuban Republic*. Chapel Hill: University of North Carolina Press, 2011.

Patterson, Tiffany, and Robin D. G. Kelley. "Unfinished Migrations: Reflections on the African Diaspora and the Making of the Modern World." *African Studies Review* 43 (April 2000): 11–45.

Patton, Venetria K. *Women in Chains: The Legacy of Slavery in Black Women's Fiction*. Albany: State University of New York Press, 2000.

Paugh, Katherine. *The Politics of Reproduction: Race, Medicine, and Fertility in the Age of Abolition*. Oxford, England: Oxford University Press, 2017.

Peacock, John. *Fashion since 1900: The Complete Sourcebook*. New York: Thames and Hudson, 2007.

Peiss, Kathy. *Hope in a Jar: The Making of America's Beauty Culture*. New York: Metropolitan, 1998.

Pentón Herrera, Luis Javier. "La dra. Ana Echegoyen de Cañizares: Líder de la campaña alfabetizadora de 1956 en Cuba." *Latin Americanist* 62, no. 1 (October 2016): 261–278.

Pérez, Louis A. *Cuba: Between Reform and Revolution*. 5th ed. Oxford, England: Oxford University Press, 2015.

———. *Cuba and the United States: Ties of Singular Intimacy*. Athens: University of Georgia Press, 1990.

———. *Cuba between Empires, 1878–1902*. Pittsburgh, PA: University of Pittsburgh, 1982.

———. *Cuba in the American Imagination: Metaphor and Imperial Ethos*. Chapel Hill: University of North Carolina Press, 2008.

——— *Cuba under the Platt Amendment*. Pittsburgh, PA: University of Pittsburgh Press, 1986.

———. *Intimations of Modernity: Civil Culture in Nineteenth-Century Cuba*. Chapel Hill: University of North Carolina Press, 2017.

———. *On Becoming Cuban: Identity, Nationality, and Culture*. 2nd ed. New York: Harper Perennial, 2001.

——— "Politics, Peasants, and People of Color: The 1912 'Race War' in Cuba Reconsidered." *Hispanic American Historical Review* 66, no. 3 (1986): 509–539.

———. *The Structure of Cuban History: Meanings and Purpose of the Past*. Chapel Hill: University of North Carolina Press, 2013.

Pérez Sarduy, Pedro. *Las criadas de la Habana*. San Juan, PR: Plaza Mayor, 2002.

———. "The Maids." In *Afrocuba: An Anthology of Cuban Writing on Race, Politics, and Culture*, edited by Pedro Pérez Sarduy and Jean Stubbs, 250–261. Melbourne, Australia: Ocean, 1993.

Pérez-Stable, Marifeli. *The Cuban Revolution: Origins, Course, Legacy*. Oxford, England: Oxford University Press, 1994.

Perry, Keisha-Khan. *Black Women against the Land Grab: The Fight for Racial Justice in Brazil*. St. Paul: University of Minnesota Press, 2013.

Pettway, Matthew. *Cuban Literature in the Age of Black Insurrection: Manzano, Plácido, and Religion*. Jackson: University of Mississippi Press, 2019.

Piccato, Pablo. *The Tyranny of Opinion: Honor in the Construction of the Mexican Public Sphere*. Durham, NC: Duke University Press, 2010.

Pignot, Elsa. "El asociacionismo negro en Cuba: Una vía de integración en la sociedad republicana (1920–1960)." *Revista de Indias* 70, no. 250 (2010): 837–862.

Pla, José. *La raza de color: Necesidad de instruir y moralizar a los individuos de color y de fomentar el matrimonio entre los patrocinados*. Matanzas, Cuba: El Ferro-Carril, 1881.

Poole, Deborah. *Vision, Race, and Modernity: A Visual Economy of the Andean World*. Princeton, NJ: Princeton University Press, 1997.

Portuondo Linares, Serafín. *Los Independientes de Color*. Havana: Caminos, 2002.

Portuondo Zúñiga, Olga. *Pensar y existir en cubano*. Santiago de Cuba: Santiago, 2014.

Posey, Thaddeus. "Praying in the Shadows: The Oblate Sisters of Providence, a Look at Nineteenth-Century Black Catholic Spirituality." *U.S. Catholic Historian* 12 (January 1994): 11–30.

Powell, Richard J. *Cutting a Figure: Fashioning Black Portraiture*. Chicago: University of Chicago Press, 2009.

Poyo, Gerald. *With All, and for the Good of All: The Emergence of Popular Nationalism in the Cuban Communities of the United States, 1848–1898*. Durham, NC: Duke University Press, 1989.

Prados-Terreira, Teresa. *Mambisas: Rebel Women in Nineteenth-Century Cuba*. Gainesville: University Press of Florida, 2005.

Pratt, Mary Louise. *Imperial Eyes: Travel Writing and Transculturation*. New York: Routledge, 1992.

Pryor, Elizabeth Stordeur. *Colored Travelers: Mobility and the Fight for Citizenship before the Civil War*. Chapel Hill: University of North Carolina Press, 2016.

Putnam, Lara. *The Company They Kept: Migrants and the Politics of Gender in Caribbean Costa Rica, 1870–1960*. Chapel Hill: University of North Carolina Press, 2002.

———. *Radical Moves: Caribbean Migrants and the Politics of Race in the Jazz Age*. Chapel Hill: University of North Carolina Press, 2013.

Quiroz, Alfonso W. "Martí in Cuban Schools." In *The Cuban Republic and José Martí: Reception and Use of a National Symbol*, edited by Mauricio Agusto Font and Alfonso W. Quiroz, 108–125. Oxford, England: Lexington, 2006.

Raiford, Leigh. *Imprisoned in a Luminous Glare: Photography and the African American Freedom Struggle*. Chapel Hill: University of North Carolina Press, 2011.

———. "Lynching, Visuality, and the Un/Making of Blackness." *Nka: Journal of Contemporary African Art*, no. 20 (Fall 2006): 22–31.

———. "Marcus Garvey in Stereograph." *Small Axe* 17 (2013): 263–280.

Ramírez, Dixa. "Against Type: Reading Desire in the Visual Archives of Dominican Subjects." *Small Axe* 22 (2018): 144–160.

———. *Colonial Phantoms: Belonging and Refusal in the Dominican Americas from the 19th Century to the Present*. New York: New York University Press, 2018.

Ramírez Chicharro, Manuel. "Beyond Suffrage: The Role of Cuban Women in the State-Building Years of a Failed Democracy (1940–1952)." *Women's History Review* 5 (2018): 754–777.

———. "Doblemente sometidas: Las mujeres de color en la república de Cuba (1902–1959)." *Revista de Indias* 75, no. 262 (2014): 783–828.

———. "El activismo social y político de las mujeres durante la República de Cuba." *Revista Electrônica da Associação Nacional de Pesquisadores e Profesores de História das Américas* (January/June 2016): 141–172.

———. *Más allá del sufragismo: Las mujeres en la democratización de Cuba (1933–1952)*. Granada, Spain: Comares, 2019.

Ramos, E. Carmen. "A Painter of Cuban Life: Víctor Patricio de Landaluze and Nineteenth-Century Cuban Politics, 1850–1889." PhD diss., University of Chicago, 2011.

Ramos, Miguel Willie. "La División de la Habana: Territorial Conflict and Cultural Hegemony in the Followers of Oyo Lukumi Religion, 1850s–1920s." *Cuban Studies* 34 (2003): 38–70.

Randolph, Sherie M. "Not to Rely Completely on the Courts: Florynce 'Flo' Kennedy and Black Feminist Leadership in the Reproductive Rights Battle, 1969–1971." *Journal of Women's History* 27, no. 1 (Spring 2015): 136–160.

Reid, Michelle. *The Year of the Lash: Free People of Color in Cuba and the Nineteenth-Century Atlantic World*. Athens: University of Georgia Press, 2011.

Riquenes Herrera, Ricardo Rey. *Guantánamo en el vortice de los Independientes de Color*. Guantanamo, Cuba: El Mar y la Montaña, 2007.

Rivera Pérez, Aymée. "El imaginario femenino negro en Cuba." In *Afrocubanas: Historia, pensamineto y prácticas culturales*, edited by Daisy Rubiera Castillo and Inés María Martiatu Terry, 225–250. Havana: Ciencias Sociales, 2011.

Roberts, Blain. *Pageants, Parlors, and Pretty Women: Race and Beauty in the Twentieth-Century South*. Chapel Hill: University of North Carolina Press, 2014.

Roche y Monteagudo, Rafael. *La policía y sus misterios en Cuba*. Havana: La Prueba, 1908.

Rodriguez, Daniel. "'To Fight These Powerful Trusts and Free the Medical Profession': Medicine, Class Formation, and Revolution in Cuba, 1925–1935." *Hispanic American Historical Review* 95, no. 4 (November 2015): 595–629.

Rodríguez, Rolando. *La conspiración de los iguales: La protesta de los Independientes de Color en 1912*. Havana: Imagen Contemporánea, 2010.

Rodríguez de Cuesta, V. E. *Patriotas cubanas*. Pinar del Río, Cuba: Heraldo Pinareño, 1952.

Rodríguez-Plate, Edna. *Lydia Cabrera and the Construction of an Afro-Cuban Cultural Identity*. Chapel Hill: University of North Carolina Press, 2004.

Rogers, Molly. *Delia's Tears: Race, Science, and Photography in Nineteenth-Century America*. New Haven, CT: Yale University Press, 2010.

Rojas Blaquier, Angelina. *El primer Partido Comunista de Cuba: Sus tácticas y estrategias.* Vol. 2: *Pensamiento político y experiencia práctica, 1935–1952.* Santiago de Cuba: Oriental, 2006.

Rolando, Gloria, dir. *1912, Voces para un silencio, capítulos 1–3.* Films. Imágenes del Caribe, 2010.

———, dir. *Diálogo con mi abuela.* Film. Instituto Cubano del Arte e Indústrias Cinematográficos, 2016.

———, dir. *Las raíces de mi corazón.* Film. Imágenes del Caribe, 2001.

———, dir. *Los hijos de Baragua.* Film. Imágenes del Caribe, 1996.

———, dir. *Nosotros e el jazz.* Film. Imágenes del Caribe, 2004.

Román, Reinaldo. *Governing Spirits: Religion, Miracles, and Spectacles in Cuba and Puerto Rico, 1898–1956.* Chapel Hill: University of North Carolina Press, 2007.

Rooks, Noliwe M. *Hair Raising: Beauty, Culture, and African American Women.* New Brunswick, NJ: Rutgers University Press, 1996.

Rosemblatt, Karin Alejandra. *Gendered Compromises: Political Cultures and the State in Chile, 1920–1950.* Chapel Hill: University of North Carolina Press, 2000.

Rubiera Castillo, Daisy. "Apuntes sobre la mujer negra cubana." *Cuban Studies* 42 (2011): 176–185.

Rubiera Castillo, Daisy, and Inés María Martiatu Terry, eds. *Afrocubanas: Historia, pensamineto y prácticas culturales.* Havana: Ciencias Sociales, 2011.

Ryan, Marveta. "Seeking Acceptance from the Society and the State: Poems from Cuba's Black Press, 1882–1889." In *Black Writing, Culture, and the State in Latin America,* edited by Jerome C. Branche, 33–60. Nashville, TN: Vanderbilt University Press, 2015.

Sabourín Fornaris, Jesús. *Juan Gualberto Gómez: Símbolo del deber.* Santiago de Cuba: Universidad de Oriente, 1954.

Safa, Helen. *Women, Industrialization, and State Policy in Cuba.* Notre Dame, IN: Helen Kellogg Institute for International Studies, University of Notre Dame, 1989.

Salinas Carvacho, Valentina. "El pensamiento social de las mujeres negras a través de la revista *Adelante* (1935–1939)." *Universum* 33, no. 2 (2018): 193–203.

Sánchez Guerra, José. *Mambisas guantanameras.* Guantanamo, Cuba: Centro Provincial del Libro y la Literatura, El Mar y la Montaña, 2000.

Sanders, James. "'A Mob of Women' Confront Post-Colonial Republican Politics: How Class, Race, and Partisan Ideology Affected Gendered Political Space in Nineteenth-Century Southwestern Colombia." *Journal of Women's History* 20, no. 1 (Spring 2008): 63–89.

———. *The Vanguard of the Atlantic World: Creating Modernity, Nation, and Democracy in Nineteenth-Century Latin America.* Durham, NC: Duke University Press, 2014.

Sanger, Joseph Prentiss, Henry Gannett, and Walter Francis Willcox. *Report on the Census of Cuba, 1899.* Washington DC: Government Print Office, 1900.

Sartorius, David. *Ever Faithful: Race, Loyalty, and the Ends of Empire in Spanish Cuba.* Durham, NC: Duke University Press: 2014.

Scarry, Elaine. *On Beauty and Being Just.* Princeton, NJ: Princeton University Press, 1999.

Schechter, Patricia A. *Ida B. Wells-Barnett and American Reform, 1880–1930.* Chapel Hill: University of North Carolina Press, 2001.

Schmidt, Jalane. *Cachita's Streets: The Virgin of Charity, Race, and Revolution in Cuba.* Durham, NC: Duke University Press, 2015.

Scott, Joan Wallach. *Gender and the Politics of History.* New York: Columbia University Press, 2018.

Scott, Rebecca J. *Degrees of Freedom: Louisiana and Cuba after Slavery.* Cambridge, MA: Belknap, 2005.

———. *Slave Emancipation in Cuba: The Transition to Free Labor, 1860–1899.* Pittsburgh, PA: University of Pittsburgh Press, 1985.

Scott, Rebecca J., and Michael Zueske. "Property in Writing, Property on the Ground: Pigs, Horses, Land, and Citizenship in the Aftermath of Slavery, Cuba, 1880–1909." *Comparative Studies in Society and History* 44, no. 4 (2002): 669–699.

Sekula, Allan. "The Body and the Archive." *October* 39 (Winter 1986): 3–64.

Serra y Montalvo, Rafael. *Ensayos políticos.* Vol. 2. New York: P. J. Diaz, 1896.

———. *Ensayos políticos, sociales y económicos.* New York: A. W. Howes, 1899.

———. *Para blancos y negros: Ensayos políticos, sociales y económicos.* Vol. 4. Havana: El Score, 1907.

Shaffer, Kirwin R. "Freedom Teaching: Anarchism and Education in Early Republican Cuba, 1898–1925." *The Americas* 60, no. 2 (2003): 151–183.

———. "The Radical Muse: Women and Anarchism in Early-Twentieth-Century Cuba." *Cuban Studies* 34 (2003): 130–153.

Shaw, Stephanie. *What a Woman Ought to Be and to Do: Black Professional Women Workers in the Jim Crow Era.* Chicago: University of Chicago Press, 1996.

Sheller, Mimi. *Citizenship from Below: Erotic Agency and Caribbean Freedom.* Durham, NC: Duke University Press, 2012.

———. *Democracy after Slavery: Black Publics and Peasant Radicalism in Haiti and Jamaica.* Gainesville: University Press of Florida, 2000.

Sippial, Tiffany. *Prostitution, Modernity, and the Making of the Cuban Republic, 1840–1920.* Chapel Hill: University of North Carolina Press, 2011.

Smith, Benjamin, and Richard Vokes. "Haunting Images: The Affective Power of Photography." *Visual Anthropology Review* 21, no. 4 (2008): 283–291.

Smith, Cherise. "In Black and White: Constructing History and Meaning in Civil Rights Photography." In *Let My People Go: Cairo, Illinois, 1967–1973*, edited by Jan Peterson Roddy, 83–94. Carbondale: Southern Illinois University Press, 1996.

Smith, Christen. *Afro-Paradise: Blackness, Violence, and Performance in Brazil.* Champaign: University of Illinois Press, 2016.

Smith, Lois M., and Alfred Padula. *Sex and Revolution: Women in Socialist Cuba.* Oxford, England: Oxford University Press, 1996.

Smith, Lou, and Karina Smith. "'The Sound of Unknowing': Theorizing Race, Gender, and 'Illegitimacy' through Jamaican Family Photography." *Journal of Women's History* (Spring 2018): 107–128.

Smith, Matthew J. *Liberty, Fraternity, Exile: Haiti and Jamaica after Emancipation.* Chapel Hill: University of North Carolina Press, 2014.

Smith, Shawn Michelle. *American Archives: Gender, Race, and Class in Visual Culture.* Princeton, NJ: Princeton University Press, 1999.

——. "'Baby's Picture Is Always Treasured': Eugenics and the Reproduction of Whiteness in the Family Photograph Album." *Yale Journal of Criticism* 11 (1998): 197–220.

——. *Photography on the Color Line: W.E.B. DuBois, Race, and Visual Culture*. Durham, NC: Duke University Press, 2004.

Soares, Kristie. "Garzona Nationalism: The Confluence of Gender, Sexuality, and Citizenship in the Cuban Republic." *Frontiers: A Journal of Women Studies* 35, no. 3 (2014): 154–182.

Sontag, Susan. *On Photography*. New York: Farrar, Straus, and Giroux, 2011.

Soto, Lionel. *La revolución del 33*. Havana: Ciencias Sociales, 1977.

Sotelo-Eastman, Alexander. "The Neglected Narratives of Cuba's Partido Independiente de Color: Civil Rights, Popular Politics, and Emancipatory Reading Practices." *The Americas* 76, no. 1 (January 2019): 41–76.

Spillers, Hortense. *Black, White, and in Color: Essays on American Literature and Culture*. Chicago: University of Chicago Press, 2003.

Stafford, Andy, and Michael Carter, eds. *The Language of Fashion*. Oxford, England: Berg, 2004.

Stavney, Anne. "'Mothers of Tomorrow': The New Negro Renaissance and the Politics of Maternal Representation." *African American Review* 32, no. 4 (Winter 1998): 533–562.

Stepan, Nancy Leys. *"The Hour of Eugenics": Race, Gender, and Nation in Latin America*. Ithaca, NY: Cornell University Press, 1991.

Stolcke, Verena (Martínez-Alier). *Marriage, Class, and Colour in Nineteenth-Century Cuba: A Study of Racial Attitudes and Sexual Values in a Slave Society*. New York: Cambridge University Press, 1974.

Stoner, K. Lynn. *Cuban and Cuban-American Women: An Annotated Bibliography*. Wilmington, DE: Scholarly Resources, 2000.

——. *From the House to the Streets: The Cuban Women's Movement for Legal Reform, 1898–1940*. Chapel Hill: University of North Carolina Press, 1991.

——. *The Women's Movement in Cuba, 1898–1958: The Stoner Collection on Cuban Feminism*. Microform. Wilmington, DE: Scholarly Resources, 1990.

——. "Militant Heroines and the Consecration of the Patriarchal State: The Glorification of Loyalty, Combat, and National Suicide in the Making of Cuban National Identity." *Cuban Studies* 34 (2003): 71–96.

——. "On Men Reforming the Rights of Men: The Abrogation of the Cuban Adultery Law, 1930." *Cuban Studies* 21 (1991): 83–99.

Storm, Anna. "Quinine Pills and Race Progress: Alice Dunbar-Nelson and the Black Women's Literary Tradition." *Legacy: A Journal of American Women Writers* 33, no. 2 (2016): 361–383.

Stubbs, Jean. "Social and Political Motherhood of Cuba: Mariana Grajales Cuello." In *Engendering History: Caribbean Women in Historical Perspective*, edited by Verene Shepherd, Bridget Brereton, and Barbara Bailey, 296–317. New York: St. Martin's, 1995.

——. *Tobacco on the Periphery: A Case Study in Cuban Labour History, 1860–1958*. New York: Cambridge University Press, 1985.

Suárez Díaz, Ana, ed. *Retrospección crítica de la asamblea constituyente de 1940*. Havana: Ciencias Sociales, 2011.

Summers, Martin Anthony. *Manliness and Its Discontents: The Black Middle Class and the Transformation of Masculinity, 1900–1930*. Chapel Hill: University of North Carolina Press, 2004.

Tabares del Real, José. *La revolución del 30: Sus dos últimos años*. Havana: Ciencias Sociales, 1973.

Talbot, William Henry Fox. *The Pencil of Nature*. New York: Hans P. Kraus, 1989.

Taylor, Ula Y. "'Negro Women Are Great Thinkers as Well as Doers': Amy Jacques-Garvey and Community Feminism in the United States, 1924–1927." *Journal of Women's History* 12 (2000): 104–126.

——. *The Promise of Patriarchy: Women and the Nation of Islam*. Chapel Hill: University of North Carolina Press, 2017.

——. *The Veiled Garvey: The Life and Times of Amy Jacques Garvey*. Chapel Hill: University of North Carolina Press, 2002.

Thomas, Hugh. *Cuba: A History*. London: Penguin, 2010.

Thompson, Krista. "The Evidence of Things Not Photographed: Slavery and Historical Memory in the British West Indies." *Representations* 113, no. 1 (2010): 39–71.

——. *An Eye for the Tropics: Tourism, Photography, and Framing the Caribbean Picturesque*. Durham, NC: Duke University Press, 2007.

Thurman, Sue Bailey. "The Seminar in Cuba." *Aframerican Women's Journal* (Summer–Fall 1940): 4–6.

Torres-Elers, Damaris A. *María Cabrales: Vida y acción revolucionarias*. Santiago de Cuba: Santiago, 2005.

——. "Santiagueras en el alzamiento de 1912 ¿Leyenda o realidad?" *Santiago* 133 (January–April): 116–128.

Torres-Saillant, Silvio. *El retorno de las yolas: Ensayos sobre diáspora, democracia y dominicanidad*. Santo Domingo, Dominican Republic: Manatí, 1999.

Trachtenberg, Alan. *Reading American Photographs: Images as History: Mathew Brady to Walker Evans*. New York: Hill and Wang, 1990.

Trouillot, Michel-Rolph. *Silencing the Past: Power and the Production of History*. Boston: Beacon, 1995.

Turits, Richard Lee. *Foundations of Despotism: Peasants, the Trujillo Regime, and Modernity in Dominican History*. Stanford, CA: Stanford University Press, 2003.

Tuuri, Rebecca. *Strategic Sisterhood: The National Council of Negro Women in the Black Freedom Struggle*. Chapel Hill: University of North Carolina Press, 2018.

Twinam, Ann. *Public Lives, Private Secrets: Gender, Honor, Sexuality, and Illegitimacy in Colonial Latin America*. Stanford, CA: Stanford University Press, 1999.

Umoren, Imaobong. *Race Women Internationalists: Activist-Intellectuals and Global Freedom Struggles*. Berkeley: University of California Press, 2018.

Urban, Kelly. "The 'Black Plague' in a Racial Democracy: Tuberculosis, Race, and Citizenship in Republican Cuba, 1925–1945." *Cuban Studies* 45 (2017): 319–339.

US War Department, Office of the Director, Census of Cuba. *Report on the Census, 1899*. Washington, DC: Government Printing Office, 1900.

Vera, Ana. "La fotografía y el trabajo a principios del siglo XX." In *Historia y memoria: Sociedad, cultura y vida cotidiana en Cuba, 1878–1917*, edited by José Amador,

188–189. Havana: Centro de Investigación y Desarollo de la Cultura Cubana Juan Marinello, 2003.

Vinat de la Mata, Raquel. *Las cubanas en la posguerra (1898–1902): Acercamiento a la reconstrucción de una etapa olvidada.* Havana: Política, 2001.

———. *Luces en el silencio: Educación femenina en Cuba (1648–1898).* Havana: Política, 2005.

Von Germeten, Nicole. *Violent Delights, Violent Ends: Sex, Race, and Honor in Colonial Cartagena de Indias.* Albuquerque: University of New Mexico Press, 2013.

Walker, Susannah. *Style and Status: Selling Beauty to African American Women, 1920–1975.* Lexington: University of Kentucky Press, 2007.

Walker, Tamara. *Exquisite Slaves: Race, Clothing, and Status in Colonial Lima.* Cambridge, England: Cambridge University Press, 2017.

Wallace, Maurice O., and Shawn Michelle Smith. *Pictures and Progress: Early Photography and the Making of African American Identity.* Durham, NC: Duke University Press, 2012.

Welch, Kim. "Our Hunger Is Our Song: The Politics of Race in Cuba, 1900–1930." In *The African Diaspora: African Origins and New World Identities*, edited by Isidore Okepwho, Carole Boyce Davies, and Ali A. Mazrui, 178–196. Bloomington: Indiana University Press, 2001.

Wertz, Julia Kim. "Fashioning Modernity: Dressing the Body in Ethiopian Portraiture." *Nka* (2017): 56–67.

Wexler, Laura. *Tender Violence: Domestic Visions in an Age of US Imperialism.* Chapel Hill: University of North Carolina Press, 2000.

White, Deborah Gray. *Ar'n't I a Woman: Female Slaves in the Plantation South.* New York: W. W. Norton, 1985.

———. *Too Heavy a Load: Black Women in Defense of Themselves, 1894–1994.* New York: W. W. Norton, 1999.

White, Shane, and Graham White. *Stylin': African American Expressive Culture from Its Beginnings to the Zoot Suit.* Ithaca, NY: Cornell University Press, 1998.

Whitney, Robert. *State and Revolution in Cuba: Mass Mobilization and Political Change, 1920–1940.* Chapel Hill: University of North Carolina Press, 2002.

Whitney, Robert, and Graciela Chailloux Laffita. *Subjects or Citizens: British Caribbean Workers in Cuba, 1900–1960.* Gainesville: University Press of Florida, 2013.

Williams, Andreá N. "Recovering Black Women Writers in Periodical Archives." *American Periodicals: A Journal of History and Criticism* 27, no. 1 (2017): 25–28.

Williams, Megan E. "The Crisis Cover Girl: Lena Horne, the NAACP, and Representations of African American Femininity, 1941–1945." *American Periodicals: A Journal of History, Criticism, and Bibliography* 16, no. 2 (2006): 200–218.

Williams, Carla, and Deborah Willis. *The Black Female Body: A Photographic History.* Philadelphia: Temple University Press, 2002.

Willis, Deborah, ed. *Picturing Us: African American Identity in Photography.* New York: New Press, 1996.

———. *Posing Beauty: African American Images from the 1890s to the Present.* New York: W. W. Norton, 2009.

Willis, Deborah, and Barbara Krauthamer. *Envisioning Emancipation: Black Americans and the End of Slavery*. Philadelphia: Temple University Press, 2012.

Wirtz, Kristina. *Performing Afro-Cuba: Image, Voice, Spectacle in the Making of Race and History*. Chicago: University of Chicago Press, 2014.

Wolcott, Victoria W. *Remaking Respectability: African American Women in Interwar Detroit*. Chapel Hill: University of North Carolina Press, 2001.

Wood, Marcus. *Black Milk: Imagining Slavery in the Visual Cultures of Brazil and America*. Oxford, England: Oxford University Press, 2013.

Wright, Michelle M. *Becoming Black: Creating Identity in the African Diaspora*. Durham, NC: Duke University Press, 2004.

Xavier, Giovana, Juliana Barreto Farias, and Flavio Gomes. *Black Women in Brazil in Slavery and Emancipation*. New York: Diasporic Africa, 2016.

Young, Iris Marion. "Throwing Like a Girl: A Phenomenology of Feminine Body Comportment, Mobility, and Spatiality." *Human Studies* 3 (1980): 137–156.

Zueske, Michael. "Two Stories of Gender and Slave Emancipation in Cienfuegos and Santa Clara, Central Cuba: A Microhistorical Approach to the Atlantic World." In *Gender and Slave Emancipation in the Atlantic World*, edited by Pamela Scully and Diana Paton, 181–198. Durham, NC: Duke University Press, 2005.

Index

TAKKARA K. BRUNSON is associate professor of history at Texas A&M University.